"Indiana history as viewed through a basketball net . . . An absorbing historical narrative, woven around modern Indiana history, using basketball as the thread."—The Indiana Historical Society

"The best book ever written on Indiana high school basketball. Hoose not only writes well, but his vignettes and anecdotes are fascinating. His chapter on Larry Bird is probably the best short piece ever written about him."—Author Lee Daniel Levine, in *Bird: The Making of An American Sports Legend*

"One of ten recommended sports books for kids."—*The Kids' World Almanac of Records and Facts*

"A thoughtful, elegantly crafted and shrewdly entertaining examination of a fascinating American subculture . . . An amusing, vital and intelligent book about a slice of America too easily ignored."—*Kirkus Reviews*

"This superbly written piece of sports journalism will alternately tickle the funnybone and pluck at the heartstrings of basketball fans everywhere."—*Booklist*

"Phillip Hoose examines the phenomenon of Indiana basketball with wit and whimsy."—*U.S. News and World Report*

"If you're a Hoosier Hysteric, call time out and go buy it; if you're not, reading Hoosiers will be like studying the strange ways of a cult that worships gym shoes."—*Playboy*

Other Books by Phillip M. Hoose

Building an Ark: Tools for the Preservation of Natural Diversity

Necessities: Racial Barriers in American Sports

"It's Our World, Too!": Stories of Young People Who Are Making a Difference

HOOSIERS

THE FABULOUS BASKETBALL LIFE OF
INDIANA

Second Edition

Phillip M. Hoose

Guild Press of Indiana, Inc.

Guild Press of Indiana, Inc.
6000 Sunset Lane
Indianapolis, IN 46208

Manufactured in the United States of America

Library of Congress
Catalog Card Number
95-77935

ISBN 1-878208-43-8

Text design by Sheila Samson

For Bob Collins

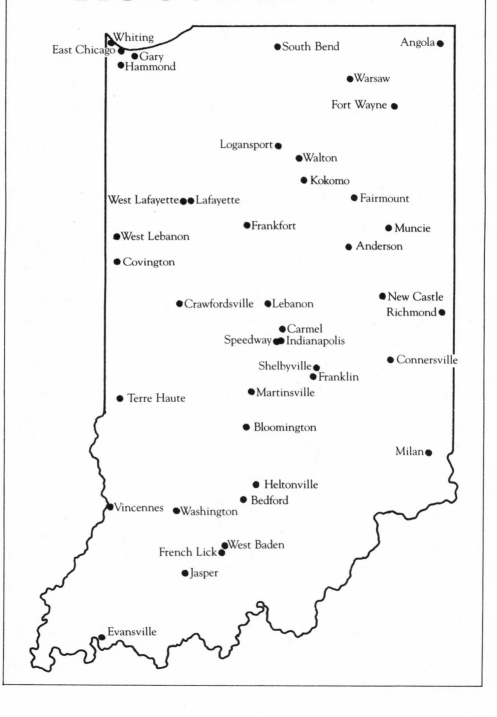

HOOSIERLAND

Whiting
East Chicago • • Gary
Hammond
South Bend
Angola •
Warsaw
Fort Wayne •
Logansport •
Walton
Kokomo
West Lafayette • • Lafayette
Fairmount
Frankfort
Muncie
West Lebanon
Anderson
Covington
Crawfordsville • Lebanon
New Castle
Richmond •
Carmel
Speedway • Indianapolis
Shelbyville
Connersville
Franklin
Terre Haute
Martinsville
Bloomington
Milan •
Heltonville
Bedford
Vincennes • Washington
French Lick • West Baden
Jasper
Evansville

Contents

Acknowledgments

I would first like to thank the more than two hundred players, coaches, fans, referees, entrepreneurs, and administrators who took the time to talk with me as I researched this book and its predecessor edition. For help with this edition, especially in Indiana, I wish to thank Darwin, Tim, and Peggy Hoose, Grace Hine, Bob Collins, Al Harden, Pat Aikman, Ron Heflin, Jim Nelson Rogers, Louis "Bo" Mallard, John Baratto, Tyson Jones, Ron Hecklinski, Tom Roach, Patricia Roy, Judi Warren, Lisa Anderson, Stephanie White, Shanda White, Kevin White, Jenny White, Kelly Fink, Murray Sperber, Ray Crowe, Bill Scott, Marcus Stewart, Jr.; Bill Hampton, Hallie Bryant, Willie Gardner, Willie Merriweather; Bailey Robertson and Bob Jewell — now both regrettably deceased; Angela Jewell, Frank Fisse, Rick and Rich Mount, Jim Jones, Tom Jones, Garry Donna, Damon Bailey, Sanford Gentry, Cloyce Hedge, David Benner, Gene Keady, and Frank Kendrick.

Ron Newlin, Wilma Gibbs, Wendell Trogdon, James Lane, Steve McShane, Gilbert Taylor, Scott Williams, and Stanley Warren are foremost among the historians and archivists who generously shared their work and/or steered me toward other important references.

Jon and Donna Halvorsen, Alan Reinhardt, Jeff Blake, and Robert Satter reviewed chapter drafts and gave me advice and encouragement. Nancy Baxter, Sheila Samson, and Guild Press have given this book a wonderful home.

All Hoosiers should thank Dr. Herb Schwomeyer for his decades of research and documentation of basketball in Indiana. Tirelessly he has preserved an important part of Indiana's cultural history.

Above all, I thank my wife, Shoshana, for giving me this book. Too often she did the work of two parents while my mind was in Milan or the Region and still, somehow, cared enough to review chapter drafts. Finally I thank my glorious daughters, Hannah and Ruby, for having the humanity to interrupt my work and bring me back to life.

Introduction

I wrote the first edition of this book ten years ago. It began as research for a feature story that appeared in *Sports Illustrated*, and then became a book proposal, and finally a book. My aim in travelling through Indiana, looking up legends and digging out stories, was to celebrate my native state's special obsession before major figures died and took their memories with them.

Like many expatriates, I didn't really understand how special basketball was to Indiana until I moved away to a neighborhood in lower Manhattan in November of 1971. Naturally, a few weeks after I got to New York, I got the itch to see a high school game. I saw a story in *The New York Times* about two nationally-ranked city powers who were playing at George Washington High, not far from me, at three in the afternoon the next Wednesday. It seemed a bizarre time to play a game, but I took the subway over, arriving early to beat the crowd.

I found the gym, but there couldn't have been a hundred people in it. Probably half of them were college scouts. Even if there had been more, there was no place for them to sit. The room was so quiet that you could hear the players talking and the coaches swearing. These were great players; if that game had been played in Muncie or Anderson or East Chicago or New Castle there would have been thousands of fans present. What a waste, I kept thinking. For the first time, I began to wonder if what I had always heard — and assumed to be talk — was really true: that I had grown up in the state where basketball meant the most.

So in 1984 when I had the chance to interview the legends and ordinary Hoosiers who made the game, I jumped. It was an amazing opportunity. I was able to talk with John Wooden, Larry Bird, Oscar Robertson, Judi Warren, Bob Knight, and Bobby Plump, the star of the team after whom the movie *Hoosiers* was modelled, and more than one hundred others.

I learned that for most of this century Indiana has been a realm of rivalries and grudges that won't die, of mythical heroes and heroines and larger-than-life coaches, a landscape dotted with lavish basketball temples built with public money to capture the home court advantage in the state tourney. At this writing, fifteen of the sixteen biggest high school gyms in the United States are in

Indiana, as well as twenty-nine of the thirty-five gyms that can seat more than five thousand fans. Almost every town has, or had, a high school gym that could seat the entire student body several times over. This is because in Indiana every school, regardless of enrollment, plays in the same high school tourney, a month-long event which has long provided a dramatic stage for teams to settle scores. Little schools regularly send teams from large urban institutions sprawling in the sawdust, especially in the early rounds.

In researching this book I learned a lot about Indiana history and more than a little about myself. I remember especially one comment that Oscar Robertson made during a long interview in an office in Cincinnati. "You know, the Klan started my high school," Robertson remarked, almost offhandedly. It caught me by surprise. I had taught English at Indianapolis Crispus Attucks High in its final year as an all-black school without ever knowing how it got that way. Growing up around Indianapolis it had always struck me as odd that there should be a racially segregated school in my city. We were in the North, not Mississippi. And the Klan?

The comment led me to research the chapter about Attucks that appears in these pages. Some of what I learned was personally painful. I discovered that members of my own family, wonderful people whom I love and who had always been kind to me, had been among the hundreds of thousands of Hoosiers who hid beneath hoods and robes in the early 1920s, swept up in a frenzy of intolerance and nativism which had indeed led to segregated schools in Gary, Evansville, and Indianapolis. I talked with many others whose families were similarly affected.

I also came to realize that a quarter century after leaving Indiana I am part of a great diaspora of Hoosiers, one of thousands who live elsewhere but who carry around in our heads a built-in tape encoded with the names of people and towns and events from Indiana that can recur in a flash. We can be watching the news on television and when the word "Lebanon" crops up, so, for a microsecond, does the image of Rick Mount. Likewise the word "Peru" registers as Kyle Macy just before it dissolves into Shining Path or makeshift cocaine airstrips. We read the word "Milan" in the news and it carries us not to Italy; but to a small, shining place that has a meaning all its own, known only to us.

I decided to write a second edition of *Hoosiers* for several reasons. For one, the first edition, published by Random House, had gone out of print. I wanted especially the historical chapters to remain available.

Also I wanted to write about places I had missed the first time around. Glenn Robinson flipped through the first edition of this book during a break at his basketball camp in Gary, and noticed one thing right away: that his school and his city, and the entire Calumet Region were missing. He handed me the book back and, eyes narrowing, asked a question that anyone who takes pride in a place would ask. "Why," he said evenly, "would anyone do that?" I could only muster a traditional answer: that the Region hadn't *seemed* like Indiana. Somehow I had also managed to overlook Purdue, with thirty-six thousand students and a rich basketball tradition.

Mostly, though, I just wanted to go back and do it again. Winter after winter, friends refused to let me lose touch with Indiana, sending artifacts from Hoosierland to my home in Maine. They sent a video of the Damon Bailey Game, in which forty-one thousand fans assembled in a domed football stadium to see a high school basketball game which followed an Olympian script. They sent me the Glenn Robinson vs. Alan Henderson game, and a clipping about girls' game played on a week night between Lake Central and East Chicago Roosevelt high schools which had attracted enough fans to fill a giant gym to the rafters. They sent an editorial cartoon which showed Stephanie White, described as the most exciting girl player in Indiana history, dragging the girls' game up a tall mountain entitled "Recognition." I couldn't stay away any longer.

And so in 1994 I went back to see for myself how the game, and Indiana with it, has changed in a decade. The verdict: still crazy after ten more years, though the symptoms are slightly different. As Garry Donna, longtime publisher of *Hoosier Basketball* magazine, put it, "If you looked at Indiana basketball as a pie, the whole pie might be even bigger now than it used to be, but the pieces would be different. The college and pro slices would be bigger, and the girls' and women's pieces would be too. There are fewer high schools now, but the boys' high school piece would still be big, and bigger than anywhere else. And of course, TV means more all the time."

Postcards from an obsession, 1994:

- In a little town south of Bloomington, I found a stonecutter chiselling the image of Damon Bailey into a carefully-selected slab of limestone, for permanent display in a rise in the center of town.

- After a game in West Lebanon, near Lafayette, sports-writers were encouraged to wait to interview Seeger High star Stephanie White until she had finished signing autographs for children. It took nearly a half hour.

- In Indianapolis, a company was distributing cream-and-crimson caskets for IU fans who could not contemplate an afterlife without the Hoosiers.

- The Indiana Pacers, all but dead since the 1960s, were now a runaway success. Bobby "Slick" Leonard, the two-fisted coach of the Pacers in their Dodge City Days, had become the radio voice of the team. His phrase "Boom, Baby!" — used to mark a three-point goal — had become so popular that he had applied for a trademark for the phrase.

- Bob Knight had become a living billboard for a vast product line from sweaters to furniture. One entrepreneur near Fort Wayne had developed a porcelain doll in Knight's likeness which was moving briskly at more than five hundred dollars per icon. (Bumper sticker on I-65: "Will Rogers Never Met Bob Knight.")

- In Gary, Glenn Robinson had used the first installment of his new wealth to set up a different kind of basketball camp, not a meat market for college scouts, but a place of instruction, free to those who couldn't afford it.

- Gene Keady, now the coach of two consecutive Big Ten champions, was beginning to crawl out from beneath the long shadow of Assembly Hall. (Banner at a Purdue game at Mackey: "Gene 3:16.")

Some things hadn't changed at all: home games still brought multitudes to the Wigwam in Anderson. The martyrs who select the Indiana All-Star teams were still receiving vicious mail (and faxes, and e-mail now), and for all the same old reasons, mainly centering around geography and race. The patterns and rhythms of the game were still a living part of any Hoosier community that had a hot team or a star player. Diehard fans throughout the state were still sizing up new players as if they were pups from a litter, observing that their feet were big or remembering that the father was fast or the mother played volleyball. Over beers at night and coffee in the morning, people were still convincing each other that the sophomore center still had one growth spurt left. It's just that now they were more likely than before to be talking about a girl.

Here, then, is the evolving story of the basketball life of Indiana as it begins its second century, at a moment when the known universe is being observed through a telescope conceived by an ex-New Albany High School basketball coach named Walter Hubbel, and when an ex-Huntingburg High wannabe named Dan Quayle ("Too slow, nice shot, very competitive," said the man who cut him) has made news by dropping out of Presidential contention, and when the late night airwaves feature David Letterman, a junior high non-starter from Broad Ripple whose florist father donated the school scoreboard.

Ever since 1893, when a Presbyterian minister taught the people of Crawfordsville to throw a ball into a feed sack which hung from a forged iron hoop, Indiana has lived and breathed basketball in the winter. This is the story of a hundred years of games and teams and heroes and villains and goats and families and towns and neighborhoods that have influenced every aspect of life in Indiana.

Before plunging, the reader has a right to know — or to be reminded — what the word "Hoosier" means. Unfortunately, the exact meaning is lost to the ages. James Whitcomb Riley, canonized as "the Hoosier poet," was often asked by nonresidents to define the word and gave what may be the most recent definition. "The early settlers were vicious fighters," Riley explained to one scribbling interviewer, "and they not only gouged and scratched, but frequently bit off noses and ears. This was so ordinary an affair that a settler coming into a barroom on a morning after a fight, and seeing an ear on the floor, would merely push it aside with his foot and carelessly ask, 'Who's y' ear?' "

For our purposes, a Hoosier is one who is drawn toward the home gym or the playground and the month of March like the tides to a full moon. As James Naismith, the inventor of basketball, put it not long before he died in 1939, "Basketball really had its origin in Indiana, which remains today the center of the sport." More than a half century later, it still is. This is the continuing story of basketball's grass roots.

Phillip Hoose
July, 1995

Stoneworkers lovingly lower into place a monument to Heltonville's favorite son. (A. J. Mast)

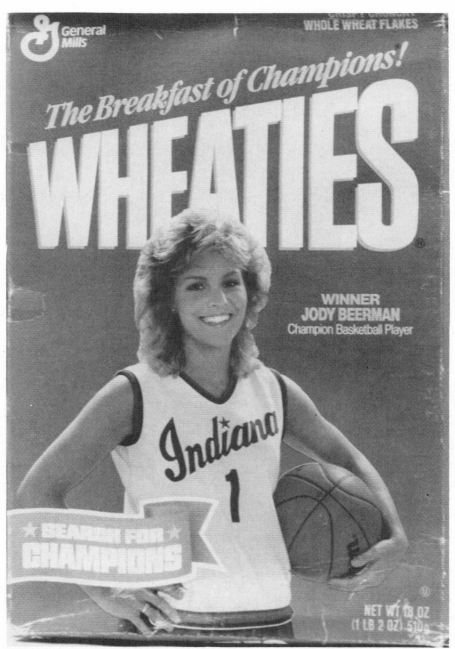

Jody Beerman, Miss Basketball, 1983. "Turns out basketball's real big out there," said a Wheaties spokesperson. (Courtesy Indiana Basketball Hall of Fame)

The former Monon Avenue, midtown French Lick. (Tom Roach)

Welcome to Loogootee. (Phillip M. Hoose)

God, Country, and IU, from a front yard in New Castle. (Phillip M. Hoose)

When you die, that's in your obit, that you were an Indiana All-Star. And it's usually in the lead paragraph.

—Don Bates, former All-Star Director. (Courtesy *The Indianapolis Star*)

Bob Knight and Gene Keady —
The Man in the Red Sweater
and the Florist's Son

The Man in the Red Sweater

Here are some things you can learn about Bob Knight during
the course of a few winter days in Indiana: Bob Knight is deep.
Bob Knight reads a lot, mainly history. He's happier now with his
second wife; she was a coach, too. He's mellowed. Bob Knight ties
his own flies. He's his own man. He didn't mean to kick Patrick —
he was aiming for the boy's chair. He didn't want to throw the
chair against Purdue but the refs left him no choice. He wasn't
really trying to head-butt Sherron Wilkerson. Calbert Cheaney
went along with the whip. Coach Knight donates fortunes to char-
ity but doesn't tell anyone. He visits sick people and sometimes
returns the calls of ordinary citizens. He's a perfectionist; impa-
tience drives him over the edge. He didn't mean the thing about
rape — he just said that to get a rise out of Connie Chung. He's
really more a teacher than a coach. He doesn't cheat. Bob Knight
is one honest SOB. He teaches the Game of Life. Each of his players graduates from IU as a Quality Person who then teaches it to
ten more. It's like Amway; the world gets better that way. The
media is out to get him.

Bob Knight, the head coach of Indiana University's men's basketball team is the most famous, most obsessively discussed, and
controversial individual in Indiana, and a national entertainment
figure as well. Knight is constantly on television in Indiana. The
residents of up to 40 per cent of all Hoosier households hunker

down to watch the IU Hoosiers play ordinary Big Ten games, contests in which Knight takes center stage and holds it like an Olivier. A really big IU game, like the IU-Purdue game of February, 1994, pulls in more viewers than the NCAA championship game, more than most telecasts of the Olympic Games and nearly as many as the Super Bowl.

His golf show, co-hosted with a local pro, often outdraws national tournaments in Indiana. His coaches' show is a long-running hit. Bars and AM morning shows hum with Bob Knight jokes ("There were these three guys, see, and one of 'em had on a red sweater . . . "; "A priest, a rabbi, and the IU basketball coach decide to play golf . . . ") Indiana newspapers faithfully report episodes of Knight's contacts with ordinary citizens, ranging from surprise visits to ailing fans to checks to charities that show up unexpectedly, to his cautionary letters to school children whose grades have dropped (Knight to Timmy H.: "Work at becoming as good a student as possible. You will be amazed at how this will help you as a basketball player.") Fans debate what to call him in front of their friends: "Bobby," the standard moniker of his early, or plaid jacket period, now seems adolescent. "Coach Knight" seems fawning. "Knight" is somehow impossible. These days it's "Bob." Bob is solid. American. Like a Buick. Which he used to endorse.

Knight's Elvis-like stature in Indiana has made him a wealthy man. His ten-month, $132,420 coaching salary is the bare tip of an income which includes sold-out basketball camps, motivational speeches to business leaders at $20,000 per oration, and his personal endorsement of a long line of local and national products. Everyone knows that Knight's shoes are now by Converse — after his turbulent Adidas period — and that his soft drink is Coke, his pizza Domino's, and his supermarket Marsh. Couches and end tables are by Bimrose Furniture in Ellettsville. Transportation is provided by Royal Chevrolet and Mazda.

Probably the most recognizable single article of clothing from Gary to Evansville is the Bob Knight Sweater. Each holiday hundreds of Hoosier men unwrap what its manufacturer, the Starter Corporation, calls "Bob Knight's Bench Pique." It is a red knit sweater with a crew neck, like the one Knight wears on TV during IU games. Available in solid red or emblazoned with a white jagged line, it retails for about seventy dollars. Men remove it from the box, struggle into it, and head straight for a mirror, tugging at the sleeves, as he does, to lift them about a quarter of the way up the forearm to expose, in his case, a wristwatch with a metal band.

Knight's fame even spawns cottage industries. Kendallville, Indiana, businessman Tom Alberts has put out a line of porcelain dolls of Knight barking out a command in his Starter sweater and Converse shoes. The doll comes with a moveable body, stuffed by clients at the Noble County Association for Retarded Citizens. The price: $545. The limited-edition item is moving rapidly. "I saw how popular IU and Bob Knight things were and realized that there had never been a porcelain doll . . . ," Alberts explained.

How did it get this way? Other Indiana University coaches have been popular, but it's hard to imagine a Branch McCracken doll or a Lou Watson sweater. Knight came to Bloomington in 1971 after coaching at West Point. He was already well-known to Big Ten fans, having been a reserve on three great Ohio State teams in the early sixties. He also came with a diva's ego and a pure gift for the outrageous, but few knew that. In his autobiography, John Havilcek reminisced about evenings at the movies with Bobby Knight in the Ohio State days: "He would eat peanuts and scatter the shells for about ten rows every direction. Then he would get up and crunch them while he stretched. Sometimes people would move about ten or twelve rows away. You'd be sitting there and right in the middle of the movie he'd yell, 'Hey John!' . . . He had no inhibitions."

Knight arrived in Bloomington with a basketball blueprint that ran directly against IU's high-scoring, fast-breaking basketball identity. Win or lose, IU fans were usually chanting "we want a hundred" at the end of the game. Point-volume was a source of statewide pride.

Knight gave them a team of probing, patient opportunists, content to pass the ball until they could create a likely shot. IU lost their first four conference games, and the crowds were practically riotous. "I saw the first conference game he ever coached at Indiana," the late IHSAA Commissioner Phil Eskew recalled. "Some

Kendallville businessman Tom Alberts surrounded by Bob Knight dolls. May they never come to life in the night. (*The News-Sentinel*, Fort Wayne, IN)

guy stood up behind me and said, 'Can't we just have *one* fast break?' At the end of one game, with the score 59–40, fans started chanting, 'We want a hundred.' "

And then Knight turned it around. Indiana won nine of its last ten games and went to the National Invitational Tournament. In 1975 and 1976, Knight built beautiful teams, consisting of strong individuals who shared a common vision of excellence, his vision. Both went undefeated until the NCAA tourney and one won the national championship.

The teams and their fiery coach caught the state's imagination. He brought a sense of military theater to each game. With Bobby Knight in command, Illinois actually *did* seem to be invading Assembly Hall. They may be scheduled for 7:30 P.M., but they could come at dawn, and to be caught unprepared was sheer folly. He demanded devotion to duty from everyone involved in the campaign, right down to the cheerleaders who were occasionally summoned to his office and dressed down for not modelling more enthusiasm.

He was toughest of all on his players, sometimes pulling them to the sidelines by their jerseys, berating them in public, benching them in disgust the instant they made a mistake. He was often compared to Patton, who dared to strike his soldiers, but in some ways he was more like MacArthur, a man who seemed to absorb the spotlight. Knight's plaid jacket and later his red sweater became, like MacArthur's muffler and riding crop, fashion statements, part of the costume of warfare and the coach, more than the players, became the show. As IU won, bigger and bigger games, and then championship games, Knight was transformed into something more than a basketball coach to those who turned on the TV set. He was offering a belief system as well as a team. In an age of shifting values and kids who didn't listen, here was an authority figure. Bob Knight believed in consequences.

For many, an IU game became soon became a referendum on discipline, a debate on corporal punishment between bleeding hearts and hard-liners. "I'd never let *my* kid play for Bob Knight," someone would declare when Knight blistered a player, his body tense with rage, his face an inch or so from the boy's ear. "Bob Knight wouldn't *want* your kid," came the stock reply.

Indiana University men's coach Bob Knight pulls DelRay Brooks to the sideline for instruction. After courting Brooks, Knight proclaimed him too slow afoot and allowed him to transfer to Providence in 1985, where he became a key player on a final four team. (John Terhune)

There were off-court explosions in the early years. In 1979 Knight was arrested for assaulting a Puerto Rican police officer and was led from the floor in handcuffs. Unflattering remarks about Puerto Rico added fuel to the fire. Two years later Knight made national news by stuffing an antagonist into a garbage can one evening in a restaurant.

The combination of the great teams and the Knight's erratic behavior made for great entertainment. Television revenue to IU soared from two thousand a game to eighteen thousand a game in Knight's first decade on the job. Watching an IU game was like watching the Indianapolis 500: get up for a beer and you might miss a spin. Cameras focused obsessively on Knight, constantly alert for a violent or theatrical reaction to an official's call or a close-up of a player's face as Knight chewed him out.

Knight became the State Dad in Indiana's favorite winter television series. Assistant coaches were familiar bit players, devoted men who often glanced up at Knight as he brooded and stormed in front of the players. In thirty or so episodes Knight gave viewers an ordered world, a setting that looked like the early sixties in which white players often wore crewcuts and black players — of which there were fewer than on most Big Ten squads — kept their hair short. There was no gloating after dunks, no messages cut into hair, no long trunks, not even names on the back of the IU uniforms. These kids knew how to behave.

The supernova, the explosion that caused the first serious examination of means and ends as they applied to Bob Knight came in a game against arch-rival Purdue in Bloomington near the end of the 1984 season. Five minutes into the contest, his team behind 11–6, Knight became angered when an official named London Bradley called a foul on an Indiana player in a scramble for a loose ball. Knight ranted at Bradley and was assessed a technical foul. Knight then picked up his chair and lofted it out over the court, where Purdue guard Steve Reid was preparing to shoot the technical. Reid froze like a deer caught in headlights as the chair sailed by. "I was going up to the free-throw line and a chair went by," he said. "I didn't know what to do."

Neither did anyone else. After the chair came crashing down Knight continued to rail and was ejected from the game. The mood got uglier as the game progressed, with fans showering coins and other debris at the officials. Purdue coach Gene Keady's wife Pat was clipped in the eye by a coin and required medical attention. The state was apoplectic. Lapsed IU fans telephoned late night talk shows to declare their intention to defect to Purdue. Hard-liners closed rank behind Knight. A few fans who flew IU flags from their home flagpoles tied chairs to the top as a gesture of defiance. Supporters and detractors flooded the newspapers with letters. "Like General Patton in World War II, Knight knows how to shape boys into men and naturally this bothers all the people who would like men to be wimps and sissies," wrote a woman to *The Indianapolis Star*. "They would prefer someone more like Alan Alda, who is sensitive, caring, supporting and vulnerable. Sorry, wimps."

Sensing a heroic opportunity, a legislator from Elkhart announced that he would introduce a resolution in the Indiana House condemning Knight's conduct. A volley of hate mail from as far away as Texas sent him diving for cover.

Some fans, though, viewed the occasion as a long-needed opportunity for self-examination: to them the event was embarrassing. *The Indianapolis Star* writer John Shaughnessy put the question to his readership with uncommon directness. "Does it ever seem to you," he asked, "that we take Knight too seriously?"

In the winter of 1985–86, Knight let *Washington Post* sportswriter John Feinstein tag along with the Indiana team for a year. The book Feinstein wrote, entitled *A Season on the Brink,* was serialized in *Sports Illustrated*, reaching more than three million readers. The opening installment reported Knight's profanity-laced hazing of a player named Daryl Thomas. Now the entire nation was hooked. The book sold millions and remained on *The New York Times* best seller list for more than six months.

The book made Knight even more controversial in Indiana. Early in 1987 the IU faculty council, a body not known for combat readiness, passed a resolution aimed at Knight that declared, "athletes shall not be subjected to physically or verbally abusive, intimidating, coercive, humiliating or degrading behavior." The vote was 18–16, and ripped apart the council and, seemingly, the town of Bloomington. Faculty members identified as supporters of the resolution in the local paper received hate mail from Knight fans. One arrived home to find a dead cat on his porch. An economics professor named Elmus Wicker, after having had his tires slashed and his sleep interrupted by threatening callers, invited the police out to show him how to defend himself. "I had never received calls like these in all my life," he recalls.

Three years later, another faculty member went even further, with much the same result. Murray Sperber, an American Studies professor who joined the IU faculty the same year Knight arrived in Bloomington, dared to examine perhaps the central article of the IU faith, namely, that almost all of Bob Knight's basketball players graduate from IU. The graduation rate is used to justify Knight's tough love and to attract the parents of talented high school prospects. As Brenda Patterson, mother of current IU player Andre Patterson put it when asked by a *New York Times* reporter why her son chose IU, "The graduation rate was something like 90 percent . . . I mean, how bad can this man be?"

The IU Athletic Department calculates the rate as the percentage of "four-year seniors" who graduate. That way you come up with over 90 percent. But Sperber wanted to know how many had dropped out before they reached their fourth year. "By the time they had stuck it out to the fourth year it would be a miracle if they didn't graduate," he says. He looked over registrar's records and NCAA records of IU players in the decade of the 1980s and found that most players recruited by IU as freshmen had left school before their fourth year. In a book entitled *College Sports, Inc.: The Athletic Department vs. the University* Sperber wrote that "Only 42 percent of Bob Knight's 1980s basketball recruits have graduated from Indiana University (only 11 percent of his black recruits), and many of his players' grade point averages were in the C range, grades often earned in the easier courses in the university." Along these lines, *Sports Illustrated* reported in 1992 that only eight of the twenty-four black players who had entered IU as freshmen to play for Knight had received a diploma from IU.

Soon after publication of his book and newspaper coverage of his findings, Sperber found himself on the firing line. "My answering machine levitated in the air for awhile," Sperber recalls. "There were even death threats but the main response was denial. It amazed me that this myth meant so much to people personally. People didn't want to know the truth. They kept saying, 'Bob Knight graduates all his players.' Their main question was, 'Why are you disloyal to IU?' "

There have been some fine IU teams recently — including a Final Four squad in 1992, but no champions since IU beat Syracuse on Keith Smart's corner jumper with four seconds remaining in 1987. At one point after a rocky stretch during the 1994–95 season, Knight seemed to hint at retirement.

However, nothing has derailed the state's obsession for the IU team or its leader. And no amount of criticism or censure has kept Bob Knight from behaving as he pleases. In these post faculty-resolution years, Knight has head-butted one player, kicked (or kicked at — this being a matter of much discussion and careful interpretation) his son Patrick who played on three IU teams, and pretended to bullwhip Calbert Cheaney, a black player. Through it all, sales are up, ratings are steady, and more and more men pull on the Red Sweater.

Nationally, Knight continues to fascinate. ESPN's Dick Vitale, a gushy fan, has given Knight a new identity as "The General" (which of course gave rise to "The General's Store" in Bloomington). Not long ago Knight played himself in a Hollywood film. Today, a computer search of magazine articles about Bob Knight (the indexing company calls him "Bobby") brings up several dozen articles sorting into fourteen major topics. They range from "anecdotes, cartoons, satire, etc." through Knight's "conduct of life" to his "quotations," to the recreational aspects of Bob Knight and all the way to Bob Knight's "social policy."

Early in 1994 an entrepreneur came up with the most enduring commercial idea of all. For years there have been funerals in which the deceased have been buried in IU sweaters or caps, and in which the entire parlor has been decked out in cream and crim-

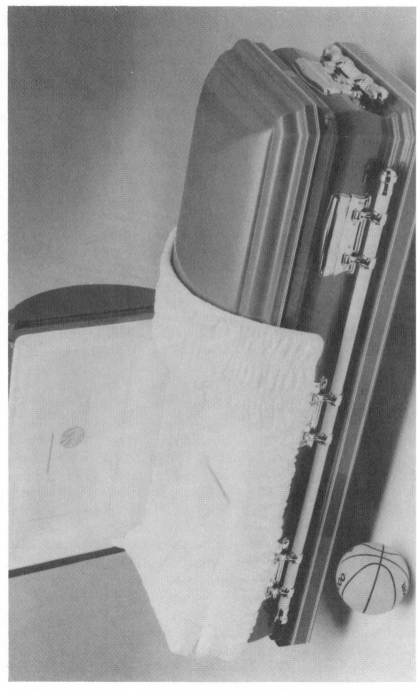

A postseason option for IU fans. At first the model had the word "Hoosiers" embroidered into the lid, but IU officials objected. The casket remains cream and crimson, IU colors. (Courtesy Oak Grove International)

son. But the problem remains: Bob Knight will be gone some day, one way or another. Will we be ready? Oak Grove International, a casket maker out of Manistee, Michigan, has found the answer. They developed a crimson-colored, fiberglass casket with a cream velvet interior. Inset into the lid is a panel depicting, in careful hand-stitching, a basketball dropping gently through an orange hoop. Nothing but net when life's buzzer sounds. Beside the ball is the simple, all-encompassing word, "Indiana." (Early models also had the word "Hoosiers," but IU officials objected). The price: $3,050.

Jerry Ellenwood, Director of the Day Mortuary in Bloomington, said his parlor sold five in the first months. He recalls the children of one family who came in to look through the casket catalog with him when it became clear that their mother had little time remaining. They paged past the Statue of the Praying Hands, past the Falling Leaves, past Old Glory, until they saw it, and pointed to the photo. "One child said, 'Mother just loved IU and Bobby Knight,' " recalls Ellenwood. "She thought that casket provided the perfect atmosphere for her mother to rest."

The Florist's Son

There is a certain color that Purdue coach Gene Keady turns when he is really worked up that makes you want to get up and adjust your set. It doesn't look like a shade that occurs in nature. "I know what you, mean," says Keady from his office at Guy Mackey Arena. "It's reddish, isn't it?" Yes, it is, sort of. Not crimson or scarlet, but more a burnished, prairie color. As Keady storms along his few feet of the sideline at Mackey, raging at an official, he appears as a thickset, brutal force, his flushed face set in a scowl, a thick cord of a vein in his neck clearly visible, the vents of his suit coat splaying out behind him; a boiler ready to explode.

Until her death a few years ago Keady's mother would call after the games, which she would watch on a satellite dish at a Pizza Hut in central Kansas. "Don't you talk that way," she would warn her son. "I can read your lips, and you weren't taught that way. Just knock it off."

And he's not that way, either. He is a broad, weathered-looking man with a self-deprecating, Irish sense of humor. He is common in the way of people who grew up on land, a man who learned to do things for himself. When a visitor runs out of batteries for his tape recorder, Gene Keady rummages through his desk drawer and, finding none, arranges his heavy frame on a tiny footstool near an electrical outlet. He remains that way for over an hour. He offers coffee, then walks past a secretary to retrieve it and pour it himself. When his guest spills it, he goes to the washroom, comes back with a wad of paper towels and gets down and starts to clean.

"Am I schizophrenic?" he laughs. "That's a good question. I know what you're talking about. I look at films of the game later and I think, How can I look that mean? I'm happy and I like coaching and I'm not thinking that stuff. I'm not out of control, I know what I'm doing. I'm not trying to bait referees, it's just that I know my players better than they do. Anyway, last year I tried to make a different image for myself. I tried to sit down more. To smile more. The way I was acting may have turned referees off. Maybe we were losing fans. My wife noticed a change. Could you tell?"

Purdue University is a massive campus with thirty-six thousand students set in the pancake-flat glacial till of West Lafayette, about midway between Indianapolis and Chicago. It is best known as an engineering and agricultural school, a place that produces the nerds with pocket protectors who will end up ruling cyberspace. Twenty astronauts are Purdue grads, including the first and latest humans to visit the moon. Neil Armstrong went to Purdue. Dr. Albert Kinsey, the sex researcher, went to IU. To many in Indiana, that about sums it up.

When Bob Knight arrived at IU there was something like parity between IU and Purdue. Purdue was coming off Rick Mount's enormous popularity and a 1969 Final Four appearance. IU was floundering. The statewide audience was split roughly right down U.S. 40, with fans to the south rooting for IU and those to the north for Purdue. But Knight, his national championships, and his camera-absorbing antics have changed much of that. Now

Purdue's television ratings are only about a third of IU's state-wide, and their fan stronghold is generally localized in the north-west quadrant of Indiana.

Still, Purdue has a frenzied local following and often turns out impressive teams. All Purdue games are televised statewide and no sports program in Indiana did better in 1994 than Purdue's local broadcasts. Fans, dressed in gold and black, wedge themselves into 14,123-seat Mackey Arena, a deafening room which has been sold out for the past three seasons.

Living in the shadow of IU and surrounded by huge and glamorous basketball programs in Michigan, Ohio, and Illinois, Keady has ("quietly," as the Purdue media guide puts it) managed to win or share five Big Ten titles in fifteen years as head coach at Purdue, and has carried the Boilermakers to eleven NCAA tourneys, twice reaching the final eight.

Gene Keady, fifty-eight, arrived in West Lafayette after twenty-five years on coaching's back roads. "I have to laugh when I read about rich coaches," he says. "I went twenty years before I made more than fifteen thousand. I coached ten years at Purdue before we paid off our debts."

Keady grew up in the farm community of Larned, Kansas, the son of a florist who worked in the same greenhouse for fifty-five years, and a mother who worked at a five-and-ten-cent store. His parents were his heroes. He remembers once talking back to his father, who, it turned out, had done a fair amount of amateur boxing. "Bam, bam. It was all over. I learned a major life lesson . . . I learned this guy has quick hands. Later he taught me to run from a fight, which he wouldn't have done."

Keady starred as a football quarterback at Garden City Junior College, then played at Kansas State. He was drafted by the Pittsburgh Steelers, but discovered that the Steelers' quarterback roster included Lin Dawson, Bobby Layne, Jack Kemp, and Earl Morral — perhaps the greatest collection of quarterbacks ever assembled on one football team. The Steelers had cut Johnny Unitas the year before. Sensibly, Keady announced that he was a pass receiver. A knee injury put an end to his NFL dreams.

He went home and coached high school basketball for seven years, then coached hoops at Hutchinson (Kansas) Junior College, winning six league titles in eight years. "Anything I know about

Purdue's Gene Keady, in a benign moment at Mackey arena. (Courtesy Purdue University)

time management I learned at Hutch," Keady says. "Coaches did everything in those days: teach, coach, recruit, scout. I was the head basketball coach and the assistant football coach. I taught officiating. I taught twenty-four hours of biology. I got up and kicked my players out of bed and made them go to class. It was wonderful."

Keady left for a job as an assistant coach at the University of Arkansas where he recruited, among other stars, the great Sidney Moncrief. Sometimes the trail led through Indiana, and Keady was always amazed by the sheer capital investment in the game. "I'd fly into Indianapolis, rent a car and go out to see my recruits wherever they were playing. You'd walk into these huge gyms, major college-sized gyms, like New Castle and Anderson. Unbelievable. You came to understand that it's just different here."

After two years as a head coach at Western Kentucky, Keady applied for the head coaching job at Purdue. Having grown up in the Midwest, Keady was well aware of Purdue's formidable basketball tradition. He had heard stories of Ward "Piggy" Lambert, who coached Purdue to glory between 1917 and 1945, and who is generally regarded as the father of fast-break basketball. Keady had seen Purdue's only appearance in the NCAA final game in 1969, when a squad built around the jump shooting of Rick Mount was taken apart by a UCLA team coached by ex-Purdue star John Wooden.

Keady applied for and was offered the head coaching job at Purdue, but people he respected kept telling him he would be crazy to take it. "Al McGuire said, 'You'll never reach the pinnacle at Purdue. You can't recruit there, you're surrounded by bigger programs, and the academics at Purdue are too tough. There are no side doors for academic underachievers. Don't do it.' I listened but finally I just did what I wanted to and took it."

Starting with a mixture of holdovers and his own recruits, Keady's first Purdue team finished 21–11, fourth in the Big Ten and third in the National Invitational Tournament. It was a pleasant surprise for Purdue fans and a year of education for Keady. A first rude shock was that he had to play back seat to IU in scheduling games on the statewide television network. "You gotta learn about this league," he says. "The travel. The crowd. It's not who you're playing next, it's what happened to them the game before. Most games are gonna be close, three-pointers. You gotta be ready, with something organized, at the last. Flying helped us. We took busses the first couple years. Then we got a plane. Indiana has their own plane and I thought that helped them. They were fresher at the end of the season. We started to charter planes. When we won the league in '84 I thought that was a big factor."

He had to learn the recruiting ropes, too. "It is hard for you to pull a player out of southern or central Indiana," says Keady. "Too many IU fans around there. They might kill the player. Same with Kentucky. It's a waste of money to recruit in Louisville, unless the player's uncle is a Purdue grad. A great player in Kentucky? No way."

But Purdue has made do, finding players in Chicago and Michigan, and as far away as California, and stockpiling them in New England prep schools where they learn to pass the SAT. There has been regular success in the Calumet Region of Indiana, for which the Purdue staff could write a detailed travel guide. "I remember one Sunday afternoon [assistant coach] Frank Kendrick and I went up there on a recruiting trip," Keady recalls. "We were at 185th Street and 94. We had to go to the bathroom and we go into this really bad pool hall. We were thinking we'd better leave our watches in the car. But it was amazing . . . everyone in the place knew me. I was safer there than in some parts of Lafayette."

The biggest catch of all from Gary was Glenn Robinson, the 1993–94 college player of the year. Kendrick, a former Purdue All-American, struck up a special relationship with Robinson during a summer basketball camp on the Purdue campus in the summer after Robinson's sophomore year. Still in shape from playing professionally in Europe, Kendrick played Robinson one-one-one before sessions began in the morning. "We'd play," recalls Kendrick, "and I'd beat him, and the counselors would be whistling that it was time to move on to another station and he'd say, 'No, no, wait, we gotta play again.' "

The next fall college recruiters followed Glenn Robinson wherever he played. Kendrick went too, but he refused to let Robinson see him as just another salesman. He wanted to be recognized as the player Glenn Robinson hadn't beaten. "One night Gary Roosevelt — Glenn's school — played Gary Wirt at Wirt High," recalls

Kendrick. "I got there just in time for the tip-off. I peeked in the gym and I could see that everybody was there: Indiana, Illinois, Georgetown, Louisville, Minnesota, Wisconsin, Ohio State — everybody. I wanted to stand out from all the others for Glenn, so I stood outside and waited until just before tip-off to walk through the door. Then he caught sight of me. I winked at him and he winked back. Then I took my seat, right behind the Roosevelt bench, not with the other college coaches. He finally beat me the summer after he signed. How did he react? He wanted to play me again."

Until last season, Keady's ability to develop a team as a season progresses had been all but unexamined by national pundits. Keady, and too often Purdue itself, had been dismissed as poor cousins to Knight and IU. Purdue's Big Ten championship and Final Eight appearance in 1993–94 were attributed mainly to Glenn Robinson's greatness. But last season's conference championship, with Robinson gone and point guard Matt Waddell injured much of the year, raised eyebrows and won Keady National Coach-of-the-Year honors. "No one gets a team ready for a game any better than Gene Keady," Dick Vitale gushed during one midseason telecast. "His practices are so impressive, so thorough."

Keady is always hustling for a new wrinkle that will give Purdue a competitive edge. After his only losing season in 1988–89, he flew to Las Vegas and asked Jerry Tarkanian, the acknowledged master, how to develop three-point shooters. "Tark really changed my philosophy. We had been fast-breaking, but only for two-point shots. Tark showed me how to get three, to work our legs harder and get our hands ready. And so much of it is psychological. Tark just tells the kids, 'Don't worry, you'll make the next one.' It got me back to the way I was in junior college. To put money in your program you gotta understand you're in the entertainment business. We get greedy now. We go for three."

In Indiana comparisons between Keady and Knight are constant. The IU and Purdue programs are similar in many ways. Both are almost always competitive in Big Ten play and both almost always make the NCAA tournament. Both graduate about the same percentage of seniors who reach the fourth year and in

Glenn Robinson scores with punctuation for the Boilermakers. (Courtesy Purdue University)

both programs, many players do not reach the fourth year. Players take roughly the same kinds of courses and end up doing about the same things after graduation, most remaining involved in basketball in some way or going into business.

And at first blush the men themselves seem similar. Both are intense, profane, theatrical on the sideline, and utterly competitive. But there are differences. While Keady's temper detonates throughout a game, and while sometimes he flings his coat and exhorts the fans at Mackey and berates the officials, he manages to keep his hands, feet, and forehead to himself. While Knight plants himself at center stage and markets the IU program around his persona as a commander — "a builder of men," as the IU media guide puts it — Keady sometimes seems almost embarrassed to be attracting so much attention. "I think the spotlight is too much on coaches anymore," Keady says. "It's the players that the fans come to see."

Keady prides himself not as a theoretician, but as a community builder, a "player's coach" who solicits the input of his players. "We have a rule here, that kids must participate in team meetings. I like for my players to have a say in things. If I don't like it I'll tell 'em to shut up, and if it's good we'll put it in. They have to do it right, but it's not about punishment. It's never personal. I don't carry grudges. I don't believe destroying a kid's confidence is the answer."

Perhaps Keady's greatest accomplishment is to survive and prosper in the same jungle with Knight. Like Knight, Gene Keady has an official shoe and an official pizza and a camp and a coaches' TV show, but unlike Knight, Keady has not achieved international fame as an entertainment figure. And outside of West Lafayette, perhaps, there is no Gene Keady cult of personality.

John Feinstein, during his year with Knight and IU, described the relationship with Keady as "civil." Bob Collins, former sports editor of *The Indianapolis Star*, remembers calling Keady the day after one of Knight's explosions. "I forget which one it was, it might have been the chair," says Collins. "Anyway, before I could even ask him anything Keady says, 'You know, every day I stand in front of the mirror and thank God for Bob Knight.' I said, 'Why?' He said, ' 'Cause if it wasn't for him, I'd be known as the biggest prick in Indiana.' "

"Given our temperaments," sighs Keady, "it's probably about as good between us as it could be. It's a battle, and on game day it sometimes feels like hate, but I know if there were an illness in my family he'd help us. Same as I'd help him. He's asked me to go fishing a lot, but I haven't. Schedule problems, mainly."

A few minutes before a morning practice at Mackey, Gene Keady gestures vaguely south toward Bloomington. "In this state it doesn't seem like you've done much, with Knight sittin' over here, you know. And Myers at DePaul and Crum down at Louisville and Michigan up here. With all that around you, the feeling of success lasts about a week. It passes so easily. You feel like unless you won a national championship you haven't done your job. And if you won one, people would be saying, 'Knight's got four.' "

Still, despite the intense pressure to keep winning, Gene Keady, the florist's son, is sometimes able to smell the roses. He especially remembers a few games in Glenn Robinson's final year at Purdue, when Mackey was going nuts and every other fan seemed to be waving a "Big Dog" (Robinson's nickname) poster, and ESPN was there, that he looked out at it all and felt lucky and sad at once. He knew it had to end, and it was so much fun. "Most years it's, Damn I wish the season was over. But sometimes that year I'd stop and look at Glenn and think, Damn, he's a hell of a player."

And there are other tiny victories, known only to him. His mom is gone, but his dad is still watching, and he's just as tough a TV critic as she ever was. Lately, the reviews seem to be improving. "If my wife likes it, and if my dad doesn't call me, or if my sister doesn't relay what he says, then it's great. Then I'm happy. Who wouldn't be?"

The Education of Stephanie White

Two hours before tip-off everyone agreed that the line behind the school at Fountain Central High was at least two football fields long. People blew into their hands and passed along thermoses full of coffee and jiggled from foot to foot to stay warm. Moments after the doors mercifully opened, four thousand people surged into the gym and packed themselves into the bleachers, shoulder to shoulder, as high as the eye could see. The crowd was a thousand more than the fire marshal's posted order permitted. Of course the fire marshal was there, too, trying not to be noticed and praying nothing would happen.

They were there to see the most exciting player to hit the Wabash Valley in many years, a player who had scored sixty-six points just the game before, nearly outscoring the other team. Now that player needed twenty-three more points for the career state scoring record for girls. Everyone wanted to see her do it.

In 1994, her senior year at Seeger Memorial High, enrollment 399 students, Stephanie White was widely regarded as the best female high school player in America, and maybe the best in Indiana's history. The summer before she had been one of only three high school girls in the nation selected to play in the U.S. Olympics Festival, a proving ground for future Olympians. In the four years she had played for Seeger, the Patriots had lost only seven games. She was averaging forty points a game.

Male scouts and coaches spoke about her as if she were a new hybrid or a technological breakthrough, The Girl Who Played Like a Boy. "Stephanie White is the first girl that people have talked about like they did Damon Bailey or Glenn Robinson," says Garry Donna, for twenty-five years the publisher of *Hoosier Bas-*

ketball magazine. "You know, where they say, 'I've just got to see her play.' " At five-ten she could spring up and grab the rim. Her movements were strong and fluid. She was an amazingly creative passer and a tough, intuitive defender. To fans watching her for the first time, she was a fascinating study in contrasts: a pretty girl with high cheekbones and clear blue eyes and an easy smile which appeared most quickly around the young children who followed her everywhere. And yet the same girl played basketball with power and aggression, and a deep, intense focus. She was well-proportioned but not bulky; it was hard to see how she could be so strong, but she often simply overpowered her opponents. She did surprising things nearly every game, especially as a passer. To those who had worked to build the girls' game in Indiana, Stephanie White was the popularizer who was bound to come someday, the girl who would be so good that hard-core basketball fans throughout Indiana would become excited.

An hour before game time, Stephanie brushed back her shoulder-length black hair and tried to look into the bleachers through the crowd of children surrounding her. Behind her she could see her parents, both sets of grandparents, aunts, uncles, and cousins on both sides, half her congregation from church and many of the people she had grown up with. They were all looking at her. She told herself for the millionth time not to lose it in front of them all when she broke the record. Television crews bathed her in a circle of hot light. Already she was drenched. Two boys came up and raised their T-shirts to show that they had smeared her number twenty-two across their chests in Patriot-blue paint. A friend came down to show off her baby. Children lined up to offer her various objects to sign. One was a jacket. "Are you sure you're not gonna get in trouble?" Stephanie asked, hesitating with her marker. The girl nodded solemnly. Stephanie signed.

In the locker room a few minutes before the game she drew back her hair and fastened it with a red holder, pulled on her red-white-and-blue uniform and thought about her opponents, the Turkey Run Warriors. The main problem would be a set of twins who seemed to like to intimidate them by playing rough. A couple of years ago there had almost been a fight outside the locker room

Stephanie White is the first girl player I ever heard men say, 'I gotta see her play' about, the way they said 'I gotta see Damon Bailey play' or 'I gotta see Glenn Robinson play.' —Garry Donna, publisher of *Hoosier Basketball* magazine. (*The Indianapolis Star*)

door after the game. She was glad her sister Shanda was with her in the lineup. Shanda, she thought, would defend her against anything.

When at last the game started, Stephanie quickly reminded the fans why they had come. She gave them wraparound passes, feather-soft three-pointers, bone-crunching picks to spring teammates for open shots, powerful moves to the hoop. At one point Stephanie raced around a screen and ran right into one of the twins, who pushed her to the floor. She bounced up, smiling inches from the girl's face, and returned the favor sweetly a few plays later with a forearm shiver that sent the girl sprawling. Shanda advanced, ready to rumble. Stephanie told her to forget it and they ran back up the court. With several seconds remaining in the first half, Stephanie needed only one point to break the record. She sprinted from beneath the basket in a tight, counterclockwise arc, received a pass, and drove for the hoop. She was fouled hard as she rose to shoot. She stepped calmly to the free throw line, thinking about using her legs to support the shot, and tossed the ball softly through the iron ring for the record.

The game was halted. Kids streamed down from the upper reaches to be near her as everyone stood and cheered. One by one, her teammates gave her lingering embraces, taking time to say something special. She had given them big games and big crowds and adventures that they wouldn't have had without her. The other team's players were applauding, too, even the twins. Her game face was disintegrating and it was becoming impossible to hold the tears back. When Kelly Fink, her four-year teammate, gave her the ball to keep, she took it into the stands and handed it to her red-eyed parents, who themselves were trying to remain composed as television cameras closed in. "I love you guys," she whispered, embracing first her mother, then her father. "It made me feel so good," Kevin White said later. "We've been so busy headed toward goals for so long. 'I love you' are words we haven't stopped to say enough to each other."

∞ ∞ ∞

From the early years it was clear to Kevin and Jennie White that there was something unusual about their firstborn. It wasn't so much that she loved to play ball games. Everyone loved to play in their family. Grandma Henry had been a basketball player in the six-girl days, and both Jenny and Kevin had been varsity athletes at Seeger. But Stephanie seemed driven to play. One evening when she was five, Kevin had hit her a milk crate full of balls after his baseball practice. She fielded them all and threw them all back and remained in position. He hit her another crate, and another. She was like one of the broomsticks in "The Sorcerer's Apprentice." She wouldn't stop, even when her father was worn down. It was hard to wear Kevin White out; he was only twenty-four.

Injury meant nothing to her. One day she broke her wrist playing basketball and was out playing soccer the next day. She explained that you didn't have to use your arms in soccer. By the time she was in second grade she was playing baseball with ten- and twelve-year-olds, then asking to be taxied straight to soccer. She often complained that her leg hurt, but she wouldn't rest. One evening Kevin and Jenny noticed that she was dragging the leg behind her as she ran, and seemed to be in some pain. They drove her straight to a bone specialist in Indianapolis, who diagnosed bone cancer. Kevin broke down in tears a few evenings later while rocking Stephanie on the porch. Stephanie was looking calmly up at him. "Don't worry Dad," she said, "I'll beat it." Luckily the problem turned out to be a stress fracture that had become badly infected from constant wear. The real struggle was getting her to rest it long enough to heal.

The closest town to the country acre on which the Whites live is West Lebanon, population nine hundred, one of a group of farming communities that straddle the Wabash River near the Indiana-Illinois line. Thirty-five miles south of West Lafayette, West Leb is in the heart of Purdue country.

For much of the century, when Indiana state basketball tourney time came around, West Lebanon High played in the sectional at Attica, a town a few miles upriver that had the biggest gym around. But in 1951, the citizens of Covington, the next biggest town, built a bigger gym and took Attica's home-court advantage away. They spent all winter to draft the blueprint in

Effray Harden's downtown barber shop and then, when warm weather came, they all went outside and built the gym together, as volunteers, on shifts after work and on weekends, the way you raise a barn or rebuild a church after a tornado. Unskilled laborers worked side by side with carpenters and glaziers and masons until finally the welders welded the baskets to the standards and the painters lined the floor. In the end it held thirty-two hundred people — four hundred more than Attica's gym.

West Lebanon High closed in 1959 as part of a consolidation with Seeger High, but the old schoolhouse, which looks much like Hickory High in the movie *Hoosiers*, still stands. The West Leb gym has been open a night or two a week for people in the community to play basketball ever since. It is here, on Wednesday and Sunday nights, among men three and four times her age, that Stephanie White learned to play basketball.

At first she begged just to tag along with her father to watch, but soon she wormed her way into the full-court games. She joined a formidable lineup. Besides Kevin White, who works as a laborer in the shipping department at Quaker Oats, the regulars included Rex Cronk, a burly, bearded six-foot-one highway worker, Tom Miller, a football coach in Lafayette, Mike Miller, whom they called "The Hacker," and Doc Greenwood, the local veterinarian, a highly-competitive ex-Seeger High guard. And now a ponytailed girl in fourth grade.

She was appealing and tough. She wanted so badly to learn the game they loved that they began to enjoy teaching her. "They showed me how to set screens to get other people open and myself open," she recalls. "And they taught me to see things before they happen. To anticipate a cut before someone goes. They kept saying, 'Throw the ball *harder* — you're playing with guys, not girls.' They told me that over and over."

They soon learned that Stephanie White meant business. "The worst thing was when they tried to baby me. It made me so mad. Once when I was in fifth grade one of them blocked my shot clean and called a foul on himself. I wouldn't take the ball from him. I said, 'Look, I'm here to improve. How am I going to get any better this way? *Don't baby me!*' As I got older they grew out of it. They would pound me and not call a thing. That helped and I never got hurt."

The Education of Stephanie White became a community project. Improvement was continual, but from time to time she did startling things. One night when she was twelve she stole the ball twice in a row from Doc Greenwood and laid it in at her end. "Dammit, Steph," Greenwood had muttered, "The second time I was ready."

Jenny White contributed countless hours of outdoor labor. She had postponed a career as a teacher to stay home with her three daughters, each of whom had her own needs. Often, Stephanie's was rebounding. "Hundreds of times I've heard her say, 'Mom, will you go out and rebound for me while I shoot?'" Jenny says. "I usually go, except in really cold weather. I've learned to throw the ball back to her just the way she wants it."

Kevin White was the project manager. Though he had blown out his knee before he could play on the Seeger varsity basketball team, he had an analytical mind for the game and tried to learn enough to keep up with Stephanie's growing talent. Along the way he developed a few teaching techniques not normally found in videos and clinics, such as firing a shotgun in the air to try to distract her as she shot free throws.

For the first year or two Kevin was the only one at the gym who would push her down to get a rebound or charge into her. He said he did it to make her mentally tough, but she thought he was showing off in front of his friends. After a while she found a way to get him back. "I learned that if I didn't react it would make him mad. It got to the point where he just couldn't take it if I'd bounce back up and not say anything. I would just smile."

Stephanie developed ways to assert her strength without losing her temper. Her composure could be disarming. "Once we were playing out in the yard and I tried to intimidate her to see how tough she was," Kevin recalls. "She was working on dribbling with her left hand and she made the same mistake three times in a row, and I grabbed her basketball and kicked it as far as I could and started yelling at her. She kept eye contact with me and waited until I finished. She said, 'Are you finished?' I said 'Yeah.' She said, 'Don't *ever* kick my ball again. It's not a soccer ball. Take care of your equipment and it'll take care of you.' She intimidated me. I felt so low."

Kelly Fink first met Stephanie White, her future teammate at Seeger High, when they were in fifth grade in a YMCA basketball program that Kevin had organized. To the girls who lined up in shorts to learn a new game, Stephanie seemed almost like a different species. "I remember she was trying to teach us how to set picks," says Kelly. "We didn't know what she was talking about. We sort of stood there looking at her. She was so advanced, we didn't know what to think. We couldn't do it."

After their games, the girls were invited to dress up as cheerleaders for the fifth grade boys' games. All but four did. Kelly and two others who didn't want to just sat down and watched the boys. Never one to sit still, Stephanie developed her own alternative. "She dressed up in this warrior costume and ran in circles around the gym whooping," Kelly says. "She got everybody psyched up. People loved it."

By the time Stephanie reached adolescence, she had given herself to the game. When she tested the limits of her parents' authority, the issue usually involved basketball. She begged them to let her ride her motorcycle to an outdoor court in the dark so she could shoot at night. No, they said, pointing out that her bike had no headlight. Well, what if she taped a flashlight to her helmet? No. And then there was the night Stephanie announced that she could no longer do the dishes because, as she put it, dishwater "removes the natural oils in my hands." That, she explained would ruin her shooting touch and destroy her chances for a scholarship. Kevin bought her a pair of Playtex gloves.

Stephanie entered the Seeger High starting lineup in her second game as a freshman and immediately took over as point guard. Point guard meant passing, and passing was her love in life. After five years at the West Leb gym, she could now whip the ball through a blur of arms and legs and make it spin right up into a cutter's hands. She could throw a bounce pass diagonally the length of the court. Working alone, she had invented her own passes, with side spin and top spin and back spin. She could throw behind her back off the dribble with either hand and hit an *X* she had taped to the basement wall. Stephanie knew passes.

The only problem was that her new teammates couldn't catch them. "They were like bullets," says Kelly Fink, who joined Stephanie on the varsity as a freshman. "I thought I was strong, but my fingers were like butter with her sometimes. I worked one whole summer on being able to catch her passes. I started playing with the men, too. After their games I would have them throw me hard, long, baseball passes. I waited till Steph wasn't around because I didn't want her to know I couldn't catch them. I was determined to do it."

Stephanie became a team leader from the beginning. She led mostly because she was so good and also because she seemed to have been born with the software of the game in her head. Everything was possible to her; she saw cuts they could make, and recognized new defenses the instant they formed. Her teammates also soon discovered what the men at the West Leb gym had known for five years now: that Stephanie White was a perfectionist, impatient with mistakes — especially her own. Her dedication was contagious. With Stephanie averaging nearly twenty points per game, the Patriots lost only three times her freshman year and did not lose at all until the tourney the following year. In both seasons they advanced to the Lafayette semistate before they were defeated by much bigger schools.

She set her sights on a college scholarship and being named Indiana's "Miss Basketball" as a senior. While not wanting to discourage her, Kevin White wondered how college scouts would ever even hear of a girl from West Leb. The newspaper that covered Seeger's games was printed across the river in Illinois; few people in Indiana read it. And Bob Knight was not about to walk into Seeger's gym to make a girl famous the way he had done for Damon Bailey and Larry Bird and other boys.

Kevin and Jenny tried their best to help her realize her dreams. They paid to enroll her in a national Amateur Athletic Union tournament and drove to Texas one summer and Utah the next, so she could play in tournaments with girls from around the nation in games witnessed by college coaches. "That's what really woke us up to her talent," says Jenny. "We wondered whether she was just a good player from a small town but she was as good as anybody at those AAU camps. She won MVP in her age group one year." After her freshman year letters from colleges began to appear. Within two years there would be letters from more than two hundred schools.

By Stephanie's junior year, nearly every Seeger girls' game was a sellout, at home or on the road. It didn't matter that girls played their games on weeknights, or really where the games were. Hoosiers love a hot team, and this was a hot team. On game nights, hundreds of people from all over the valley piled into vans and cars and pickups and followed them wherever they went. The guys from the West Leb gym were among the Patriots' biggest fans. Rex Cronk signed on to drive the team bus and sat as near as possible to the court so Steph would be sure to hear him yell, "Throw it harder!" Ministers wove the Patriots into sermons and announcements, usually praising the way they carried themselves in a big game. "Sometimes our team even makes the Praise List at our church," says Kelly Fink. "That's the list of things to be thankful for, like recovering from surgery or a new baby."

It was about this time that the starters, particularly Stephanie, began to attract a permanent cloud of children who shadowed their every move and asked them to autograph whatever objects they could produce. Stephanie loved the chance to matter so much to younger kids, but it took a lot of time. The local McDonald's helped by sponsoring autograph nights when they could all just sit together and eat and sign things for an hour or so. Success brought the Patriot girls closer and closer. Often they played hide-and-seek in the locker room after practice. On weekends they drove around together, often in the Whites' blue Probe, to catch games around the valley.

It wasn't always easy for the boys to stomach all this. Stephanie's boyfriend was fine — he went to another school and played three sports himself — but Seeger High can be a fishbowl. Especially in Stephanie's junior year, when the girls were undefeated and the talk of the valley, an atmosphere of tension set in at school. "They'd say stuff to us when we walked down the hall, or in class," Stephanie recalls. "Stuff like, 'The girls' team isn't really that good.' They thought they were getting cheated because we got more recognition than they got. We thought the behavior was immature and we let it go. We'd worked for this. If they had worked that hard they would have got there too."

∞ ∞ ∞

In Stephanie's junior year the Patriots were eliminated from the tourney in the Lafayette semistate by Lake Central, a talented, well-coached, and nationally-ranked team from a school near Chicago. "They were intimidating," recalls Kelly Fink, who was by now a starter. "They were much bigger than us. The younger players were really scared." Seeger had led by six points with two minutes remaining, but then took hasty shots and lost the ball again and again. "It slipped away so fast at the end," says Stephanie. "I tried to get people together at the free throw line and say things, like 'let's be patient,' but it didn't work. It's frustrating to watch the tape of that game. I gave the ball up sometimes when I shouldn't have. I keep saying, 'Why did I do that, why didn't I just keep it?' I was silly."

The next year they dedicated themselves to getting through Lafayette and on to Indianapolis in the tourney. They were closer, stronger, and better balanced. Kelly and Stephanie had been playing together for four years, and by now she could catch any pass Stephanie could throw. Stephanie continued to improve on her own as well. Each morning she got up to lift weights before school with the swim team. She still played twice a week with the guys in the gym, and by now they had trouble keeping up with her. She startled them all again one evening by swatting one of Rex Cronk's shots out of bounds. It was the first time they could remember her having blocked a shot with such authority. "I was back on my heels," he explains. "Otherwise, she'd have never got it."

Perhaps best of all was that the White sisters seemed to have worked out their differences. Shanda, two years younger than Stephanie and herself a fine athlete, had the distinction of being the only Seeger Patriot whom Stephanie would criticize in front of the others. Shanda hated it. "She was always saying I wasn't trying hard enough, or that I didn't want it badly enough," Shanda says. "I would tell her, 'Steph, I just don't see all those cuts like you,' or 'I'm not fast enough to catch that pass,' but she wouldn't listen." At home, Shanda had found subtle ways to defend herself against hard-driving Stephanie, just as Stephanie had learned to overcome her father's mind games. The best was sweetly simple.

"We'd be playing outdoors," Shanda recalls, "and sometimes I'd just walk off the court and go in the house. That'd really get to her."

In the last ten games or so of the 1994–95 season, Shanda became a much more aggressive player, averaging about twenty points and ten rebounds per game. Shanda says she just grew into it, while Stephanie says she seemed to "want it more," but neither quarreled with the result. The new Shanda helped make Seeger a statewide power. During the regular season, Seeger was able to beat Lake Central in a close game on their court. Going into the tourney, the Seeger girls believed this was their year.

Practically speaking, it probably came to an end when, during the sectional final, Kelly Fink put all her weight on one knee as she was trying to save the ball from going out of bounds and felt something pop. She had torn her anterior cruciate ligament, and faced surgery. They braced her up so she could play the following week in the regionals, but she was more like a mummy than the old, athletic Kelly Fink.

The season died on a single play the next week at Lafayette, and, of course, against Lake Central. With Seeger behind by three points and less than a minute remaining, a Lake Central player missed a free throw. It clanged off the rim on the opposite side of the basket from Stephanie, and a Lake Central player knifed in and stole the rebound. That was it. Stephanie fouled out with fourteen seconds remaining in the game. She had scored thirty-nine points, collected fourteen rebounds, and stolen the ball six times against a team which had been ranked third nationally by *USA Today* at one point in the season. And this time, at least, Stephanie had gone down shooting, having scored seventeen of Seeger's last twenty points.

When she walked slowly off the court, despondent and exhausted, six thousand people rose to their feet as if jerked up by a puppeteer, in a final tribute to a great player. "That ovation was the one of the most thrilling moments I can remember in having watched girls' sports in Indiana," says Patricia Roy, a commissioner of the IHSAA, who has dedicated her career to the development of athletic opportunities for girls.

Nearly an hour later, Stephanie was the last player out of the locker room, a ball cap reading "Basketball is Life" pulled low over her reddened eyes, blaming herself for the loss. She answered reporters' questions until they left and children surged in to fill the vacuum. The kids seemed to make her feel better. She signed until even they were gone.

A few weeks before, a Lafayette editorial cartoonist had set out to draw what Stephanie White had come to mean to girls' basketball in Indiana. He found himself sketching a mountain, with two puzzled looking boys on the summit. Coming at them was a long chain of girls, being pulled toward the top by a ponytailed player with "Seeger" on her jersey. The mountain was called, "Recognition." "Come on . . . ," Stephanie White is saying. "We're getting there."

Kelly Fink, for one, is a believer. "I heard something I couldn't believe this morning," she said a few days after their season had ended but while the boys' tourney was still on. "One of the boys on the team comes up to Stephanie in class and says, 'Did you see our game last night?' Steph says 'yeah.' He says, 'Well they called me for charging into a guy and he didn't have his feet planted. Aren't you supposed to have your feet planted?' It was the first time I had ever heard a guy ask a girl to explain a rule."

Now Stephanie is on her way to Purdue, less than an hour from her home. Her father would have preferred Stanford, but Stephanie had her way as usual. This way the kids from Benton and Warren counties can still crowd up to her after the games, and her grandparents can see her, and so can her Seeger teammates who stay around the valley. The guys from the West Leb gym can elbow each other knowingly when she rifles seeing-eye passes toward women who know when to cut and whose fingers are as strong as theirs. Fans from several counties away are already buying season tickets to the Purdue women's season. A fine student, Stephanie will major in aeronautical engineering. Her bedroom walls are papered with photos of airplanes. Officially she says she may want to be a pilot. Secretly, maybe she'd like to be an astronaut.

But there are other goals first. She wants to coach. And even though she realized one of her dreams by being named Indiana's Miss Basketball, there's a little stretch of that mountain left to climb. "Yeah, there are still things to do," she says. "I want to change the girls' game so it's more like the guys' game. I want it to

Pulling the girls' game up the mountain of respect. (Dave Sattler, *The Journal and Courier*, Lafayette, IN)

be more exciting. I want to be a point guard who can rebound and shoot as well as pass. I want to put a little showtime in it. People like Judi Warren [the first Miss Basketball] started it and molded it. They helped it to become what it is now. We're just adding on to what they did. I want to be one of the people who will help it to be what it is in the future. I think I can."

Anderson, Indiana —
Basketball Town

If I had to take a disbeliever to just one place I'd take 'em to Anderson High School.

—Herb Schwomeyer, the Hoosier Hysteria Historian

Ron Porter's ear is mashed against a telephone receiver. "Turn it up, Earl!" he screams at the bartender twelve hundred miles away. Between the bedlam at the Olympia Lounge back in Anderson and the noise at the Astrodome, where the Boston Celtics are playing the Houston Rockets, Porter can barely hear.

It is February, 1982. Driven from Anderson by the collapsing auto industry, Porter and his roommate, Ron James, arrived in Houston six months before, looking for cars to sell. The summer and fall were all right, but now it is winter — although it doesn't feel like it — and back home the Indians are playing Highland in the Wigwam right now, right *now*, for the sectional title. As Larry Bird and Moses Malone go at it, Porter is thinking, My God, this is the first Indiana high school basketball tourney I've missed since 1954, when I was ten. As the game goes on, the monkey bears down harder and harder on Ron Porter's back.

By halftime, he can't take it any longer. He leaps from his seat, sprints up the stairs two at a time to a phone booth, jams some coins in a slot and dials Earl Alger at the Olympia Lounge. Alger knows exactly what to do, for he's known Ron Porter a long time, and he's had cases like this before. He places the receiver tight against a radio, turns up the broadcast, and goes back to mixing drinks. Porter never returns to his seat.

At that time Ron Porter was one of a diaspora of Anderson High School alumnae — "Old Indians," they are called — who depend on these long distance radio hookups each March during the tourney. They pile up monstrous phone bills when the Indians survive into the tourney's advanced rounds, as they often do.

But Porter, now fifty, knew he couldn't continue to live that way. Starting the next year, he set out to restructure his life so that his seasonal movements could match those of the Indians. Now, each year, usually around Christmas, Porter buys a low-mileage GM used car that he thinks he can sell for a profit in Indiana — something like a Buick Park Avenue — flings his bags into the spacious trunk, punches the cruise control, and settles back for a journey to Anderson. The distance is 1,025 miles, door-to-door. His best time is a radar detector-assisted sixteen hours.

As he motors eastward, he is only vaguely aware of the changing landscape or fluctuating sunlight. His heart is filled with the romance of Wigwam, his mind dancing with images of last year's underclassmen. By the time he bypasses Naptown on I-465 and swings north onto I-69, with Anderson less than an hour away, he is once again brimming with hope. If everyone plays up to his potential, if the center grew, if they study, if the freshmen jell and the new coach is as good as he's cracked up to be, this could be the year. In fact, it probably will be. No doubt, really. This time it will all be worth it. As the Redbud City fills his windshield, Ron Porter is certain that this year, when he returns to Houston after the tourney, it will be later than ever before.

Anderson, Indiana, is the hottest grass roots basketball town on earth. It is a tough, blue-collar city whose many auto workers live from contract to contract, a family town where drugs and weapons and crime have become increasingly worrisome, and a place where high school basketball is still celebrated on Fridays after sundown much as it was three-quarters of a century ago. Families have held season tickets to Anderson High School's games since the Great Depression. The townspeople have dressed up in red and green — Indians colors — to share popcorn and cheers and dances and songs that haven't changed for longer than anyone can remember. Many Andersonians can most easily mark the events of their lives by remembering what grade a star player was in at the time, or how the Indians did in the state tourney, year after year.

Travel around Indiana and ask coaches and players to name the hotbed of hotbeds, and you will hear a lot of replies like, "We have great fans, but those people in Anderson are crazy."

For much of its history Anderson, thirty miles northeast of Indianapolis, has been a one-industry town whose residents have cranked out headlights and windows and doors for several GM parts factories. With a large and stable labor force and low taxes, Anderson was briefly promoted as "the next Detroit." But in the late seventies and early eighties, when high interest rates and foreign competition crippled the U.S. auto industry, Anderson nearly collapsed.

Seemingly overnight, GM laid off five thousand workers, Nicholson File and Anaconda Wire moved out, and small-job shops dried up. By 1984 Anderson had the highest unemployment rate in the nation, over 22 percent. While welders and assembly workers stayed home, salespeople like Ron Porter took off for places like Houston, looking for showrooms with some action. Daybreak found the citizens of Anderson clinging to "The Game."

In that desolate winter the bleachers became pews. Anderson High School sold fifty-six hundred season tickets, nearly twice as many as the NBA's Indiana Pacers, and crosstown rivals Highland and Madison Heights each sold several thousand more. When all three schools had home games on the same night, one of every four Anderson residents was in a gym, sheltered in tradition. In the Wigwam, four generations huddled together in warmth and light and ritual. For a few hours the old problems — how to break Kokomo's press or contain Muncie Central's guards — left no room for brooding about the next paycheck.

Even jobless families could afford eighteen dollars for a season ticket, a pass to twelve winter evenings of blessed relief. "I mean, things were bad around here," said Tom McMahan, then mayor of Anderson. "I'm talking about real human needs. But basketball was the great stabilizing factor. I'm very serious about this: even if they didn't have a job, people could look forward to the games. When snowstorms closed down the city government and the library, I've seen people walk down the railroad track in two feet of snow to get to the gym."

Elders of the Tribe at the Wigwam. (Norm Johnston)

Anderson High had already outgrown two gyms by 1925, when the doors were opened to the original Wigwam. Anderson's children hoarded pennies to buy bonds to pay for the Wigwam, the gym which would at last be big enough for everyone. The bonds were hawked with the fervor of the World War I bond drives of the previous decade. Seating over five thousand, the Wigwam was to be the Gym To End All Gyms.

It was too small from the first whistle. The town lived with it until the winter of 1958, when it burned to the ground. Many believe it was finally torched by a citizen who could not get in one Friday night too many. A new Wigwam began to rise from the ashes almost at once.

Today, from across Lincoln Street, Anderson High School itself — a practical, red brick institution built in 1910 — looks something like a snail peeking out from beneath an oversized shell. The shell is, of course, the Wigwam. Best examined from the parking lot behind the school, the Wigwam is a mammoth mint-green cube with an Indian's head emblazoned on the side. Judging from the size of the building alone, it is plain to see that this time the townspeople got it right.

It is more a temple than a gym. Seating 8,998 fans — nine times the enrollment of Anderson High — the Wigwam cost over two million dollars even in 1960. Ron Hecklinski, who became head coach of the boys' basketball team in 1993, takes a few moments before practice to guide a visitor briskly through the Wigwam's weight rooms and video rooms, past an Olympic-sized pool and into the locker room for a glimpse of pantries full of new shoes and practice uniforms and bright orange balls.

Voices lower when one steps into the gym itself. This is the second largest high school gym in the United States, containing a mere 327 fewer seats than New Castle's Chrysler Fieldhouse, about thirty miles away. (Gym size is a raw nerve in this part of Indiana, one that New Castle fans skillfully tweak by stretching a wall-to-wall banner across their gym proclaiming it, "The largest and finest high school fieldhouse in the world.")

The eye rises to meet seemingly endless sections of brightly-painted seats. A four-sided, NBA-style electric scoreboard is suspended high above a gleaming floor. A brave's head in full head-dress is painted into the center circle. It is a room much larger and

Friday Night Fever: nine thousand fans attend a home game at the Wigwam. (John E. Simon)

better-appointed than those in which most NCAA Division I teams play their games.

Ron Hecklinski, tall, angular, a bank of straight brown hair halting in an even row above thick spectacles, is already hoarse five minutes into practice on an early November afternoon, a week before the Indians' first game against Indianapolis' Manual High. There is too much to teach in too little time. Five of his players are freshmen, and their inexperience often shows as they scrimmage. Four assistant coaches, a team statistician, and a video coordinator patrol the margins of the court, tracking and recording every action. Again and again, Hecklinski stops play to lecture and instruct, his neck arching forward to reach out for volume in the huge room. The players listen carefully and repeat the mistakes. Hecklinski loudly banishes one player to the custody of an assistant for not warning another that a pick had been set. Head down, the player begins to run laps as Hecklinski's lips move in a private prayer.

Hecklinski, thirty-eight, beat out sixty-two other applicants for the job of the Anderson Indians' head coach. Eleven of the applicants for the job were, like Hecklinski, college assistant coaches, and another was a head coach. Hecklinski had been a key assistant at Ball State University during a six-year period in which the men's basketball program became nationally prominent. The part he hated the most were the endless trips that kept him apart from his wife and young daughter. Having grown up in Indiana, Hecklinski saw the Anderson High job for what it was: a unique chance to live the life of college head coach, but without the family-killing qualities of life on the road.

The position had suddenly became available when Anderson coach Norm Held suffered a heart attack and resigned. Held had been an entrepreneurial leader who ran the program with the flair of an evangelist. He had taken the Indians to four state championship games in his eighteen years. All were lost, and Held is remembered by many in Anderson not for the journey but for the outcome of those games. Each of the three huge runner-up trophies were carried quietly to a back corner of the coaches' room where no one could be reminded of the shame.

Shortly after arriving in Anderson, Hecklinski was invited to play golf with a trio of Indians fans. At the tee, one asked

Hecklinski if he had heard they named a street after Norm Held. He felt their eyes hard upon him. "Yeah," said the fan, "they named it Second Street." No one laughed. "All I could think was, What's my street gonna be — Sixty-seventh Avenue?" Hecklinski recalls. "I mean, Norm did it all here."

Hecklinski inherited an amazing business package: besides Norm Held's team, Hecklinski took over his radio show, his shoe contract with Adidas, his paid staff of assistants and a cable TV deal. He could bring in his own basketball camp, or take Norm's. There was also a booster club which generated ten to fifteen thousand dollars per year for team equipment.

After practice, Hecklinski remains for awhile in the Wigwam bleachers, winding down. "There's something a lot of people don't understand," he says. "This facility, for a thousand students, is probably better than three-fourths of the university facilities we played in when I was at Ball State. The community really takes care of this place. I've been all over and I don't think there's a better high school coaching job anywhere. Maybe not a coaching job of any kind. Basketball still matters here. Sure we have problems in Anderson, guns and gangs and drugs and whatever. But on Friday and Saturday night we come in here and we pretend none of it exists. On those nights, it's just ball."

Anderson High was the only school in town for three-quarters of a century, until the mid-fifties, when Highland High was annexed into the city of Anderson and Madison Heights High was created to educate the sons and daughters of an expanding GM management. Although the Indians didn't welcome the prospect of competition, the threat at first seemed harmless enough, for Anderson High still had the most students.

A decade later, the civil rights movement transformed everything. School districts were redrawn, the most dramatic change splitting a large, predominantly black neighborhood, the source of many of Anderson's best players, almost in half. Students living south of Twenty-second Street were assigned to Madison Heights; those to the north went to Anderson. Still other residents were bused to Highland, and for the first time there was authentic competition in Anderson.

Anderson's Norm Held, who built a major college-scale
program at Anderson. (John E. Simon)

Most Hoosiers now rate the Anderson sectional as among the toughest of all the sixty-four sectional tournaments. Sectional week is the most passionate time of the year, a few days in mid-February when three Anderson schools and three smaller local schools go hand-to-hand for the right of only one to survive to go to the regional round. Hostilities simmer within acceptable limits throughout most of the year, but at sectional time Anderson can feel like Ulster.

It was only a generation ago that everyone in town went to Anderson High, so there are many families with parents who bleed red and green and whose children and grandchildren go to Madison Heights or Highland. During sectional week there are a lot of unfinished meals.

"My daughter was a cheerleader at Anderson High, and so was her best friend," said Brenda Weinzaphel, a lifelong fan and former treasurer of the Indians Booster Club. "But her friend's mother was a secretary at Madison Heights and her dad taught at Highland. She'd get into it all the time with her parents. Finally it got so bad she had to come to stay at our house during sectional week."

The tension seems to grip adults harder than kids, who get to mix at parties and in back seats and on outdoor courts. But much of Anderson's service club life revolves around basketball in the winter, and it is harder for adults — especially Old Indians, who still regard the other two schools as bratty newcomers — to forgive and forget. There are those who will not shop in rival neighborhoods.

An hour before game time the fragrance of fresh popcorn already fills the Wigwam. The Indians boosters are busy at their table, unboxing high school basketball's most complete product line. Tonight's assortment includes sweatshirts, T-shirts, posters, license plates, pennants, buttons, ballpoint pens, mugs, window stickers, and window shades. "Anything that's red and green," says a smiling booster.

After a while, fans start to trickle, then flow, then surge into the gym. Young families and guys in ball caps arrive first to begin their long trek upstairs to aeries that call for keen eyes. Then older, nicely-dressed quartets, the boys steering the girls with a light touch on the back, dawdle momentarily at courtside to watch layup drills and then finally ascend into the top and middle seats of the floor level. Everyone seems to know everyone else.

Below them is a block of boosters, many of them elderly women decked out in red and green outfits. Some are wearing red and green lipstick. Finally, arriving fashionably late, are the town's gentry, including the ex-mayor (the current jobholder is a Highland graduate), members of the school board and the managerial elite. One of them turns out to be Carl Erskine, Class of '45. The old Dodger curveballer today is president of the First National Bank of Madison County.

Erskine swears he is remembered locally more as a set-shooter than as a major league pitcher. "Hardly a day goes by when somebody doesn't stop me on the street and say 'Carl, hey, uh, remember that game when you . . . ' and I think they're gonna talk about the Yankees. Then they'll say, 'I was in the old Wigwam that day you made that one from the corner against Kokomo. Here I'm not a Dodger — I am an Indian."

As tip-off time draws near, the opposing cheerleaders are squatting around the center circle, passing a peace pipe. Suddenly the lights go out. Everyone leaps to their feet, whooping in the dark as the Wigwam reels with the thunder of tom-toms. All at once a spotlight falls upon an Indian brave in full headdress, arms folded across his bare chest.

He dances in wide circles around the gym, then cuts abruptly into the center circle as the spotlight broadens. There, kneeling, is a maiden. The crowd noise would mute the Concorde. As the two hold a long, unblinking stare, she rises and they begin to dance slowly together, mingling rather sensually for high school fare in central Indiana. He bolts loose for a final circle, breaks in again and leaps over her. They stride from the spotlight together and the crowd cuts loose with one last great whoop.

The Dance of the Brave and the Maiden is a sacred tradition in Anderson, perhaps fifty years old. Competition for the roles of the brave and the maiden is said to be as keen as that for starting forward on the team. The dance is believed to have an intimidating effect on the opponents, some of whom remain in the locker room until it is done.

Because the ceremony of the game means almost as much here as its playing, cheerleaders, majorettes, band members, and dancers have long been respected at Anderson as they are in few other places. "I was a cheerleader at New Castle High," recalls Brenda Weinzaphel, "and to come to Anderson and see the maiden and the brave dance and pass the pipe, that was the high point of the year. At Anderson High a cheerleader really means something. When my daughter made cheerleader here, I was in ecstasy."

The lights come back on, and, when vision and hearing are again possible, a neighbor points out that all that the best seats in the house are occupied by very old people, mainly, it turns out, by members of seventeen families who have held season tickets for over fifty years, along with the interlopers who sat down thirty or forty years ago.

Season tickets for those seats are Anderson's crown jewels. You work your way down toward them row by row, year by year, throughout the course of your life. At the Wigwam you begin at the top and descend when someone dies or moves away or forgets to renew. The players get closer as your ability to see them gets worse. From the young families up in the clouds down to the gerentocracy at courtside, Anderson's human geology is recorded in the strata of the Wigwam.

Word that one of these tickets has become available is whispered among family members and trusted friends, like word of a vacant rent-controlled apartment in Manhattan. These tickets surface from time to time in wills, and Indians athletic director Jack Macy has three times been summoned to testify as to their proper custody in spiteful divorce hearings.

Dan Quickel, ninety, has what seems to be the best seat in the house, front row center. He is happy to share the story of his marvelous descent. "I started out in the top of the old Wigwam in the student section," he recalls. "I bought my first season ticket in 1928, when I was a freshman. I had to sit with the students until I graduated in 1931." When he came home from Cornell and law school at the University of Michigan, opportunity knocked, hard. Waiting was the break of a lifetime.

"My father had become team physician. Because of that, he could get us into all the games, row three." From there it was all downhill, so to speak. "Then we were in the second row when the

The Maiden and the Brave stare down the
opponents during the pre- game ceremony.
(John E. Simon)

new gym opened. We had three seats together. Then Father died at the age of ninety-nine. He was getting ready to go to the ball game when he fell down the stairs and couldn't come anymore. After that Charlie Cummins, the athletic director, put us in the first row, section D, down by the stage. Finally, two seats opened up front row center, and we were delighted to take them."

The Indians hold a drawing to distribute tournament tickets. To enter "Lottery Night" you hand in your regular season ticket stub one weekday before the sectional — during Red and Green Week, when everything in town looks like a Christmas package — and then return to the Wigwam at eight that night for the drawing.

Actually, you could show up at nine for the drawing, because it is preceded by at least an hour of inspirational speeches and fight songs and syncopated cheers. Each team member gets to shuffle up to the mike amid riotous applause for a few defiant words, and the booster product line appears once more.

Finally, one blindfolded student cranks the drum and another yells out a number. There's a shriek and a woman in a red blouse and a green skirt bounds down the stairs to claim her tourney ticket. For more than an hour down they come, in every combination of red and green, until the drum is empty.

Although Jack Macy insists he's never been offered a bribe for a tourney ticket, that doesn't mean every rabid Indians fan is content to trust the tournament to blindfolded students. Ron Porter remembers scoring eight tickets for the state finals one year by stapling six season ticket stubs from the previous year to his two current tickets, and then getting lucky in the drawing: "And then I was walkin' out of the gym and a guy said, 'R.P., I'll give you a hundred dollars apiece for 'em.' I said, 'No way, no way.' "

Though Anderson High celebrates the game ritually and in multitudes, though the faithful have twice passed the hat to erect a truly flattering place of worship, though the prayers are earnest and the faith unbroken, the gods have not smiled on the Indians since 1946, when a five-foot-eleven center named Jumpin' Johnny Wilson, a pioneer dunker, led the them to their only Indiana championship.

Since then, the Indians have escaped their cutthroat sectional — which surely can be likened to the Valley of the Shadow of Death — many times. They have captured regional and semistate crowns, and three times have reached the final, *final* game for the championship of all four hundred Hoosier schools, only to lose by four points, and then two, and finally *one* excruciating point.

"We're snakebit," explains Ron Porter glumly. "There's no other way to explain it. Year after year we have the statistics, the superstars, and something always happens." Porter can tell the story firsthand, for no matter where he has been or what has been going on in his life, he has been with the Indians in spirit or flesh every year since his graduation in 1962, and he has even made a little spending money on the side. A sampling of key events in Ron Porter's postgraduate years leaves no room for doubt about the intensity of his faith:

"In '68–69 I was at the top of the gym when we got beat by Highland in the sectional. We were down by one point with about forty-four seconds to go, and Artie Pepelea shot a shot from the ten-second line that went over the backboard and into the stage. I just went wild. I was so mad I left my ex-wife at the gym. I was screamin' and cussin' and stomped down those stairs and out of the gym and got in my car and drove to my buddy's house and got drunk. It was one of those days.

"In '73–74 we were 27–0, ranked fifth in the *nation* by some magazine. We had to play in the Fort Wayne semistate. I went up to northern Indiana and bought five hundred tickets from the different schools in the semistate. Me and four other guys, we left Anderson at midnight and drove to Elkhart and bought a hundred and fifty tickets for four dollars apiece and I was sellin' 'em for twenty. That night we played Fort Wayne Northrup and we lost. Unbelievable.

"Let's see, seventy-nine is when I thought I had the heart attack. We were in the state finals and this girl and I were drivin' to Indianapolis for the afternoon game. I was workin' for Stupes Buick and I made him give me a light-green-and dark-green Regal to drive to the game. Then I started havin' chest pains. She had to drive me back to the hospital. I'm missin' the game, I'm pissed, so I make 'em put it on the radio in the emergency room. Then the guy comes in and says, 'There's nothin' wrong with you, but tonight I want you to come in and get an upper GI.' We beat Argos in the afternoon and so I just got dressed and drove to Indianapolis. I went to Steak and Ale, had dinner, went to the finals, and we got beat."

The game, the one that sent Porter and nearly every other Indians fan combing back through the collective past for traces of some unpaid karmic debt — like, maybe somebody really *did* burn down the first Wigwam — was the one-point loss to Connersville for the 1983 state title. The game boiled down to one shot, a shot that high-scoring guard Troy Lewis took from eighteen feet.

The final seconds of the Connersville game remain hauntingly clear to all who were there: behind by one point, the Indians took the ball downcourt and held it for about thirty-five seconds. With three seconds left, Lewis dribbled it into the middle and shot a jumper. Norm Held remembers watching the flight of the ball, convinced that all his trials were over. "The ball looked dead-center, but it hit the front of the rim and bounced up and off . . . it just didn't go in."

Ron Porter was listening to the game by telephone from Houston with his roommate, Ron James. "I just went numb. My roommate was on the phone at the end, I couldn't take it. With about thirty seconds left, he says to me, 'Listen, I can't stand this, Norm's holdin' the ball for the last shot.' When Lewis missed, I just went numb. We were bigger than them, we could've gone inside and got fouled or got a last-second shot . . . I couldn't believe it."

Brenda Weinzaphel was stricken. "I cried all the way home. My husband didn't know what to do with me. When that shot didn't go in, I went into the lobby at Market Square, and I don't even remember being out there. I cried all the next day. Even today, I can be in the car driving, I can think about it and I'll be there again. It hurts."

Fifteen-year-old freshman Tyson Jones takes a pass from a teammate in a preseason practice game and breaks for the middle of the court. Two players fan out to flank him as three defenders backpedal furiously. A step past the free-throw line, Jones fakes to his right with the ball and his hips, drawing a defender to him, then splits the defense with a burst of speed, maintaining his dribble. As hands flail to reject his shot, Jones smoothly passes the ball behind him to a trailing player who banks the ball in the hoop. The tension in Ron Hecklinski's face dissolves. "I love to watch that kid," he says to no one. "He is just so skilled."

Tyson Jones was born to be an Indian. He is the son of a father who was a star at Anderson High in the late fifties, and a mother who has followed the Indians faithfully since her graduation from Anderson. Tyson has two stepbrothers who were also AHS stars and who played at major colleges. He lives with his mother in a large house in a racially mixed neighborhood which he describes as increasingly dangerous.

Like many young people throughout the United States, Tyson grew up dreaming of playing basketball for high stakes in great arenas before massive television audiences. But unlike most young athletes, Tyson knew he could do this before he left high school. As a young boy his heroes were not Magic or Michael or Larry, but Artie Pepelea the third, Tim Westerfield, Archie Fuller, Vince Tatum, and of course, Terry "Kojak" Fuller. Real dreams came true in the Wigwam.

Tyson grew up listening to the Norm Held show on Monday nights. Many times he heard coach Held explain to callers the reasoning behind Troy Lewis' last-second shot, and once he even met Troy Lewis. Like Dan Quickel and the other old-timers, Tyson Jones remembers the day that someone moved and he and his mom got tickets closer to the Wigwam floor.

Tyson went to as many of Kojak's games as possible, even some on the road. Kojak Fuller was short, like Tyson, a wonderful ball handler and an explosive scorer. Tyson was in Indianapolis' Hinkle Fieldhouse for both of Kojak's semistate losses to Indianapolis' Ben Davis. After the first disaster, Tyson shut himself in his room and repeated the excuses he heard adults make: the refs stunk. Injuries killed us. The second time, when Kojak scored forty-seven and the Indians still lost, Tyson just sat in a car where no one could see him and sobbed.

One day Tyson was at a recreation center and Kojak walked in. Before long, somehow, they were playing one-on-one, just the two of them outdoors. Even when rain came, they kept on playing. Finally, drenched and laughing, they walked in together.

Ron Hecklinski councils the Braves: "There is no better coaching job in the U.S." (Brian Drumm)

Freshman Tyson Jones begins his career, hoping he can be as good as his heroes. (Brian Drumm)

Last summer Tyson began to hear rumors that he and perhaps four others from his undefeated eighth-grade team might make the Anderson High varsity as freshmen. At the beginning of the school year, when Ron Hecklinski named the squad and gathered them for team photos, it came true.

In the days before the Indians' first home game it began to hit Tyson that the biggest moment of his life was at hand. Soon he would step out onto the stage where his father, his stepbrothers, and his greatest heroes had performed, like their heroes before them. The prospect brought a faint smile to his face in the locker room after a preseason practice. "The other night my mom said, 'Do you know, Tyson, ever since I've been in high school, I get so excited when I hear that school song play and I watch the players come out on the floor. I can't imagine what I'll feel like when I hear that song and see you run out on the floor.' She said, 'You won't be able to imagine it either till it happens.' Well, she's right, I don't know how I'll feel. I know I'll be nervous . . . but I can't wait."

When he heard about the five freshmen on this year's team Ron Porter was thrilled. "Now that's just what Hecklinski should do," he said by phone from Houston. "Cut his losses from last year and invest in the future." And as the new year approaches, Porter has added a new wrinkle of his own. "This year I'm gonna take four cars back in a hauler," he says. "I'll get someone to drive it and I'll follow in my car. I think I can move that many. Indiana is GM country. Besides, if those freshmen are as good as people say, I might need to stay longer this time. You never know . . . This could be our year."

The Region —
Hoops in the Other Indiana

I see a city rise as if by magic, in proportions vast and splendid, with a hundred busy marts of traffic and of trade, with palatial homes unnumbered and seats of learning multiplied.

> — Governor Frank Hanley, in his speech at the first
> banquet of the Gary Commercial Club, 1907

People come to Gary expecting to be shot.

> — Glenn Robinson, 1994

A sixteen-mile-long strip of Indiana known as "the Region" is considered by many Hoosiers who don't live there to be a different planet. Catholic, Slavic, Polish, Democratic, black, unionized, contentious, and driven by racial and machine politics, the Calumet Region seems to have little in common with the rest of Indiana. The Region is even in a different time zone from everywhere else in Hoosierland.

Hugging Lake Michigan, the Region is a land of steel mills and meat packing plants and smokestacks that discolor the sky and sour the wind. Its four major cities seem to have more in common with Chicago than Anderson or Jasper. The phone books of East Chicago, Hammond, Whiting, and Gary are columns of surnames with postponed vowels and silent consonants. The yellow pages are filled with mosques and temples and ethnic restaurants. The Region is a place where every day could be a feast day.

Gary, the third city to the west, has come to represent much that many downstate Hoosiers fear and scorn, and has been isolated in the collective consciousness even from other cities in the Region. East Chicago or Hammond means unpronounceable. Gary means black. Gary means poor. Gary means danger. Even the Jackson Five, people say, left Gary as soon as they could get to LA and never came back. To basketball fans, Gary is *Hoop Dreams* to downstate's *Hoosiers*. It is racehorse ball, city ball, playground ball, black ball, rough ball.

Gary Roosevelt High School, alma mater of Purdue and Milwaukee Bucks star Glenn Robinson, is perhaps the most identifiable institution of African-American life in Indiana, now that Indianapolis' Crispus Attucks High has become a middle school. Forty years after the U.S. Supreme Court ordered America's schools to integrate, not a single white student is enrolled at Roosevelt. Some downstate coaches candidly express their fear of visiting Roosevelt High, a fear "to go in there," as they put it, as if Gary were Beirut. "We had a coach here for the first time not long ago," says Ron Heflin, the coach of Roosevelt's boys' basketball team. "And all he could talk about was how surprised he was that our windows weren't broken and that he didn't see graffiti."

To many fans in the Region, and particularly in Gary, downstate — everything in Indiana south and east of the Region — means bias. Biased refs, bad calls, bleachers full of people who are set against them before they enter the gym, people who are prepared to hate them before having met them. There have been flare-ups, such as the state championship game in Bloomington in 1972 between a Gary school and a downstate school that ended in a brawl along racial lines. But there had been tension long before that. "I remember one game in the fifties between Gary Froebel and Lafayette Jefferson at Purdue when it really got rough," recalls Cyril Birge, a retired official. "I ejected two Gary players and I thought the sky was going to come down. The next day I read in the paper that a legislator from Gary started a petition drive to get Gary out of Indiana and into Illinois, where he said the officials were fairer. The IHSAA Commissioner L.V. Phillips called me up one night the next week to hear my side of the story, and I happened to mention the petition drive. Somehow, he hadn't heard about it. I remember he didn't say anything for a minute, and then said, "You know, Cyril, that wouldn't be a bad idea."

And yet, there are enduring basketball ties that bind Gary like ligaments to the Region and the Region to the rest of Indiana. There are huge high school gyms in the Region, like the mammoth rooms you find in Muncie or Kokomo or Anderson. Children who grow up in Gary or East Chicago have a chance to grow up watching or becoming local heroes among multitudes of their neighbors, just as they would downstate. This is a distinctively Hoosier opportunity that doesn't exist in Chicago or Detroit.

And each March the tourney brings the Indianas together, at least temporarily interrupting the estrangement for better or worse. Players from the Region journey south to Lafayette and sometimes to Indianapolis as the tourney advances, flashing across cultures week after week, entering new dimensions, struggling mightily to concentrate on passing or defending as they adjust on the spot, trying to look proud and composed and to concentrate on the game.

The tourney has always offered a way to settle scores and gain revenge, but for the people of the Region it has perhaps an even greater importance. Especially for players and coaches in central Gary, the tourney offers a chance to mingle with Hoosiers who simply don't visit anymore. Above all, despite everything that has happened, the tourney offers all Hoosiers a chance to remember that schools from Gary, and from the Region, are brilliant threads within the tapestry of Hoosier Hysteria.

∞ ∞ ∞

"I only saw my father work once," recalls Bo Mallard, eighty-four, who coached football, track and basketball at Gary Roosevelt between 1938 and 1968. "One day I went to the Gary Works when I was in high school. Until that day I was thinking about the mill myself, because the wages were good. My father was what they called a 'heater' in the tin mill. He picked up rolls of iron with these long tongs and put them in the blast furnace, and then took them back out when they were red hot. He could stand the heat for about two or three minutes. That was all I needed to see." Besides steering the boy away from steel as a profession, the visit explained something about his father. "I had always noticed that one side of his face was lighter than the other," he says. "That was the side that faced the furnace."

Alphonso Mallard, Bo's father, took his family to Gary from Magnolia, Mississippi, when he heard that they needed workers to make steel for shells and tanks in World War I. In 1906, the year the U.S. Steel Company decided to build a steel mill on a seven-mile-long strip of sand between the Calumet River and Lake Michigan, there were but a few thousand people scattered across the bare dunes of lake Michigan in the towns of Hammond, East Chicago, and Whiting. Overnight, the company trucked in acres of black dirt from Illinois and spread it over the dunes. Then, hastily, they laid out the fourth town in the Region, which they named Gary, after Judge Elbert Henry Gary, the first board chairman of U.S. Steel.

When U.S. Steel's Gary Works opened in 1908, all sorts of people flocked in, American and foreign-born, first living in bunk houses and tents, then in windowless boarding houses south of the Wabash Railroad tracks. Since the furnaces ran continuously, furnace tenders worked twelve-hour shifts seven days a week. Recruiting agents placed ads for workers like Alphonso Mallard in *The Chicago Defender*, a black newspaper which was circulated widely throughout the deep South. Thousands took the Greyhound up Highway 61 from the Mississippi Delta to work in the mills.

Blacks and Eastern Europeans who had been rural peasants but a few years before lived together, often in squalor, on the Southside. When an observer criticized U.S. Steel for throwing up slum houses too close to the mills, an official snapped, "We're not in the summer resort business."

Gary's grade schools were racially segregated in 1908, but Bo Mallard and about a thousand other black students studied with whites at Froebel High School on Gary's Southside until September of 1927. That month, twenty-four black students were allowed to report to all-white Emerson High, which was closer to where they lived. Thirteen hundred white students, many encouraged by their parents, promptly walked out in protest and stayed at home until a settlement could be negotiated. Its key provision was the appropriation of six hundred thousand dollars to build Gary Roosevelt High for black students and teachers on the Southside.

Bo Mallard was tall, well-built, and highly competitive, a valuable commodity to Froebel as a three-sport athlete. He and a few of his black classmates were allowed to continue their studies at Froebel even after Roosevelt opened in 1928. Mallard lived one block from Roosevelt, but chose to walk two miles each way to Froebel to remain with his friends and teammates. Roosevelt, like Crispus Attucks in Indianapolis, had been denied membership in the Indiana High School Athletic Association, and could not play against white schools or in the state basketball tourney.

At times he wondered if he'd made the right choice. He was constantly separated from whites. There were separate proms and commencement ceremonies even for the few of them. When Froebel's basketball team left Gary, Mallard and his two black teammates were forced to stay in a room by themselves, except for the time they were smuggled one at a time through the freight elevator into their teammates' hotel. Fans heckled them, trying to throw them off stride. Once, during warm-ups in a game at LaPorte, a man rose and led his section in the song, "Three Black Crows."

The Froebel High swimming pool was strictly off-limits to the black students. It was as if school officials thought whatever made their skin dark might seep into the water and contaminate them. "We just had to stand around and watch the whites swim," Mallard recalls. "Except this one day someone pushed a black kid into the pool. So they hauled everyone out and drained the pool. They couldn't swim until all the water was replaced. It made you feel like a dog. It made you feel lower than a dog."

The swimming pool became an issue again in the autumn of 1945, when about a thousand white students at Froebel walked out — strikes being by now a time-honored tradition among their parents — to protest the "pro-Negro policies" of their new principal, which included allowing blacks to swim in the school pool one day a week. A year into the strike a local committee brought in one Frank Sinatra to talk sense into the teenagers. On November 1, the thirty-year-old crooner faced several thousand students in the Froebel gym at eight o'clock in the morning, which must have been a dreadful hour for him. "Believe me, I know something

Frank Sinatra appeals to striking students at Froebel High School, who objected to the presence of black students among them in 1945. "This is a bad deal kids," the crooner said. Sinatra went home and the strike went on. (Calumet Regional Archives, Indiana University Northwest)

about the business of intolerance," Sinatra told a hushed audience. "At eleven I was called a 'dirty guinea' back home in New Jersey." "No, Frankie, no," answered a chorus of female voices. Sinatra held them spellbound for an hour and left. The strike continued until the following spring.

The high school basketball teams of the Region got off to a slow start in the state tourney. Only four times in the tourney's first twenty-eight years did a team from the Region make it to the final round, losing each time. Immigrant parents had no time to attend games and needed their children at home. There was little basketball tradition in a town as new as Gary. Most of the Region's schools had small gyms, others had none at all. There were no junior high programs or paid junior high coaches. Gary Roosevelt played most of its games against black schools outside of Indiana until the early forties.

Football was king, anyway. Michigan and Michigan State had giant football programs and Notre Dame was just a few miles away in South Bend. Knute Rockne, the legendary coach and athletic director at Notre Dame, wrote letters to Arthur Trester, commissioner of the Indiana High School Athletic Association, ridiculing his high school basketball tournament as unmanly.

And yet kids from the Region still plugged into Hoosier Hysteria by virtue of a statewide radio network which let them hear about Johnny Wooden or Fuzzy Vandivier and other heroes downstate, and by the tourney, which brought all but the black and Catholic schools together. By the 1930s skilled players and fierce rivalries began to develop. The North Carolina State squads of the early 1940s were stocked with boys from the Region, imported by State's coach, Everett Case, a native Hoosier.

In 1940, Hammond Tech produced the first team from the Region to win the state championship. The team was a microcosm of the Region, with Serbs, Poles, and a black player named John Thomas, who was the star of the team. Tech was hardly a pretourney favorite. They had lost six times, and barely slipped by three other tough teams from Hammond in the sectional. They beat Froebel by a single point in the regional final, then headed

The 1940 Hammond Technical High team, the first team from the Calumet Region to win a state championship. It was the melting pot at its best, a lineup which included Bicanic, Shimala, Kielbowicz, and Abatie. (Courtesy Indiana Basketball Hall of Fame)

Fifty thousand of Hammond's seventy thousand residents greeted the Hammond Technical state championship team at ten o'clock on a Sunday morning. (*The Indianapolis News*)

south to become the nightmare of every downstate radio announcer.

After winning the Logansport semistate easily, they took a train to Indianapolis the following Saturday, carrying, as one Hammond sportswriter put it, "the prayers of Hammond, of Lake County, of the whole Northern Indiana Conference, and that sector of Northwestern Indiana between Logansport and Lake Michigan."

In the afternoon semifinal they played Lapel High, from a farm town of about a thousand near Anderson. Hammond led by two at the half, steadily built a cushion in the third quarter and then began to fall apart as the game wound down. People throughout northwestern Indiana leaned closer to the radio as the play-by-play man stumbled over lines like "Kielbowizc to Bicanic . . . Shimala scores!" Tech hung on to win by two points and, led by Thomas, defeated Mitchell easily in the final game.

When the championship buzzer sounded, everyone grabbed their coats and headed for Hammond. Parades jammed the downtown streets all night long, blocking all major Hammond intersections completely. Railroad ties were jerked from the railyard, piled up, and set ablaze. The train bringing the team home from Indianapolis was delayed by fans who repeatedly attempted to board it before it could reach the station in Hammond. At ten o'clock on a Sunday morning, fifty thousand of Hammond's seventy thousand residents, many of whom had not slept, gathered to greet their champions. Hammond Tech's principal made the most of his few moments at the microphone. "Basketball will bring to Hammond something it has needed for a long time," he proclaimed. "A new school building!" The multitude erupted at the good news. Hammond's city officials, probably still hung over, dutifully appropriated funds the following morning.

∞ ∞ ∞

John Baratto gazed around his rickety, nine-hundred-seat gym at East Chicago's Washington High for the first time in September of 1943 and wondered why anyone would want to play in such a dump. No wonder their schedule was so pathetic, and they only played teams from around the Region. Who could blame a coach from Muncie or Kokomo for not busting his butt to come up here and play in this place? There was no money to be made, no excitement to be had, no glory in the offing.

Baratto had come to coach at Washington from downstate, where he had been plugged directly into the juice of Hoosier Hysteria. His baseball coach and mentor at Indiana State Teachers' College had been none other than the immortal Glenn Curtis, who had been Johnny Wooden's coach at Martinsville High. Curtis had helped Baratto get his first coaching job, at a schoolhouse near Terre Haute with a grand total of sixty-four students. Baratto had cheerfully led them to two straight sectional championships and then asked Curtis to see if he could help him find something a little bigger.

So Curtis drove Baratto up to East Chicago to look into an opening. When they crossed the viaduct over the Calumet River, Baratto caught his first sight of the gigantic smokestacks of Inland Steel belching fumes into the sky. He got cold feet. He mumbled something about turning around. "Look John," Curtis reassured him, "It takes a lot of big strong men to make that steel, and they have sons who'll play basketball for you."

So here he was. East Chicago was bigger all right, but it was a football town in a football Region. At least he had a gym. Some of the schools in Gary didn't even have that.

But John Baratto felt at home in the melting pot of the Calumet Region. He had been born in Texas and moved to Indiana as a young boy, when his Italian father got a job in a coal mine near Terre Haute. He had grown up among Slovaks and Serbs in the little camp towns like New Goshen and Clinton. One of his early squads at Washington had five Serbs in the starting lineup. He enjoyed visiting the homes of his new players, sampled dishes from their home countries, and was happy to celebrate their feast days. He knew a few words in many languages.

And Curtis had been right: they were good players. He had no trouble with discipline; those strong, steelmaking fathers were happy to tell his players that one wise-ass remark or slipup at practice and there was a job waiting for them at the mill, starting Monday morning. Cocky, personable, full of laughter, Baratto cut the kind of figure that tough people responded to. Polio as an infant had left him with a limp on the left side and made him talk

East Chicago Washington's coach John Baratto in the huddle. "I just *looked* tough," he later said. (Courtesy Indiana Basketball Hall of Fame)

out of one side of his mouth. He looked like a permanent wise guy, a tough guy in a tough town. When a parent complained that his son wasn't getting enough playing time, Baratto found out where and when the father drank and simply took the stool next to him. "Sometimes we crawled out of those places," Baratto recalls, "But we crawled out together."

He set out at once to build a major program like the powers downstate. He filled up the little gym and beat the other teams around the Region, then went to the mayor and asked for a real gym. He didn't want a bond drive, he wanted an appropriation. He would build a winner, but there was no way the major powers, the money makers, would come up to play in that sorry excuse for a gym. And besides, what sense did it make for Washington to travel over to Gary to play the regional tourney there? How could you win that way? You needed a home-court advantage. He would give East Chicago a winner, but they had to help him. And in 1952 they built him an eight-thousand-seat showcase, as splendid as any gym in Indiana.

When it came to finding players, Inland Steel was always there to help the community achieve its goals. "Foss Mayberry was the general superintendent at Inland," Baratto says. "We had an area they called Sunnyside, with a lot of homes. Mayberry would say, 'John, if you have a player you think oughta move in, just get him in to see me and we'll have a job for his father Monday morning.'"

As Baratto's players improved and high statewide rankings became commonplace, as the great teams arrived at the new showcase and the city began to get some respect, the purse strings loosened. The city gave him money for a defensive coach and placed paid coaches throughout East Chicago's grade schools from the fifth grade on, all of whom reported to Baratto. Baratto did well, too, in some years earning nearly fifty thousand dollars. He was simply mimicking the successful coaches he had seen downstate, although his private stable of harness horses, which he kept at the local track, added a certain unusual flair.

It was important to Baratto that wherever the East Chicago Washington Senators went, they went first class. No burgers on the road for them. Again, when you needed help, you turned to the community. "In East Chicago we had the 'Big House,' which was the biggest gambling casino in Indiana," says Baratto. "They'd bus people in from the Palmer House in Chicago to play. It was right in the harbor, there. Dr. Fletcher, our team physician, was a member of the syndicate that ran the casino. He was always there for us. I'd say, 'Doc, will you feed the kids tonight?' and he'd say, 'Whatever you say,' and we'd go to Bill Smith's or whatever. He took care of everything. He dressed our boys up in blazers and slacks. Full outfits. 'I'll take care of it,' he'd say."

Nineteen sixty was the breakthrough year. No team from the region had won the tourney since Hammond Tech twenty years before, though Baratto had taken Washington to the Final Four in 1947 and Gary Roosevelt had made it to the championship game in 1955. Baratto had a typically tough blend of blacks, Serbs, Slovacs, and Hispanics.

His star center, Jim Bakos, was a classic Foss Mayberry special. Bakos was already well over six feet tall in eighth grade, and tough. But his parents were Catholic, which meant he might be headed to Bishop Noll, the Catholic school in Gary. This concerned Baratto. Enter Mayberry. "One night Foss and I were having a martini before dinner, and I said, 'Foss, does Jim Bakos (the player's father) work for you?' He said, 'Oh, yeah, I know old man Bakos.' " Baratto told him about the tall son with a difficult choice ahead. "Foss said, 'I'll talk to old man Bakos.' Foss calls him over the loud speaker at Inland Steel: 'Mr. Bakos, please come to the superintendent's office.' Bakos came, wondering what was wrong. Foss said, 'I understand you've got a son that's a good basketball player. Well, Mr. Baratto's a good friend of mine and he's interested in him and he'd like to have him to go to Washington instead of Bishop Noll.'

"Two or three days later Bakos goes back to Foss and says, 'My boy's gonna play for Baratto.' That was fine, except pretty soon the word got around. One day I was leaving the Elks and I saw the priest over at Bishop Noll. I said, 'Uh-oh. This guy's lookin' for me.' He was, too. When he saw me he started right out, saying, 'I never thought you'd stoop so low as to threaten a man's job just to get a basketball player.' It was the wrong thing to say. I hopped all over him. I said, 'Father, you make a living selling religion and I make a living selling basketball. But I never threaten anyone's job to get a basketball player.' "

From the start of the 1960 season Baratto knew he had a team that could go all the way, so that at the beginning of the season he tried to predict who they would be most likely to face in Indianapolis in the final game. He poured over lineups and records and schedules and kept getting the same answer: Muncie Central.

So eight times throughout the season Baratto drove to see Muncie play, often slipping off by himself when Washington had no game. "I went a couple of nights in below-zero weather, travelling late at night, all the way to Muncie or wherever. And in the end, we knew them better than they knew us."

Muncie Central was favored by nineteen points when they met East Chicago Washington at Butler Fieldhouse for the state championship. Muncie Central was undefeated and had won its games by an average margin of thirty points. Ron Bonham, their best player, was scoring nearly thirty points per game. Before the game, Baratto was extremely nervous and so hoarse from yelling at practice that he could barely whisper. He told his players to get physical, and to try to wear Muncie down with a pressing defense. "When you're playing in the state tournament," he says, "in the finals it's a matter of who's the strongest. Who can last. They can all shoot by the time they get to Butler. And we were physically stronger than they were. I figured we would have beaten them in a street fight nine times out of ten."

Early in the game, Jim Bakos smashed a Muncie player to the floor while scrapping for a rebound and took him away from the middle for the rest of the game. By the end, Bakos, elbows flying, had hauled in fifteen rebounds and Washington had pulled off one of the biggest upsets in the tourney's history, winning by sixteen points.

It was the Region's first win since Hammond Tech's 1940 championship, and the team, its attitude, its class, the blazers, and their dead-end toughness stirred the pride and spirit of the Region. It was a team that looked like the Region: tough, unvarnished, a beer-and-a-shot team with a cocky coach. It was a cultural statement, an exclamation point of a win against a glamorous downstate team.

When they got back, John Baratto's angels took care of him as never before. After one dinner they gave him a ticket to the Rome Olympics and the keys to a new Cadillac. It was of course under the table, but who in the Region was going to hold it against him? Other coaches reported to the IHSAA. Johnny Baratto worked for the Region.

It got easier after that. Before he retired in 1968, Baratto ended up taking six teams out of steel country to Indianapolis. Today, Baratto winters in Florida and summers in Indiana. And today, when East Chicago players suit up, they take the court in the gleaming, eighty-one-hundred-seat John A. Baratto Auditorium and Civic Center, built in 1986. Now seventy-seven, he looks back fondly on the two-fisted steelworkers and their sons who gave him his best years. "Was I tough?" he repeats, chuckling. "No way. It just looked that way."

∞ ∞ ∞

From the time Bo Mallard took over as head basketball coach at Gary Roosevelt in 1957 and long before as an assistant coach, he and his wife Mary Elizabeth had been scavengers. His players were the sons of good, strong, struggling people, but poor people. There were few fathers in their homes. And it was a simple fact that no kid could play the running game Bo Mallard coached without food in his belly.

The Mallards organized a network of golfing buddies, faculty colleagues, merchants, coaching associates, and neighborhood women to help the players. Bo talked the cafeteria crew at Roosevelt into letting his players bus lunch, which gave them one extra meal.

The Mallards hoarded clothes, surplus welfare tickets, anything that would give the players a few more calories and threads on their back. "Our basement looked like a secondhand store," laughs Mallard. "We had one electrician who stood six-foot-one who brought in I don't know how many suits." Mary Elizabeth helped the gangly boys slip on suit coats and taught them how to knot a tie. After a while some of the players had several outfits. "We had one kid who changed clothes all the time," Mallard said. "We had to teach him to pace himself."

Mallard nearly landed his center of the future through his basement store. One day Mallard saw an amazingly tall boy whom everyone called "Big Bird" walking down a Gary street wearing galoshes on a blazing summer day. Realizing that the kid probably had no shoes, Mallard took him home, rummaged through the basement's shoe department and came up with a spare pair of black wing tips. The happy boy jammed his feet into them, and sure enough, came out for basketball the next fall. Mallard was certain he had anchored the middle of his defense with a pair of shoes. Wrong. "The kid had hands of iron," Mallard says ruefully. "Couldn't catch a cold."

Bo Mallard even scavenged time. From the thirties through the sixties, all Gary high schools practiced and played at Memorial Hall, a drafty old municipal civic center built in 1928. Each school was allotted an hour and a half to practice, but Mallard was always looking for ways to get more. When Roosevelt's practice was finished, Mallard would ask the next coach if they could just run up and down the stairs and around the bleachers while his team warmed up. "At first they'd laugh at us," Mallard recalls. "They'd say, 'You out for track?' But that was fifteen minutes of conditioning, each day."

Sometimes Mallard took oranges to practice just in case another school didn't claim their practice time, as often happened on the coldest days. That way he could feed his kids right at Memorial and use the unclaimed time. "We'd have us a picnic right out there," he says. One custodian at Memorial, a diehard Panthers fan, could sometimes be convinced to shovel one extra load of coal into the furnace at the end of the evening so they could keep playing.

By the early sixties, Roosevelt was Gary's dominant team. Mallard was able to fend off competition for black players from the other Gary schools mainly by developing a sense of pride and a winning tradition. Kids who had been in trouble got a second chance at Roosevelt if they could follow Bo Mallard's strict code of conduct and appearance and make their grades. "I told kids, 'Forget your former troubles,' " says Mallard. " 'You have a new day with me.' " Making the team meant a chance for glory, a chance to play in the footsteps of Dick Barnett and Jake Eison, who had led them all the way to Indianapolis in 1955. Gary boys could listen to a flamboyant broadcaster named Johnny O'Hare as he called the games on WWCA, imagining they were Reggie Lacefield or Loren Thompson or the great Manny Newsome. "I had kids, hungry kids, kids who went without breakfast and sometimes lunch, kids who would run for hours after school in our workouts," recalls Mallard. "They wanted to play for Roosevelt so much."

Each year the two Indianas — the Region and downstate — collided in Lafayette like frontal systems. The weekend after the East Chicago regional, winning players found themselves in a coach's car streaking south on Highway 41, smokestacks vanishing behind them, flat fields coming into view south of Crown Point, blurring rows of beans or corn tapering to the horizon from either side of the car, then slowing down to pass through little towns with names like Enos and Morocco and Ade, where white people chatted idly on the sidewalks.

When Roosevelt won, Bo Mallard usually took the starters in his car to talk some serious strategy. It was a mixed blessing. "Riding with coach Mallard could make you a nervous wreck," recalls Jim Rogers, who played as Jim Nelson in the late sixties. "He drove fast down 41, and a lot of the time he was turned completely around, talking to the players in the back seat. You had to have one eye on him, but you also couldn't help trying to look out the windshield."

The Saturday semistate games were played at the Purdue fieldhouse. Coaches from the Region prepared their players for two foes: the opponent and the shock of a being in a different world. "In the early years I made the mistake of going down there the night before," says John Baratto. "Kids weren't used to it. Everything was so different, even staying in the hotel. The black kids would go down and stand in the lobby just watching people. I had to keep them in their rooms. After the first year, we waited till the morning, had a good breakfast, and then drove down there. And we went straight to the gym, got dressed and played."

Usually the foe was Lafayette Jefferson High School, or "Jeff," as it was called, the largest high school in Tippecanoe County. Locally, they were all but invincible, winning twenty-three straight sectionals in one amazing stretch. Jeff's coach, Marion Crawley, was the most admired and resented coach in Indiana. He was a straitlaced, immensely disciplined man who was widely believed to recruit the fathers of good players from far and wide through an arrangement with a Lafayette-based manufacturer of prefabricated homes. But Crawley's greatest sin, as far as the other coaches were concerned, was that of being hard to beat. "Crawley was like a wolf down there," says Mallard, "just lickin' his chops."

The Lafayette semistate was Crawley's court and Crawley's crowd. "Crawley knew all the tricks," recalls Mallard. "You'd have an outstanding player and he'd have one of his worst players taunt him to get him off his game. Get him mad. Get him to lose control. They'd say everything — 'Nigger' — racial things. You try to prepare the kids for that but it's just too much for some guys."

Even in the years when they were eliminated in Gary or East Chicago, Mallard drove his underclassmen to Lafayette, just to prepare them for what it would be like the next year. They would sit together in navy blazers and dark grey slacks, a small island in an ocean of white people, often profoundly uncomfortable as they saw themselves through the eyes of others. It was hard not to feel different and unwelcome.

The games were hellish for referees. "Just by his presence on the bench, Crawley was one of the game's biggest intimidators," recalled a veteran official, Don McBride. "He didn't have to say anything or do anything to get your attention." Most officials were from downstate, and unused to refereeing the rougher, faster game played in the Region. "It was farmhorses versus race-horses," says Jim Rogers, "and since the refs were from down-state, it was farmhorse rules." Downstate coaches taught their players to stand in front of a flying player from the Region and take the charge. No one called that play an offensive foul in Gary. No one didn't in Lafayette or Logansport. Officials thought the Lafayette semistate was among the roughest of assignments. You couldn't win.

Teams from the Region, after having prevailed in the Darwin-ian struggle to get out of their own regional, often found them-selves headed back to Gary or Hammond or East Chicago empty-handed, trying not to blame the refs, or the crowd, or even Crawley, trying to think of some silver lining. Homecomings could be rough. In each of the two years before East Chicago Washington won the state championship, they were upset by Jeff and Crawley in Lafayette. The second year when they returned to the school parking lot they were greeted by effigies of themselves hanging from a light pole.

At fifty-seven, with thirty years in at Roosevelt, Bo Mallard had already made up his mind to retire at the end of the 1968 season. Gary, and coaching, and just about everything, for that matter, had begun to change. It was getting harder to maintain authority. The seniors were part of what was to be one of the largest graduating classes in Roosevelt's history, in a year of upheaval in the United States. Richard Hatcher, a Gary Democrat, just become the first black mayor in U.S. history. Muhammad Ali was champ. Black Power was important in Gary. Some players seemed a little less willing to run through a wall for Roosevelt.

Some issues were easy to deal with; as for Afros, Mallard simply told his players they could wear their hair as long as they wanted, providing it wasn't longer than the stubble atop his head. Other problems were more troubling. Early in practice, it became apparent that Roosevelt's best guard had developed a drug problem. Mallard tried to help as best he could, but had little experience. Finally he felt he had no choice but to dismiss him from the team. Not only was he in agony for the player, but now his starting guards were five-five and five-six. All season long he struggled to find ways to give them help against taller players.

His greatest asset was a big, experienced front line, averaging about six-foot-five in height. Forwards Cornelius McFerson and Aaron Smith could both shoot, though Smith, oddly, could hit consistently only from one corner. Jim Nelson, the center, was skilled but inconsistent, highly intelligent but not easy for Mallard to understand. He seemed to drift in and out of focus, and Mallard didn't always know how to bring him back. He loved basketball, having grown up tutored by neighborhood Roosevelt heroes, but he had other interests as well. He liked poetry. While most Roosevelt players were raised by their mothers and grandmothers, Nelson's father was very much in the picture. He had worked his way into a white-collar job at U.S. Steel and wanted Jim to join U.S. Steel's work-study program. When the coaching staff first spotted Jim Nelson as a stork-like adolescent, they had to convince the father that the Gary Roosevelt basketball program could teach his son life's important lessons — sticking to goals, finishing the things he started, having his work stand up to inspection — just as well as could United States Steel.

All year long the Roosevelt team walked a tightrope. They were never out-rebounded and rarely outshot, but any team with big, good guards had a chance against them, and it was a year of exceptional talent throughout the Region. Roosevelt lost six times during the pre-tourney season, including their last two games. But the team jelled for the sectional and struggled past East Chicago Washington in the Regional final. When they got to the Lafayette semistate, Jeff had already been eliminated, and only small-town teams remained at the gate. Roosevelt crushed a school called North Miami 91–30 for the semistate title, and made ready to go to Indianapolis and the state finals the next weekend with a full head of steam.

The following Saturday they beat Vincennes in the afternoon game and prepared to face Indianapolis' Shortridge for the state championship. Shortridge had won their game on a last-second shot by their star, Oscar Evans. In the few hours between games Mallard primed his defenses to shadow Evans and went over plays designed to get Aaron Smith the ball in his corner.

To Mallard, the championship game hinged on a single moment involving Jim Nelson, who was playing passively. Late in the first half, with Shortridge ahead and pulling away, Mallard called time out and put his finger in Nelson's chest as soon as Nelson reached the bench. Mallard glared straight into the eyes of his center. "I told him he was loafin'," Mallard recalls. "I said, 'You're in another world. Get in this one.'"

Nelson went back out and stuck two jumpers which seemed to turn the game around. Aaron Smith drilled shot after shot from

Gary Roosevelt coach Louis "Bo" Mallard cuts down the nets after Roosevelt won the 1968 state finals in Indianapolis. (Courtesy Indiana Basketball Hall of Fame)

the corner, ending with twenty-eight points. Roosevelt won by eight. The team stayed in Indianapolis that evening, then drove back home through Lafayette and back up 41. The farther north they got, the more families came out to wave at them, and the more signs of congratulations they saw on the lawns of the rural families. For a while, at least, a team of black players and coaches from the south side of Gary now represented all of northwest Indiana.

It was the sweetest of the hundreds of drives Mallard had made up and down 41, from the years when they couldn't play in the tourney to now, when he could retire a champion at the end of the school year. Some things had remained constant: in thirty years he had never made more than three thousand dollars as a coach, even when he had coached three sports. They had joined hands in prayer before each game. And through all the civil rights movement and the official integration of Gary's schools, he had never coached a single white player or taught a white student at Gary Roosevelt High. It was a wonderful way to go out: he had fed his players and clothed them and scavenged for them and his wife and daughter had even taught some how to use silverware on the road, and now they were champions. The towns flew by and the people kept waving until the smokestacks of the mills came into view. He even found himself slowing down a little. "I had worked so hard," he remembers. "I had to pinch myself."

∞ ∞ ∞

Glenn Robinson slides down against the wall of the Mallard gym at Gary Roosevelt and sits on the floor by himself. Fixing an impassive expression on his oval face, he tries his best to concentrate on the young players who are attending his summer basketball camp. Before him are several hundred boys, scattered in groups of twenty-five or so throughout the gym, going through ball-handling drills and one-on-one tournaments. Most sneak peaks at him whenever a counsellor isn't looking.

The phone in Roosevelt coach Ron Heflin's office rings constantly for Robinson's agent, Charles Tucker, who is never far from it. Everything is still up in the air: Which shoes will Glenn wear? Which sportswear company will he sign with? Which team will he play for? Will he even play? Earlier in the summer, Robinson was selected by the Milwaukee Bucks in the NBA draft. He was the first college player chosen. Tucker, who also represents Magic Johnson, promptly announced that it would take $100 million to employ Glenn Robinson. Herb Kohl, the Bucks' owner, half-jokingly proposed that he just sell Glen Robinson the team and let him run it. Later Robinson signed a multi-year contract with the Bucks for $68.8 million, one of the biggest sports contracts ever. It is an almost cartoonish sum of money where Glenn Robinson grew up. On this day he is not yet twenty-two.

Glenn's mother, Christine Bridgeman, was an unmarried teenager when Glenn was born. Though she was poor she was determined to give her son the best. As soon as he was of high school age, she moved them into a small frame house on Harrison Street from across Gary Roosevelt High, which had been her school. She felt that Roosevelt, where strong teachers and counsellors constantly remind their students that it is a good and proud thing to be an African-American, was an important gift she could give her son.

He would need all the help he could get. Then as now Gary had one of the highest per capita murder rates in the nation and an unemployment rate twice the national average. Guns and drugs are everywhere, and much of the action centers around Twenty-fifth Street, a main artery of Southside Gary, which everyone calls "Two-five." Roosevelt is on Two-five. Trouble is all around. "Glenn's just like I was, and like every other kid who grows up around Two-five," says Ron Heflin. "He could have wound up on either side of that street, with a life of trouble or a life with possibilities. It all depended on who he listened to."

At first uncertain of his skill, Glenn did not go out for basketball until his eighth-grade year. He made the junior varsity as a freshman. When Glenn tried out for the varsity as a sophomore, Heflin noticed his toughness before his ability. "One day we were going through workout drills at practice. We call 'em 'suicides.' I ran them for about forty minutes straight. The rest of the kids were grabbin' their stomachs and complaining but he didn't bend over and he didn't say nothin'. I got interested. I said to myself, I'm gonna see what it takes to break this guy. I couldn't do it. He always came right back to the starting line. That night I went home and told my wife, 'I got a special kid here.' "

Robinson started on the Panthers varsity as a sophomore, but didn't get the ball much. "We thought he should have been the first option but he was the last because he was the youngest on the starting five," says Rickie Wedlow, a teammate. "He didn't complain."

When his grades slipped in the second semester, Christine marched him into Heflin's office. "She said, 'Coach Heflin, I wanna talk with you. If his grades drop any more' — she put her finger up in Glenn's face — 'you won't be playin' basketball any more. *Do you understand me, Glenn Allen?*' Here's this guy towering over his mom, and he just says 'yeah'. Total control. You don't want to cross Christine. I still tease him about it."

In his junior year Glenn took over leadership of the team. He was an explosive scorer and rebounder, a disciplined player with a versatile game. He loved to dunk. He loped down the court, arms down by his thighs, his face expressionless, in a way that seemed to lull opponents into complacency. Then he would strike. He did things nobody at Roosevelt had seen. "I remember this one time Darryl Woods, one of our guards, threw him an alley-oop when he was coming down the left side," recalls Rickie Wedlow. "We all thought Darryl had overthrown it and we were getting ready to go back on defense. Glenn leaped and caught the ball at the top of the square above the rim and jammed it down over Judah Parks of East Chicago Roosevelt. We were just shocked."

Gary Roosevelt lost only seven games in Glenn's three years. By his senior tourney, though all defenses were keyed on him, he was unstoppable. He hit the winning basket in both the regional and the semistate. "Everybody in the gym knew where the ball was going both times," Heflin says. "It didn't matter. Nobody had a chance. He can focus better than any athlete I've ever known." He led Roosevelt to the 1991 state championship, winning a heralded showdown with future IU star Alan Henderson in the final game. Glenn was named "Mr. Basketball."

After a brilliant three-year career at Purdue — during which a custodian gave him the name "Big Dog" — Glenn decided to postpone his senior year and enter the NBA draft. He announced his decision to the nation's sporting press at Gary Roosevelt High, in

Glenn Robinson listens to a camper's question at his Big Dog Basket-ball Camp at Gary Roosevelt High, 1994. (Todd Panagoupoulos, *The Times*, Gary, IN)

the gym whose walls sported bigger-than-life cutout figures of him and his 1991 teammates. "One thing's sure," observed Ron Heflin. "His mom will make sure he gets that degree."

Gary has lost one-fourth of its population in the past fifteen years. The steel industry has been crippled both by foreign competition and by its own inability to adapt to rapidly changing circumstances. The exodus from Gary to the suburbs has included thousands of whites and many black professionals. But not Glenn Robinson. "Anyone who puts Gary down," he says defiantly, "doesn't know Gary. Gary is a good place. I want to give something back."

The first installment turned out to be Glenn's basketball camp, staged in August of 1994. Summer basketball camps are a major industry in Indiana. There are jump shooting camps, big man camps, defensive camps, IU camps, Purdue camps, boys' camps, girls' camps, celebrity camps, and meatmarket camps where college prospects are trotted out in groups of ten to play before college coaches who inspect them like plantation owners at a slave auction. What most camps have in common is that they are expensive.

Robinson's camp is different. Three hundred campers, almost all of whom are black and from the Region, paid ninety-five dollars for four days, but only if they could. About a quarter of them got in free.

On the first morning of camp they gathered near an entrance to Roosevelt High and then Robinson blew a whistle, leading them out of the shade and into the sticky heat for a mile run on the school's track. Some were looking at each other and muttering complaints. He paid them no mind. Then they practiced ball-handling drills outdoors on the new surface that Glenn had purchased for the school and shot on new rims he had given them. Finally they entered the Louis B. Mallard Gymnasium, the room in which Glenn Robinson learned to do the things that have made him a millionaire, for a talk about discipline. They listened.

At twenty-one, Glenn Robinson had become the one player in a million that these boys wanted to be. His success had given him the means to see the world, to take up golf, to buy cars and condos and open businesses in his name. But that morning, as he divided the campers into teams, he was taking advantage of a bigger chance. It was the chance to instill among a group of boys a sense of pride in the part of Indiana, overlooked and scorned by so many, that is the real Hoosierland to him. And for a morning, at least, it seemed to be working. "I like Glenn better than Michael Jordan," said one camper. "I like him because he's here."

Farm Boys —
How Indiana Became
the Basketball State

Round my Indiana Homestead
(as they sang in years gone by)

Now the basketballs are flying and they almost hide the sky;
For each gym is full of players and each town is full of gyms
As a hundred thousand snipers shoot their goals with
      deadly glims.

Old New York may have its subway with its famous Rum
      Row trust,
And old Finland with its Nurm runs our runners into dust,
But where candlelights are gleaming through the sycamores
      afar
Every son of Indiana shoots his basket like a star.

      — Grantland Rice
      "Back in 1925"

    The cold fact is that basketball didn't start in Indiana. It should have, but it didn't. It has taken Bob Knight to find a face-saving explanation: "Basketball may have been invented in Massachusetts," Knight explained in 1984, "but it was made *for* Indiana."

    The vector of "Hoosier Hysteria" has been identified as the Reverend Nicholas McKay, a Presbyterian minister born in England. In 1893 McKay was assigned to a YMCA in Crawfordsville, Indiana. En route, he visited Dr. James Naismith's YMCA camp in Springfield, Massachusetts, where a new winter game called basketball had been invented two years before.

McKay gave it mixed reviews. It was active enough but there were still bugs to shake out. After all, It was only by sheerest happenstance that they weren't playing "boxball." Naismith had told the janitor to bring out two boxes, but all he had been able to find were peach baskets. They had nailed the baskets to a balcony railing that went around the gym and placed a stepladder under each basket. After every goal someone had to climb up and toss down the ball.

Reverend McKay knew he could do better. After he found space above a tavern in Crawfordsville for his YMCA, he hired a blacksmith to forge two metal hoops, sewed coffee sacks around them and nailed them to the walls. It did not occur to him to slit the sacks so the ball could fall through, but at least they no longer needed a stepladder as long as they had one tall player. "It became my job, right off, to jump up each time a goal was made and knock the ball out of the sack," Dr. James Griffith, the tallest player in McKay's first organized game, later wrote. "The thing I remember most vividly is having a pair of bruised knuckles next morning."

Basketball was indeed made for Indiana. It was a game to play in the winter, something between harvest and planting, something to do besides euchre and the lodge and church and repairing equipment. At the turn of the century, when Indiana was a landscape mainly of small towns and crossroads hamlets — settlements of a few houses, a church, a schoolhouse and maybe a lodge — basketball was a godsend.

Most towns were too small to find enough players for a football team and too poor to buy all the pads and helmets anyway. But it was easy enough to nail a hoop to a pole or a barn, and you could just shoot around by yourself if there wasn't anybody else, just to see how many in a row you could make.

Basketball was epidemic in Indiana within a year after McKay carried it in. In Madison they played in the skating rink; in Carmel they played in the driveway of a lumber yard, with spectators hooting from atop skids of walnut. Other towns shoved the pews back against the church walls or dragged the desks from the schoolhouses out into the snow.

In the early days, games were played everywhere: churches, skating rinks, schoolhouses, driveways. This 1913 game between Newberry and Switz City High Schools was played outdoors on a warm October day. (Courtesy Indiana Basketball Hall of Fame)

Rules, such as they were, were highly customized. The town of Amboy surrounded its court with chicken wire, so that the ball would always be in play. In Clinton shooters were allowed to bank the ball in off the ceiling. Brawls were common, and in the Dodge City days, an athletic supporter was someone who came to watch you play.

∞ ∞ ∞

Each March since 1911 Hoosier schoolboys have played in the State High School Basketball Tournament. The first "tourney," as it has always been called, was sponsored by the Indiana University Boosters' Club, who viewed the occasion mainly as a chance to recruit players away from Purdue and Notre Dame.

The club invited each of Indiana's thirteen congressional districts to send its best team to Bloomington, no questions asked. Usually, local play made it clear who was best, but sometimes there were mitigating circumstances. For example, South Bend High School once informed the Boosters that Rochester High had compiled the best record in season play only because one of their forwards was really a Notre Dame student who came home on weekends. The Boosters held themselves above this ugliness, perhaps because they knew that the boy, Hugh Barnhart, was also the son of the local congressman.

When news reached Crawfordsville that their very own Athenians had won the first tourney, citizens ran shouting through the streets, men with their coats turned inside out. Church bells tolled throughout the town. Everyone danced around a mighty bonfire until a train whistle was heard above the clamor. Then they all sprinted to meet the Monon, steaming in from Bloomington. It took several minutes at the platform for them to realize that the players weren't on the train. Exhausted, they had spent the night in Bloomington.

Indiana's first superstar was a farmboy named Homer Stonebreaker. He played in 1913 and 1914 for Wingate High School, a crossroads schoolhouse whose enrollment included only twelve boys. Like many Hoosier schools at the time, Wingate High was a single room with a stove, a place in out of the cold where a few kids might learn something useful until the ground could take a plow. Having no gym, they practiced outside, except for the one evening a week when Coach Jesse Wood hitched up a team and cantered six miles to a gym at New Richmond.

"Stoney," as the boy was called, was a square-shouldered, six-foot-four center who scored most of his points from far outside, by squatting suddenly and spinning up long, looping underhand shots. It is said that opposing coaches ordered their players to pick up Stoney at midcourt, but often even that was too late.

The Wingate players were ridiculed in Bloomington. While everyone else wore monogrammed tank tops and short pants, the Wingate boys took the court in sweatshirts, baseball pants, and long socks.

The laughter stopped once they stepped onto the court. Wingate won four games — three by lopsided scores — and then faced South Bend High School for the state championship. The game was a classic; Wingate won 15–14 on a shot by forward Forest Crane late in the fifth overtime period.

Stoney and the "Gymless Wonders," as they were called, became instant folk heroes. Challenges came from all over the state the next season. Great convoys of Model Ts formed in the town square, and out over the fields they rumbled. Five hundred fans chartered a train for the Kokomo game alone.

Wingate repeated as tourney champions in 1914, with Stoney scoring all of Wingate's seventeen points in the closest game, against Clinton. Not many are left who saw him — coach Wood outlived all his players — but Stoney's memory shines bright. "I used to ask the old-timers if there were any players from the early days who could still play today," said Bob Collins, former sports editor of *The Indianapolis Star*. "Three names usually came out: Johnny Wooden, Fuzzy Vandivier [who led Franklin High School to three consecutive championships], and Homer Stonebreaker."

To cope with the tourney's explosive growth — entries increased twentyfold in the first ten years — officials in 1915 divided the tourney into local, single-elimination tournaments called "sectionals." Winners met for the state championship.

With local bragging rights at stake, sectional games became even more intense than the games at Bloomington. These were mythic events, played on hallowed battlegrounds with maple floors, where martyrs fell and true heroes emerged. Losses were seeping wounds that festered in coffee shops all summer long.

The sectionals were organized basically at the county level, and in Indiana counties typically amounted to several hamlets connected by pure rancor to the local Kremlin, the county seat. The litany of complaints against the county seat became a part of Indiana's special script, as even and soothing as a chorus of locusts on a summer night. It was common knowledge in the provinces that the school in the county seat typically had the following advantages:

1. The home court in the sectional.
2. An amoral coach.
3. A county all-star team, full of players who should have been going to other schools.
4. A pair of forwards who had voted in the last election.
5. A center in his third year as a junior.
6. A network of grade school teams, controlled by the varsity coach, that would shame the Yankees' farm system.

Winning was everything; amateurism was a cynical joke. Merchants rewarded winning coaches with bonuses — once a Pontiac sedan — and players with gold watches. Coaches went after the parents of any tall boy who could shoot a lick, promising the father a better job in their town.

"It was just dog eat dog," recalled the late Phil Eskew, former commissioner of the Indiana High School Athletic Association (IHSAA). "The basketball players were important kids in anybody's town, and they could go anywhere they wanted. There were married and overaged kids playin' kids that hadn't passed a subject."

The minutes of the early years of the IHSAA, formed in 1903 to regulate high school sports, read like a police docket: damage claims for broken windows, referees assaulted, brawls, illegal rewards, and more brawls. One letter from Anderson High accuses rival Cicero High of "re-oiling" its players in a 1916 contest. Regrettably, the author did not provide a description of the crime, nor did he explain why the original oiling went unpunished.

In 1916, the IHSAA hired a lawman. Arthur L. Trester, thirty-eight, a veteran school principal and superintendent, was the stern, uncompromising son of Quaker parents. He had grown up on an Indiana farm and worked his way through a master's degree in education at Columbia University, where he formed a close friendship with the famed educator John Dewey. Trester was a huge, lantern-jawed man, almost always formally dressed, puritanical, shrewd, and intimidating. He was given a free hand to clean house.

At once, Trester set about straightening out the association's financial records, codifying its existing rules, and making new eligibility standards for players and teams. Then he turned to the matter of enforcement.

Overnight, Trester's office became the state's woodshed. Anyone accused of violating an IHSAA rule received a letter from Commissioner Trester stating the charge. The defendants had the entire trip to Indianapolis to reflect on the matter, confidence ebbing by the mile. Hearts hammered against their ribs as the groaning elevator lifted them to the eighth floor of the Circle Tower Building. There they faced the Commissioner and stammered explanations through dry lips. They were usually found guilty and often suspended from competition. "The rules are clear, the penalties severe," he would say curtly to those who sought a discussion.

Strong personalities tested him. Charles O. Finley, who, as the owner of the Oakland Athletics baseball teams of the 1970s, made a reputation for bedeviling Baseball Commissioner Bowie Kuhn, cut his teeth on Arthur Trester. As a high school student, Finley was accused of enrolling in a Gary high school to play a sport without changing residence from a nearby town. He was summoned to Circle Tower. Trester heard him out and banned Finley from competition for a year. The rule was clear, the penalty severe.

As the tourney grew, the Indiana legislature repeatedly tried to take over the IHSAA and its huge booty of basketball revenue. It galled the lawmakers that they could not deliver tourney tickets to their constituents. When the challenges came, Trester would

Arthur Trester and his showplace, 15,000-seat Butler Fieldhouse. James Naismith, inventor of basketball watched the 1925 tourney at Butler and wrote, "The possibilities of basketball as seen there were a revelation to me." (Courtesy Dale Glenn)

stay up all night, phoning and telegraphing coaches and principals to come to Indianapolis for "their" association. Trester sat silently through hearings, letting others defend him against charges of greed and gross megalomania. Then, when the bell rang, he rose to leave and the lawmakers scrambled out after him, begging for tickets.

Trester was even the chief referee. In the 1932 Muncie regional tournament, with Muncie Central leading New Castle by one point, a New Castle guard named Vernon Huffman heaved the ball toward the basket from midcourt at the buzzer.

Unbelievably, the ball swished through the net, but one official was signaling that the goal had counted and the other was gesturing no basket. As fans poured onto the floor, the referees made it into the dressing room and managed to push the door shut.

Soon they were able to agree, but there was no way they were going to announce their decision before talking to Trester; he signed the cards that *made* them referees. They called him again and again. No answer. So they drove off to Yorktown for a bite, leaving thousands in anguish. At six that evening Trester returned the call, listened to the story and told the officials he would back their decision against the storm that would surely come. Not until then did the two feel at ease to announce New Castle's victory.

In 1925 Dr. James Naismith, the inventor of the game, visited the Indiana state finals as Trester's guest. The two men sat among fifteen thousand screaming fans and watched a superbly-played game. Naismith was stunned. He could not believe what had happened to the winter diversion he had started three decades before with two peach baskets. Thousands of fans had been turned away for lack of space. And this for a high school tournament. "The possibilities of basketball as seen there," Naismith wrote in *Spaulding's Basketball Guide* when he returned home from Indiana, "were a revelation to me."

Until Henry Ford began to mass-produce affordable cars, Hoosier engineers dominated the American auto industry. At least 375 models have been made in Indiana, most of them in the first third of the century. Spring would come, and the tinkerers would

Barnstorming *Indianapolis News* reporter William Fox and Butler University coach Tony Hinkle prepare to board a Stutz Bearcat for their annual tour of the sixteen final schools in the tourney. During the final years of their circuit they raced an airplane. (Courtesy Herb Schwomeyer, Hoosier Hysteria and Hersteria, Inc.)

push back their shop doors and roll out elegant custom touring cars like the National, with its push-button electric gearshift; the Cole, with its revolutionary V-8 engine; and the Waverly, advertised as the darling of the ladies with veils and linen dusters.

High school basketball was important to the small-town life of several Midwestern states in the early part of the century, but the game exploded with greatest force in Indiana in part because Indiana was such an easy state to get around. Hoosierland is small and mainly flat, and an early, statewide network of roads was built to carry and test the great roadsters. Soon a statewide newspaper, *The Indianapolis News,* emerged, and one barnstorming reporter named William Fox, Jr., made it his mission to bring the tourney personally to every Hoosier. His scheme was to give fans a dateline and a story from each of the sixteen regional tournament sites before the state finals. He had four days to do it.

Each year between 1928 and 1936, Fox and Butler University coach Tony Hinkle vaulted into a donated Stutz Bearcat at the final buzzer of the Indianapolis regional afternoon game, raced to Muncie for the evening final and tried to make it all the way to Fort Wayne for their tourney celebration.

After that they had three days to crisscross the state from Lake Michigan to the Ohio River in order to make Fox's deadline. Hinkle drove by day and Fox wrote by night; they rarely saw each other awake. But it worked. "Shootin' 'em and Stoppin' 'em" became every Hoosier's column. Fox's turgid dispatches from the sixteen fronts gave those whose world view ended at the county line a surpassing knowledge of statewide geography.

Unlike its neighbors, Hoosierland had no major-league franchises to distract fans from its obsession: Illinois was the Chicago Cubs and Bears and White Sox; Ohio the Cleveland Browns and Indians and Cincinnati Reds; and Michigan the Detroit Lions and Tigers. Indiana was the Frankfort Hot Dogs, the Vincennes Alices, the Delphi Oracles, and the Martinsville Artesians.

Fox magnified local heroics into mythical events. Players and coaches achieved almost scriptural stature. Johnny Wooden, who three times played in the state championship game, probably came to mean more to a kid in Indiana than Ty Cobb to a kid in Michigan. "Wooden, to the kids of my generation, was what Bill Russell, Wilt Chamberlain, and Lew Alcindor were years later," broadcaster Tommy Harmon has said. "He was king, the idol of every kid who had a basketball. In Indiana, that was *every* kid."

Fox's gravel-filled accounts and predictions became so popular that *The News'* chief rival, *The Indianapolis Times,* hired an airplane to race Hinkle and Fox around Indiana.

"Don't take basketball season or life too seriously," advised Fox in one column, perhaps thinking about the increased weight of Hinkle's foot on the pedal as he glanced nervously toward the heavens. "Both are too short."

While New York City tried to scrape the skies with office buildings of Hoosier limestone, back home they piled it up against the schoolhouse. Even small towns built gyms that could hold everyone around, for everyone went to the games.

"I've been in places where I was having dinner on Friday night," says Bob Collins, "and the owner would shout 'Fifteen minutes and we're closin' up!' and everybody cleaned their plates, settled up and went to the basketball game."

Friday night was the perfect time to rob a small-town Indiana bank. "The game was the only activity in town," says Collins. "They had the bake sale at the gym, and the mothers conducted their raffle. I remember one time I went to a game in a place called Grass Creek and watched a kid play tuba in the band. Then he showed up in the reserve game a few minutes later, still dripping wet from his shower after the band quit playing."

"These gyms are our nightclubs," explained Fox to the nation in *The Saturday Evening Post*, "and we don't have to import any Billy Roses to put on our shows. At any ordinary high school game you will see bedizened and bedimpled drum majorettes leading bands through intricate formations before they toss their batons over the baskets in big league football game fashion. Our floor shows are second to none."

Along with the standard two- to three-thousand seat gymnasiums in little towns — structures built only for basketball and capable of seating far more fans than the population of the town — genuine monsters began to shadow the snowscape as well, facilities bigger than all but a few college gyms. The incentive was simple: the team with the biggest gym got to host the sectional round of the tourney. As more and more high schools entered and new sectionals were added, Hoosierland erupted into gym wars, with communities emptying their building funds and floating bonds to finance bigger and bigger gyms.

"No distinctions divide the crowds which pack the school gymnasium for home games and which in every kind of machine crowd the roads for out-of-town games," wrote sociologists Warren and Helen Lynd of Muncie in 1929. "North Side and South Side, Catholic and Kluxer, banker and machinist — their one shout is 'Eat 'em, beat 'em Bearcats!' "

During a 1929 meeting in which a motion to put up an extra three hundred dollars to hire a librarian was voted down, the Muncie City Council decided to reward Muncie Central's 1928 champs by spending a hundred *thousand* dollars for what was to be the "biggest gym in America." School administrators pressured teachers to buy construction bonds costing fifty dollars, or two weeks' salary. Today, with its 6,576 seats, the seating capacity of the Muncie Central gym is surpassed in the U.S. by only fourteen high school gyms in Indiana and one in Texas.

Other Indiana communities turned the Great Depression to their advantage. President Franklin D. Roosevelt created the Works Project Administration — or, as many Hoosiers called it, "We Piddle Around" — as a way to get America's laborers back on their feet by giving them things to build. "I attended grade school in Spurgeon, that's eight miles south of Winslow," says Eugene Cato, a former IHSAA commissioner. "I can remember we'd go outside on the playground to play basketball and these gentlemen would be working on the gym. A lot of them were black, and I doubt if we had a black living in Pike County."

FDR may have had roads and sidewalks and bridges in mind, but Hoosier politicians knew what was essential. Hell, went the reasoning, you could always build a road.

In 1930 the first black player appeared on a tourney championship team. His name was Dave Dejernette. It would have been Dave Miller, except that at the age of sixteen his grandfather had been sold from one slavemaster named Miller to another named Dejernette.

Dave's father, John, was a railroad worker who had grown up in rural Kentucky. One day in 1913 a white man came through offering twelve cents an hour for "good colored workers" who would travel to Indiana and help dig the B&O Railroad out from a flood. John went and the next spring came back for his wife Mary and their two young children. They moved to Washington, Indiana.

David Dejernette, the third of John and Mary's six children, grew up in the early twenties, at a time when nearly half the white males in rural portions of Indiana were members of the Ku Klux Klan. A few black families — the Ballous, the Cotts, the Johnsons, and the Dejernettes — most of them headed by railroad workers, lived together on the west side of town. There they had their own small Methodist church, with Mary Dejernette as pastor. They lived in an atmosphere of tension. John made a point to talk clearly to the children about how to handle themselves in town and at school. "He told us always to be respectful," says Basil Dejernette, Dave's younger brother. "He said, 'Keep to your books and learn everything you can. And don't go making wisecracks.' But he said, 'Don't let anyone hurt you, either. If someone tries to hurt you, stand your ground.' "

One on one, Dave Dejernette would have stood his ground well. He grew to be six-four-and-a-half in high school and weighed 225 pounds. He was an intimidating basketball player, usually the fastest runner and almost always the most powerful rebounder on the court. He was widely regarded as the best player in Indiana.

The week before the 1930 tourney, Washington was to play Vincennes High School, whose team Washington had already beaten twice that season. A few days before the game a letter arrived at the school, addressed to Dave. It was a death threat warning him not to play against Vincennes and signed "the KKK." Dave took the letter home to his parents.

That evening his coach, Burl Friddle, walked out to the Dejernette home. John appeared at the door and Friddle got right to the point. "You going to let John go to Vincennes?" Friddle asked. "No, I don't think he'd be safe," John Dejernette replied. "You let him go and I'll protect him," said Friddle. "How?" "I'll see that he's protected." According to Basil, it took Friddle most of the

The 1930 Washington Hatchets with Dave Dejernett, Indiana's first great black player, at right. In small towns like Washington, children of black families attended public schools. In Evansville, Gary, and Indianapolis separate schools were built for black students and teachers. (Courtesy Indiana Basketball Hall of Fame)

night to convince John, and John until dawn to convince Mary. The next morning John told Friddle that Dave could go, but he was going too.

John took a pistol to Vincennes and watched closely from the bleachers. There was no attempt on Dave, although during the game there was a commotion in the bleachers when an over-wrought fan died suddenly of a heart attack. When John and Dave got home, Mary was waiting up. Shocked, she saw John remove the gun from his coat. "What happened?" she asked, eyes wide. "Well," said John, unable to resist, "a man died in Vincennes to-night."

The tourney grew and divided again and again through the Great War and the Great Depression. So many new schools entered that two more weekend rounds — called regionals and semistates — were added to the tourney. By 1936, with almost eight hundred schools entered, the tourney took a month to play.

For the country schoolhouses, the regionals and semistates expanded the universe. To play a game before a multitude in a great house in Fort Wayne or Evansville, with the press corps taking up one entire end of the court, was like a field trip to a foreign capital. The new rounds gave the big schools a chance to dress up and look their intimidating best.

IHSAA officials struggled constantly to find a fair way to satisfy the demand for tickets. Fans would do almost anything to get in. Tickets for the 1940 Kokomo regional were to go on sale at the school on March 12 at 7:00 A.M. The first customer appeared at 5:30 the afternoon before. By midnight there were six hundred in line. They made blanket tents and tried to deal euchre and canasta with frozen fingers around kerosene heaters. Enterprising kids shuttled coffee and short order meals to those in line. At 4:00 A.M., police, fearing a riot, forced school officials to open the ticket windows. All the tickets were gone within a half hour.

Despite the odds against the little schools, Hoosiers chose not to divide the tourney into classes by enrollment, like most other states, when the tournament became unwieldy. Though more than half the teams entered represented small-town school-houses, everyone deserved a chance for the big prize. The tourney had become a perfect metaphor for the Hoosier outlook: it gave everyone a chance but no one a handout.

In 1928 Butler University, a small college known for its pharmaceutical program, built America's largest basketball fieldhouse, seating fifteen thousand, to give Arthur Trester a home for the state finals. Trester gave Butler a hundred thousand dollars for ten years' rent. "We sure never had any trouble building a great schedule," laughed the late Tony Hinkle, Butler's coach at the time. "Teams would come through from the west, headed for Madison Square Garden, but they always wanted to stop here, just to play in this building."

The finals were held in Butler Fieldhouse, now renamed for Hinkle, until 1971. Perhaps no building has meant more to Indiana, and perhaps none has provided a better place to watch a basketball game. In the afternoon, the sun pours down through mammoth windows onto a mirrorlike hardwood floor. The seats are painted in bright pastels. There are no columns to obstruct the view of play. "When other schools started building fieldhouses, architects used to come in here all the time," said Hinkle. "They said they liked the way the space flowed out."

A ticket to vintage "Hoosier Hysteria" — as Fox called the tourney — was a pass to the "Sweet Sixteen." Between 1921 and 1936, before the tourney's semistate round was created, the winners of sixteen regional tournaments met in a dawn-till-midnight two-day elimination to decide the state champion. It was like a marathon dance. Teams that made the Sweet Sixteen were said by Fox to pass through the "Pearly Gates of Butler Fieldhouse"; those that survived probably felt ready to meet their Maker.

Almost all the tickets went to the high schools of Indiana, who honored their best senior athletes with a trip to Indianapolis. When the sunlight struck their brilliant letter sweaters, the bleachers blazed with color, like autumn in Vermont. "Ah, it was just a *beautiful* sight," recalled Hinkle.

Herb Schwomeyer, seventy-eight and known throughout Indiana as the "Hoosier Hysteria Historian," saw the first of his sixty-two consecutive state finals — a Sweet Sixteen — as a high school junior in 1932. "That Friday was the only day in my whole school career that my parents ever let me miss school without being sick," Schwomeyer says, smiling at the memory. "My dad bought that ticket for me for three dollars — that's three dollars for fifteen games, Friday and Saturday. He gave me three more dollars and told me to buy a ticket for him for Saturday if I could.

"So my mother packed a big twenty-pound grocery sack full of lunch for me and I went out. At eight-thirty in the morning Vincennes, which was highly favored, got upset by Cicero. Soon as the game ended I went down to Gate Three to try to buy a ticket for my dad. The Vincennes fans were already going back home. I was able to buy twelve tickets for a quarter apiece, and another two people *gave* me their tickets.

"I saved the best ticket for my dad and at noon I went outside and sold thirteen tickets for three dollars apiece. That's thirty-nine bucks." Schwomeyer, in the telling, still seems to be marveling at such a fortune. "That's more money than I had ever had in my life. I remember I went back in and watched the rest of the games with my hand in my pocket so the money wouldn't get stolen. I haven't missed a tourney since."

"People would hide in here the day before," Tony Hinkle said a few years before his death, gesturing toward the upper reaches of the great room. "We'd have to have the police come in and sweep the fieldhouse. Once I caught a guy climbing up a drainpipe toward a window. I said, 'What are you doing up there?' and he said, 'Oh, just trying to see if I could make it.'

"I remember once telling Arthur Trester, 'If you want, I'll put in another five thousand seats for you at two dollars per seat,' " says Hinkle. "He just laughed. He said, 'No, Tony, five thousand would just make things worse. If you can figure out how to squeeze in another hundred thousand, let me know.' "

By the 1940s Indiana smoldered with basketball "hotbeds," clusters of settlements where three generations of rivalry had made basketball the strongest thread in the community fabric. The thump of cowhide against maple had become the drumbeat of the Hoosier tribe.

Dubois County, an unlikely pocket of German and Dutch settlements, was as hot as a hotbed got. The towns have names like Holland, Jasper, Huntingburg, Schnellville, Bretzville, and St.

Marks. Many residents are connected by a common Bavarian heritage, but they recognize distinctions, especially at sectional time: the good burghers of Jasper were said to speak "Low Dutch," while folks from Ferdinand, eight miles away, spoke "High Dutch."

Likewise, Jasper was Catholic, Huntingburg Protestant. After a contest between the two, the winners grew to expect a call from the losers in the middle of the night. A voice would scream "Catlicker!" or "Potlicker!" — whichever the occasion demanded — into the phone, and then it would go dead.

It could get nasty. When Holland upset Huntingburg in the 1952 sectional, the citizens of Huntingburg nearly starved Holland out by canceling deliveries of milk from the Holland dairy. In the sixties, when the Holland and Huntingburg schools consolidated — a move violently opposed by Holland, which lost its high school — the lone Holland school board member who voted in favor of the merger found his barn in flames one evening.

In 1951 Huntingburg went for the groin. In a successful attempt to become the host — and gain the home court advantage — of what had always been the Jasper sectional, they built a gym big enough to hold everyone in Dubois County. Even then it wasn't big enough. Each year at sectional time they had to build temporary seats to hold the overflow crowds. This led to perhaps uniquely Hoosier liability problems.

One year, an elderly man reached down behind him to find his seat in the temporary bleachers. His finger became caught between a board and a crossbrace. After the National Anthem, his entire row sat down and the man's fingertip was severed. "He came into school the next day looking for his fingertip," says Dale Glenn, the Huntingburg coach at the time. "His wife told him to go find it, but he didn't want to miss the game. He was hoping we'd kept it for him."

The ticketless would try almost anything to get inside. Glenn remembers two men who walked past the ticket window, each with a fifty-pound block of ice slung over his back between wooden tongs. "Concessions," they mumbled, heads down, ball caps pulled down low over their brows. Once past, they ditched the ice — and the tongs — in the restroom and headed upstairs. The halftime mob had to wade to the urinals.

Fifteen of America's sixteen biggest high school gyms are in Indiana. In 1951, the year of this photo, the Huntingburg gym could hold twice the town's population and twenty times the student enrollment. (Chase Studio)

The seat of Dubois County is Jasper, a town from the Rhine that somehow turned up in Hoosierland. Nearly all the restaurants feature sausage and *Bier*. The streets are lined with prim red-brick houses which stand in contrast to the white frame dwellings in surrounding towns. The Jasper phone book is a marvel of vowel postponement, especially at the S's.

"While I was growin' up, Jasper was 95 percent German, Catholic, and Democratic, and 100 percent white," says sixty-four-year-old sportswriter Jerry Birge. "I remember the Greyhound'd stop at Wilson's Drug Store, and now and then my buddies'd come runnin' back to me sayin', 'Hurry, there's one in there eatin'.' All us kids'd climb up to the window to watch a black guy eat. That'd be a big event."

Birge was in fifth grade in the year of the Miracle. It started the night before he was to return from Christmas vacation to St. Joseph's grade school, run by the Providence nuns. A few hours before dawn, the town's Wildcat whistle woke his family. Sirens sounded everywhere. In nightclothes, the Birges scrambled to the crest of a hill and watched the grade school burn to the ground. Three days later, the nuns had arranged for the children to share Jasper High School, the teenagers attending in the morning and the children in the afternoon.

"Come February, when the sectional started, it was really exciting for us little kids to see all the halls decorated, and all the signs sayin' 'Good luck, Wildcats,' " says Birge. "But we were almost laughing about Jasper's chances to win the sectional. Winslow was undefeated. Huntingburg was ranked. Holland had a great team.

"Well, this one nun, Sister Joan, stood up in class and said, 'Kids, don't worry, I've got it all figured out.' She was a real sports nut, had all sorts of Notre Dame stuff on her desk. She said, 'Jasper's going to win the state championship this year.' We thought she'd finally lost it. She said, 'Look on the calendar. The state finals are going to be on St. Joseph's feast day.' She was right, March 19. We said, 'So what?' 'Well,' she said, 'we're from St. Joseph's school, and God's going to reward Jasper High for lettin' us use their school.' "

No one could have blamed Birge and his pals for laughing. Jasper High School had finished the 1949 regular season 11–9, fourth in their local conference. They had lost four of their last five games. It would dignify their status to say they were unranked.

The Wildcats were coached by Leo C. ("Cabby") O'Neill, a former baseball and basketbAll-Star at the University of Alabama. Cabby had the courtside manner of a drill sergeant. He believed that basketball boiled down to fundamentals: if you learn it right in practice, you'll do it right in the games, he often said.

The Jasper squad had its share of rough kids. Some of them had a hard time taking O'Neill's regimen. One who could take anything Cabby could dish out and seemed to want even more was named Bobby White. White was a good shooter with a nice head for the game, but he'd stopped growing at five-foot-six and 135 pounds. Cabby cut him from the team as a freshman and sophomore, but White kept hanging around the gym after school, pestering O'Neill for at least a chance to scrimmage with the teams.

Cabby gave in and kept him but rarely used him as a junior and had no special plans for him as a senior until after the first game of the season. It was then that someone reported to Cabby that one of his regulars had been seen smoking a cigarette. Cabby summoned the player, extracted a confession and stripped him of his uniform.

The next game, when Bobby White's name was announced in the starting lineup, the gym thundered with boos, a great rolling wave of disapproval that functioned as a pointed finger. Many townspeople felt certain White had ratted on the dismissed player to gain a spot in the lineup. They couldn't prove it, and he denied it again and again, but that didn't matter. Evidence was not a factor. To them, it was strange-looking Bobby White. White was, in the vernacular of the day, a "clean Gene," one who didn't hang out, an outsider who had moved into Jasper too late to have grown up on the grade school teams with the other kids. He kept his nose in his schoolbooks, and, worst of all, the nuns seemed to love him.

They knew he went to Mass every day, but until later they didn't know what he was discussing with God. Every morning for years Bobby White had asked God for a chance to improve himself that day so he could help Jasper High School win the state championship when he was a senior.

His life was focused like a laser. "I'd go to Mass, go to school, and go to practice," White recalls. "Then I'd get off from practice about four, get a sandwich and go back and play until about nine." For ten years the prayer was the same. "The concept was to *win* the state championship," he says. "I prayed to improve myself so I could contribute more."

"I was in a play with his mother, Louise, once," recalls Jerry Birge, "and we got to talking about Bobby. She said she told him, 'Son, if it doesn't happen, please don't lose faith.' She said he told her, 'Don't worry, Mom. We'll win.' "

Two headlines juxtaposed in a mid-February Jasper *Daily Herald* convey Jasper's priorities as the 1949 tourney approached:

Winslow Draws Tournament Bye
and
Munich Spy Trials Partially Opened

The Wildcats somehow beat Dubois, Holland, and Huntingburg in the first three games of the sectional. When they fell behind the Winslow Eskimos 24–14 at halftime of the final game, Jasper fans were thinking that at least they'd have bragging rights all summer long. Again, there were things they didn't know.

"I remember Cabby O'Neill walking up the ramp to start the second half and saying to me, 'I want you to take it over and make it happen,' " recalls Bobby White. As the next morning's *Daily Herald* put it, Jasper roared from behind to beat Winslow 48–39 "on the sensational hard driving of little Bobby White." Quietly, after the sectional win, the other Catholic boys on the squad began to go to Mass with Bobby.

Tourney fever had consumed Jasper. The next Saturday's headlines tell the story:

Battle Today for Regional Title
and
Employee of Justice Dept., Russ. Diplomat, Seized

They nipped Monroe City 57–55 for the regional title, again coming from behind. *The Daily Herald* reported that "the first three rows [of Jasper fans] went repeatedly onto the floor to protest calls." The following morning, Bobby White noticed a throng at Mass, including, to his surprise, a few Protestant teammates.

The next week, forward Bill Litchfield, a poor shooter, banged a shot home at the buzzer to beat Bloomington for the semistate title. Most of the town dragged themselves out of bed and went to Mass that morning. Something unusual was definitely happening.

Jasper's local radio station, WITZ, had broadcast the Wildcat games all year long, but a huge forty-eight-station network out of Indianapolis had the license to broadcast the tourney. It was infuriating for Jasperites to hear the big-city announcers make repeated fun of the German names. *Schutz schoots!* was only so funny after the hundredth time.

The WITZ engineers decided to do something about it. License or no license, the Wildcats were in the finals, and God knew when they'd get there again. Very illegally, they pirated a frequency assigned to a Canadian clear-channel station that had already signed off, summoned the local announcers, and put WITZ back on the air over a four-mile radius.

The Friday before the state finals, *The Daily Herald* featured ads like the following:

> "NOTICE: Our office will be closed Saturday, March 19, to give our employees a chance to boost the Wildcats to victory.
> — Link Twins Loan Co. (Over Flick's Drug Store)"

On March 19 Jasper roared from behind twice to win the Indiana state championship, the final game a 62–61 thriller against Madison. The Jasper-Madison final is still remembered as one of the best games ever played in Indiana. The lead changed constantly; the pressure was crushing. In the final minute, Cabby O'Neill glanced over at his rival coach, Ray Eddy, and found Eddy looking back at him. In the heat of it all, each had seemed to realize how special that moment was, that maybe there would never be another like it, and had turned to catch sight of the only other person who could know in the same way. Cabby winked, and Eddy winked back.

Jasper won the tourney by rallying from behind in eight consecutive tourney games. A few smaller schools had won the tourney, but no champion had ever entered the tourney with a poorer record and less momentum.

How did they do it? It seemed like everyone in Jasper had a hand in it. Maybe it was because Mrs. Dr. St. John Lukemeyer had kept her vow never to stop pacing during the tourney until Jasper had won. Maybe it was because Bill Litchfield's dad never took off his hat until the final buzzer against Madison. Maybe the numerologists who found a clue in the three consecutive nine-point sectional victory margins had it right. Sister Joan had no doubts about what had happened; the tourney was indeed won on St. Joseph's feast day. And it seemed no accident that Bobby White, who seemed to contribute more with each game, scored twenty points in the final contest. His prayers had been answered. He was right: there had never been any reason for his mother to worry. A few days later, the nuns of the local order gave Bobby a plaque bearing Rudyard Kipling's poem "If" in recognition of his influence on the religious life of the community.

Cabby O'Neill was asked not long before he died if he thought God had a hand in the 1949 tourney. He professed little expertise in the area of miracles. "I know more people came to church when we started winnin'," he said, "but I wasn't at the door countin' heads. That wasn't my line of work."

"Let Joy Be Unconfined," blared *The Daily Herald*, "for we have crashed the circle of the basketball elite. This morning, the former Jasperites who are living in almost any part of the U.S. can point proudly to the sports pages or the front pages and say to anybody within earshot, 'Brother, that's my hometown, good old Jasper.'"

Hoosier basketball chauvinism reached a peak of sorts during World War II, which gave soldiers from Indiana a grand occasion to spread the gospel to other GIs. To hear some of them tell it, they spent much of their noncombat time teaching non-Hoosiers how to play.

"In 1944, when I was in the Navy," says Bob Collins, former sports editor of *The Indianapolis Star*, "we had a barracks basketball team. Most of the guys were from Ohio and Minnesota. They were big, rawboned kids, and they played that same highpost game, a couple of fakes and the center shot." Collins illustrates this style expertly with leaden gestures.

"We played about three games and just got larruped. I went back to the barracks and said, 'I want to talk to everyone here from Indiana.' Some guys came up, and I said, 'Did you play? Did you play? Did you play?' Some had played in high school, some just in the schoolyard.

"I said, 'All right, we're going to be a team and we're going to play a game. We got one rule. The ball does *not* touch the floor.' We went out and beat those guys something like 75–30. We gave 'em Indiana basketball. When it was over, I said to those other guys, 'Now you know what basketball's about.' "

There was good reason for pride. To America's colleges, Indiana was "the basketball state," which annually produced a bumper cash-crop of playmakers, sharpshooters, and rebounders. Scouts came in from everywhere at harvest time.

One year in the early 1940s, all of Michigan State's starters were Hoosiers. In 1938, seven of the ten University of Southern California Trojans came from Indiana. When USC invaded the University of California that season, the Berkeley band struck up "Back Home Again in Indiana." Bobby White, who after Jasper played for Vanderbilt College, remembers a game against Ol' Miss in which twelve of the twenty players came from within a fifty-mile radius in southern Indiana. "It was like a homecoming," says White.

For a while it didn't hurt so badly because the emigrants cast glory back on the Homeland. Besides, some of their own were doing the harvesting. Nine coaches of Indiana high school champions had moved straight into head coaching jobs for major colleges. Everett Case, an Indiana high school coach who spent much of the 1920s and 1930s in Arthur Trester's doghouse for recruiting high school kids away from their hometowns, later established and popularized college basketball in Dixie by filling his North Carolina State lineups with players from Indiana.

But in 1948 it went a little too far. That year, while Indiana University finished in the Big Ten cellar, Kansas University stole away six-foot nine-inch Clyde Lovellette, the state's best college prospect. Everett Case took several others. After the University of

LIFE

BEST BASKETBALLER

JANUARY 15, 1940 **10** CENTS

In 1938, seven of the ten USC Trojans came from Indiana, nationally known as "The Basketball State." One was ex-Frankfort Hot Dog star Ralph Vaughn, proclaimed by *Life* magazine in 1940 as the best player in the U.S. (Courtesy Indiana Basketball Hall of Fame)

Kentucky won the 1948 NCAA championship, their head coach, the despised Adolph Rupp, rubbed it in. "Indiana has not only lost its leadership as the top basketball state," Rupp gloated, "but the South has replaced the Midwest as the home of basketball."

Indiana University coach Branch McCracken promptly declared war. He announced that henceforth he would recruit only five boys a year, those being the five best Indiana high school seniors. Furthermore, he asked the state's high school coaches — his lieutenants in this crusade — to identify and bring forth those very special young men. To speed up the transition, he organized clinics and taught high school coaches the "McCracken system," a pell-mell fast break style ridiculed in the East as "firehouse basketball." Wherever they went, the best seniors heard people tell them, "You're too good to play anywhere but Indiana." And in 1953 it all bore fruit: Indiana won the NCAA championship with ten small-town boys from Indiana.

It seemed like a wonderful dance, one that had gone on for three generations and would go on forever. Until eternity, little towns would mill out thick-waisted sharpshooters who would walk out of fields and from under hoods and into college lineups. No matter how many wars and depressions, at least Indiana would always produce the most and best basketball players: Indiana would always be a small town, and it would always be Friday night.

But seeds of change were already in the wind. In 1940, Hammond Tech won the tourney. It was a big-city school from the Calumet Region, a place that always seemed to belong to Chicago. Hammond's players had strange-sounding surnames: Bicanic, Shimala, Kielbowicz, and Abatie. Like Lebanon or Martinsville, Hammond had a victory parade, but its parade drew a crowd of fifty thousand on a Sunday morning.

In 1951 the world shrank again. WFBM in Indianapolis began to televise the tournament. The next year WTTV began its immortal telecasts of the Indiana University games, which began with announcer Paul Lennon holding up a bag of Chesty Potato Chips and stating, "I've got my ticket; have you got yours?" Suddenly kids in Bloomington and Indianapolis could see the images of players from Wisconsin and Ohio without leaving their homes.

By the early fifties, black players were no longer lone figures in small-town team photos but instead appeared in groups of four and five — and were often the best — players on city teams. Indianapolis' Crispus Attucks High, one of three all-black schools which had been banned from the tourney until 1942, made the state finals in 1951. Their players seemed to play a different game, faster, less patterned, somewhere up in the air.

In the early fifties Jim Dean, a nice little guard from Fairmont High who in 1949 had beaten Gas City with a last-ditch shot in the Marion sectional, turned into James Dean, a bigtime movie star who, to many Hoosiers, seemed to become famous by sneering back at everything that had made him. *Rebel Without a Cause* summed it up pretty nicely.

∞ ∞ ∞

In the late 1940s, Indiana townships began to consolidate their rural schoolhouses into larger schools in an effort to provide a better education for Indiana's rural children. Few movements have caused such turmoil in Indiana. When one community in a two-community township had more power than the other, it simply annexed the other's school, name, team, and tradition and kept its own. There was genuine panic in the hamlets; lose your high school, lose your basketball team, and you stood to lose your very identity. For a small town, to consolidate was to be erased.

Some communities defended their schoolhouses as if they were the Alamo. In the summer of 1950, Township Trustee Virgil Turner announced that the high schools of the towns of Onward, population 171, and Walton, population 835, were to be consolidated beginning in September. Walton would be the high school, Onward the grade school. Onward residents refused to surrender their school and their basketball team. They set up a round-the-clock defense brigade, surrounding the schoolhouse with trucks, chaining the school doors shut, and stationing children inside the building against any attempt to remove the desks and chairs. State troopers stormed the building and were repelled until Governor Henry Schricker called them off to avoid bloodshed. The state switched to a strategy of attrition, refusing to pay teachers and discontinuing state aid. Residents kept their school alive for

Fairmount High's clutch-shooting guard James Dean, later the "Rebel Without a Cause." His mother was also an Indiana high school player. (Fairmount Historical Museum)

nearly two years, financing operations through chicken dinners which drew supporters from surrounding counties.

Before long it was happening everywhere. In 1954 Wingate High School — Stoney's school without a gym — simply disappeared, inhaled with five other little country schools to form something called "North Montgomery."

It was all changing, and too fast. For a half century's winters the excitement had crackled on Friday night. Going to the games had been little different from going to church. You came together in a room built wide and high enough for the spirit to swoop and soar. Each space had its iconography, the saints or apostles in one room and the team photos in the other. Winter after winter, the prospect of glory or vengeance had brought the community together on Friday night and the hope of redemption had reconvened it at daybreak on Sunday.

In March, 1954, the curtain came down on the farmboy era that had begun when Reverend Nicholas McKay had crossed the Indiana-Ohio line with a new game. After the 1954 tourney, fourteen of the next seventeen champions were to come from big-city schools. And after 1976, the girls who had also been playing since the turn of the century, but usually without funds or the support of their school's athletic department, had a tourney of their own.

The final act of classic Hoosier Hysteria took place on March 20, 1954, in the Butler Fieldhouse. It was seen or heard by nearly everyone of age in Indiana, and was to be the most remembered sporting event in Indiana history. It was high drama worthy of everything that had gone on before.

In 1950 the citizens of Onward, Indiana, learned that township officials planned to consolidate their high school into another, thus taking away their basketball team and their identity. Refusing to give in, they chained the doors, stationed students inside the building and set up a round-the-clock vigil against any effort to remove the desks and chairs. (*Life* magazine)

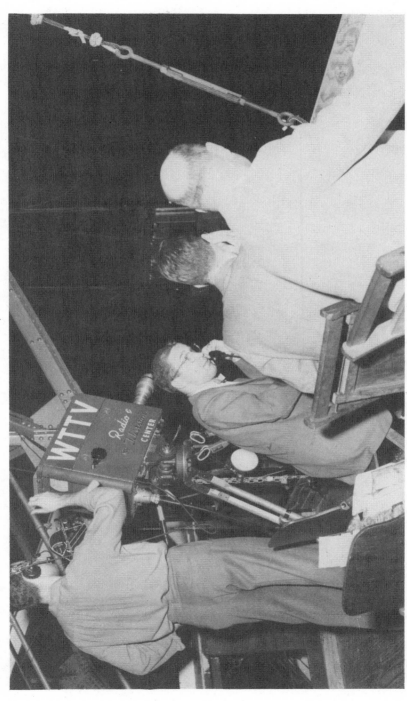

The Hoosier Village expanded forever one night in 1952, when Indianapolis station WTTV first televised Big Ten college games. It was then that announcer Paul Lennon (in bow tie) first held up a bag of Chesty Potato Chips (on chair behind him) and uttered the immortal words, "I've got my ticket; have you got yours?" (Courtesy WTTV)

Milan High School —
The Dream

The telephone shatters Bobby Plump's deep sleep. His fingers encounter the receiver on the third ring. Plump drags it across the pillow to his ear. There is country music. Laughter. He glances at the clock: 2:15 A.M. "Hello, man . . . is this Bobby Plump?" The caller's voice is thick. This is not an insurance call. It's the other call, about the game.

"Yes, it is."

"Are you the one that hit the shot?"

"Yeah."

"Well, we was bettin' here whether the score was 31–30 or 32–30 when you did it. Can you help us out?"

Each year busloads of schoolkids visit the Indiana Basketball Hall of Fame Museum in New Castle, Indiana, about forty miles east of Indianapolis. Boys and girls from Muncie and Anderson, Plymouth, Gary, Fort Wayne, and South Bend race around the rooms full of trophy cases, automated exhibits, and yellowed headlines. They laugh at basketballs stretched and laced like corsets over inflated bladders, inspect the primitive shoes in which only a god could have dunked, and then settle down to watch a video of an Indiana state championship game.

Among the most popular choices is a half hour of scratchy film labelled "Milan v. Muncie Central, 1954." They know it as the game on which the Hollywood film *Hoosiers* was based. There are few young people in Indiana, especially those who play on organized sports teams, who have not seen the movie about the farm kids who beat the big-city team in the Indiana state finals.

"Well," say their adult guides, popping in the videocassette, "here's what it really looked like." The lights go out, and what flickers before them isn't like *Hoosiers* at all. The film is silent and the images are in black and white. The players seem to play in slow motion, pushing chest passes at each other and lifting prehistoric-looking set shots and one-handed jump shots toward the basket. Kids giggle. No one dunks. For a long while at the end no one does anything at all; everyone just stands around.

Finally, a slender, crewcut white player wearing the number twenty-five on his dark jersey bounces a basketball very steadily, while being guarded intently by a taller black player wearing the number twelve. All teammates on both teams seem to have disappeared. Suddenly the offensive player fakes to the right, dribbles the ball hard, cuts to his left, and releases a soft, one-handed jump shot over his defender's outstretched hand. The ball falls through the net and the film expires.

Captured on that video is the Hoosier dream. The images surely would find a place in any time capsule intended to show survivors what Indiana was like in the mid-twentieth century, and before. The event they capture reminds all Hoosiers that old-fashioned values — hard work, boldness and imagination — will still prevail in a fair fight. And if the world no longer seems a fair fight, the State Tournament still comes around each March to remind everyone what it once was like before the deck was stacked.

All other states but Delaware and Kentucky have divided their state basketball tourneys into classes by enrollment. Typically, big-city schools play in one tourney, medium-sized and rural schools in events of their own. In Indiana little country schoolhouses confront great city institutions named Washington and Central and Lincoln in the same tournament. Not as many players get trophies in Indiana, but, if you can win, you wake up not as the champ of Division II-A but as the ruler of all Hoosierland.

But only once have Hoosiers had a chance to savor the upset the event was designed to produce. That was in 1954, when Milan High School, with an enrollment of 161 students — seventy-three boys — brought down Muncie Central High School, a school ten times as big, to win a tournament in which 751 schools were entered. The game was won on a shot with three seconds left by a boy named Bobby Plump.

It has been estimated that on that March evening, 90 percent of all Indiana families were watching or listening to the Milan-Muncie Central game. The contest is one of the most remembered events in the lives of many Hoosiers, along with the events of World War II and the births, deaths, and passages of loved ones. Milan struck a blow for the small, the rural, the stubborn; Milan stopped the highway, saved the farm and allowed many to believe that change was still merely an option.

By hitting a fifteen-foot jump shot, Bobby Plump delivered the dream to which many grateful Hoosiers still cling. That is why his sleep is interrupted by strangers, why many of his personal belongings from the early fifties are preserved in various museums, and why a few moments in his late adolescence are enshrined in New Castle for everyone to see.

Bobby Plump grew up in Pierceville, Indiana, population forty-five, about thirty miles northwest of Cincinnati. He is the youngest of six children, raised by his father and eldest sister after his mother died when he was five.

It was not an easy life, but the Plumps were not the kind to complain about what they didn't have. Bobby's father taught school for a while, but when the Depression hit he took on a chicken route to Cincinnati, selling eggs until he found factory work in Lawrenceburg.

There was a good roof over their heads, but nothing unnecessary under it. There was never running water, and no electricity until Bobby was twelve. Four years later they were finally able to bring home a refrigerator, but phones and television sets were always to be for others. It was a warm and supportive family, and Plump today recalls his as a wonderful childhood.

"I may have run the world's smallest paper route," he says, "but I always had some money. I think I delivered eighteen or twenty papers. We had it for twenty-four years. When you got six kids, after the two brothers came back from the war, you could always get a card game up. We used to play pinochle with an Aladdin's

Milan's cheering section — most prominently Bobby Plump's sister and brother-in-law — fourth quarter, 1954 state finals. (Courtesy Bob Plump)

lamp. Dad did the trading — that's what he called it — in town every Saturday. He'd go to the Oddfellows Hall, and if we had a dime we'd go to the movies, five cents to get in and five cents for popcorn. Then we'd meet him back over at one of the stores and ride back to Pierceville. It was a wonderful time."

"Town" was Milan, a center for Ripley County's hog, tobacco, poultry, and cattle markets, whose population was about eleven hundred. Though it was named after the Italian city, it is pronounced *My-lan*. One can also find Athens, Cairo, Paris, Rome, Shanghai, and Vienna without leaving Indiana.

A town of eleven hundred could seem like a jungle to a Piercevillian. "I remember getting lost in Milan in fifth or sixth grade," recalls Plump. "I went to a movie and couldn't find anybody. I was standing there crying and a man working in a furniture factory saw me and picked me up and brought me home. I just didn't know my way around."

When Bobby was in fourth grade, his father nailed a backboard to a shed for him on Christmas Day. Bobby spent most of the day shooting at it, entranced. He soon could hit the basket regularly. Better still, before long he found that he could freeze whoever was guarding him with a fake and a quick stride to the basket.

In 1949 the boy heard his first Indiana high school basketball tournament on the radio. He and Glenn Butte, who lived across the tracks, made it a grand occasion. They strung up some lights out back and together they choreographed the play-by-play, imagining how the players looked and moved.

In the final game, Bobby was Madison's Dee Monroe and Glenn played Jasper's Bobby White. Thirty years later, when Plump was introduced to Bobby White at a Hall of Fame banquet, he was astonished to discover that White was only five-six. Only then did he realize that, assuming White was much taller, they had choreographed the shots all wrong.

Even in a community of forty-five, it was easy to get ten or twelve players up after dinner, when everyone came home. You played with the older kids, your brothers, fathers, and in-laws. The games were rough, especially on a gravel surface; "No blood, no foul" was the Pierceville code.

Bobby and Glenn and two other pals named Gene White and Roger Schroeder played together constantly. After a while, they

developed a common experience of each other, each one under-
standing what the others were going to do on the court, the way
voices in family quartets seem to reach for each other and blend.

Roger's family, the Schroeders, were the town merchants —
they owned the one store in town — and day or night their place
was the hub. At first everyone played in the barn behind the store,
but the roof slanted down so you had to angle a shot from the corner too much. Besides, a nearby manure pile seemed to exert a
magnetic pull upon the ball. So they moved the goal outside,
trapped two shovels under a sheet of tin and strung electric lights
between them; that way they could keep playing until midnight.

In the winters everyone went into Milan to see the Milan High
School team play basketball. Milan's was not a glorious tradition.
Over the decades the school had won two or three sectional tourneys but had never won a game in the regionals. Batesville, one of
the other big schools in Ripley County along with Osgood and
Versailles, beat Milan so regularly in the county tourney that it
became a sort of custom, something you expected.

The Pierceville kids were especially attracted to a Milan player
named Bill Gorman. Rather than lifting his leg mechanically and
hoisting up one-handed push shots like everyone else, or stopping
to twirl the ball like a squirrel sizing up a nut and then lofting a
two-hand set shot, Gorman leaped in the air on the run or off the
dribble and fired up the first jump shots anyone around had seen.
Gorman, an Air Force pilot, died in in a plane crash in 1962, but
he left his legacy in his jump shot.

From the first grade on, they all went to school in Milan. That
meant a three-mile walk or bike ride home, unless somebody's
parents could find the time to go in and pick them up. They felt
clumsy and ill-dressed around the Milan kids, who seemed to
have a zest for ridiculing them.

Plump was painfully shy and easily embarrassed. He tells a
story about two Milan kids tearing off his new green coat and
throwing it in the snow. The memory still brings color to his
cheeks and causes his voice to break. He became a legend at
Milan, but he remains a Piercevillian at heart, and to him there
remains a huge, living difference between the two.

Glenn Butte, Roger Schroeder, Bobby Plump, and Gene White in downtown Pierceville. This photo has become a postcard in Indiana. (Courtesy Bob Plump)

Four Piercevillians — Plump, Schroeder, Butte, and White — made the eighth-grade team at Milan. Here at last was a way to shine. Milan, too, had skilled players who had grown up together. The team lost only one game all year and began to attract the attention of the town. In Milan's coffee shops it was said that these kids were "comers." The stigma of being from the country meant nothing in such quarters; you could be from Mars and it wouldn't matter as long as you could shoot or rebound.

Milan's varsity coach was Herman "Snort" Grinsted, a veteran high school coach whose nickname derived from his explosive temper. Grinsted quickly recognized Plump's shooting ability and began to plan for the future. Though one-handed shots or even overhanded free-throws had been forbidden in grade school, Grinsted told Plump as a freshman to perfect one move: start with the ball on one side of the court or the other, dribble across to the free throw line and then stop and shoot the one-handed jumper.

By the time Plump was a sophomore, he and two other classmates were dressing for the varsity games, but not really expecting to play much on a team with seven seniors. Then, early in the season, county rival Osgood humiliated Milan 85–38, and after the game Snort erupted. Red-faced, he banished all seven seniors from the team and moved three sophomores, including Plump, into the starting lineup.

No Ripley County team beat Milan again for the rest of the season, and twice they avenged their loss to Osgood. The team was the toast of Milan. Plump remembers being late for class one Monday after he had played especially well. He approached the classroom door, embarrassed as usual about his clothing, in mortal terror of standing out. He hesitated for a few moments outside the door, then gathered himself and opened it. When he appeared, his classmates stood up and applauded. "It was then I really knew I had something going for me," he says.

Grinsted, on cloud nine, rewarded his young charges by buying everyone new uniforms at the end of the year, without permission from school officials. When the word got out, Milan's principal was furious. He summoned Grinsted and pointed out that the athletic fund was now bankrupt and this time Snort had gone way too far. Shaken, Snort offered to pay for the uniforms himself, but it was too late. Like his seven exiled seniors, he was a man without a team.

There was a good reason for all the grumbling you could hear around Milan in the summer of 1953. Snort was gone. Some thanks after the year he'd had. And to make matters worse, the guy they hired to replace him was only twenty-four years old, two years out of college and, rumor was, he was a set-offense man.

Indiana at that time had achieved a national reputation as the heart of "racehorse" basketball. Most high school coaches took their cues from Branch McCracken's Indiana University squads — the "Hurryin' Hoosiers" — whose greyhounds usually won games by scores like 102–99. To slow the game down on purpose was worse than soft; in Ripley County it was near treasonous.

After Grinsted, the new coach, whose name was Marvin Wood, was indeed going to take some getting used to. He was a soft-spoken, highly disciplined and religious young man. In all the years Bobby Plump was to know Wood, he heard Wood raise his voice in anger only once, and on that occasion — after the team turned in a sloppy performance in a tournament game — Wood kicked a medicine chest and injured his foot.

Wood was convinced that these smart, sharpshooting kids could win by using the offensive system he'd learned from Tony Hinkle, his coach at Butler University. He knew firsthand that its inherent order could neutralize faster and taller players. Hinkle's system amounted to fourteen variations of a single pattern involving two players. The trick was to execute the plays perfectly. On your first day at Butler you began to learn the fourteen patterns. On your last day you were teaching them to the freshmen.

Wood had been all set to sign a contract to coach at Bloomfield High when his high school coach told him of the sudden opening at Milan and advised Wood to go check it out. Word was, there was some real talent down there.

So one summer morning Wood drove to Ripley County, sat down on a basketball and watched two groups of youngsters, one in Milan and one in Pierceville, play game after game. They were small but quick, smart and good shooters. Above all, they were obviously close friends, kids who acted like they had been playing together a long time. Though the money — four thousand dollars to teach and coach — wasn't as good as the Bloomfield job, Wood applied for and won the job at Milan.

Wood's first challenge of the 1953 season was a personnel matter: fifty-eight of Milan's seventy-three boys tried out for the team. And, as much as Wood disliked zone defenses, that was the only way any of them had ever played. At first Wood tried to force them to play man-to-man, but he soon gave up and asked the junior high coach to show him how they had learned to play defense.

Wood imposed few rules, but he enforced them relentlessly. He set a ten o'clock curfew during the regular season, but on New Year's Eve he let the players stay out till 1:00 A.M. On that evening Bobby Plump and a teammate were double-dating. A flat tire stalled them, but the quartet managed to pull up to Plump's house at the stroke of one, at least according to Plump's watch. Wood was waiting for them; his watch said they had just missed. There was no debate. As Plump recalls it, Wood said quietly, "I'm going to make an example of you." Plump did not dress for the next game.

The next-to-the-last game of the regular season, Milan was drubbing Osgood again when play started getting rough. Wood called a time-out. Explaining that he didn't want anyone getting hurt before the sectional started, he told the team to try something totally new.

He stationed Plump in the middle of the court, put Ray Craft and Bob Engels deep in the corners near midcourt and told Gene White and Ron Truitt to stand in the corners down under the basket. He instructed Plump simply to hold the ball until someone tried to take it away from him. When that happens, he said, someone come out and meet the ball so Bobby can get rid of it and everybody else cut toward the basket and look for a pass. When the players asked him about it later, it turned out Wood had even coined a name for the scheme; he called it the "Cat and Mouse." Hoosiers proudly claim it as the forerunner of all spread offenses today.

Entering the tourney, everyone in Ripley County knew Milan had a fine team. They'd had to move their final few home games to a bigger gym, and, for the first time in a long while, the school was forced to raffle sectional tickets to meet the demand. There were great displays of civic pride. Chris Volz, Milan's GM dealer, stood up at one rally and promised to provide the team a fleet of Chevies to drive to the sectional round of the tournament. There was a lusty cheer. Volz held up his hands for silence. "That's not all," he said. "It's gonna be Pontiacs for the regionals, Buicks for the semi-state, and Cadillacs for the finals." Though the statement produced bedlam, the Caddies must have felt secure on the lot: in more than thirty years Milan had never won even a regional game.

Milan breezed through the sectionals and took the road in Pontiacs to the Rushville regional tourney. There they got lucky. In a cliffhanger against Morton Memorial, Milan fell behind by two points with twenty-eight seconds left. The ball went out of bounds, and while it was being retrieved the timekeeper forgot to turn the clock off. When play resumed, Milan's Bill Jordan was quickly fouled, and when he looked at the clock, he was amazed to see that there was no time left. Calmly he hit both free throws and tied the game. Morton appealed without success. Plump won the game for Milan with two free throws in a second overtime.

Milan went all the way to Indianapolis before losing to South Bend Central in the afternoon semifinal game. Plump had a great tournament, scoring nineteen of Milan's thirty-seven points against Central. For the first time, he began to believe that basketball might carry him to college; that all the hours in back of Schroeders' and in town might actually pay off. It had been an unbelievable season, highlighted by one of the most remarkable coaching jobs in Indiana high school history: a rookie coach had taken a school with seventy-three boys to the state finals. Snort Grinsted was now all but forgotten, and Marvin Wood had every right to feel like a king. Instead, he felt like a failure.

All summer he blamed himself for having let his team down. They deserved more, he told himself. Maybe a more experienced coach could have given them the chance for which they had worked so hard. He thought about quitting.

There was a Biblical quality to his torment. One summer evening Wood was approached by a man who owned a tavern in Milan. He said he had a son who shot well and stood six-foot-four.

At the moment the boy was living with his grandparents in Lawrenceburg, but one word from Wood and the boy could live with him in Milan. He reminded Wood that Milan's center was graduating and that Wood was going to be left with Gene White as a five-eleven pivotman. The move would hardly have drawn censure; in fact the practice was something of an Indiana tradition. Marvin Wood declined politely, explaining that it wouldn't be fair to the kids who were already there.

Wood pulled himself together and took the reins again.

The 1954 group bolted off along the same path as their predecessors, losing only twice during the regular season. Seven hundred and fifty-one schools entered the tourney that year, and again few took Milan seriously. A schedule that included Rising Sun, Napoleon, Aurora, and Montezuma simply did not excite the Indianapolis sportswriters, whose hearts were hardened against the favorite-son teams which dissolved annually before big crowds in exotic cities.

But this team was for real. Milan rolled through the sectional and regional rounds of the tournament, flattening its first five opponents by an average of nineteen points. In Chris Volz's big Buicks, they cruised into Indianapolis for the semistate tourney with something to prove.

They beat Montezuma 44–34 in the afternoon semifinal, then went back to the Pennsylvania Hotel for a nap before the night game against Indianapolis' Crispus Attucks, an all-black high school. The Milan players had played against very few black opponents, and though Ripley County was hardly free of racial prejudice, Plump was surprised by the intensity of fan response in Indianapolis. "When we went out to dinner that night," he recalls, "an unusual number of people followed us around. One of the frequent remarks we heard was, 'C'mon Milan, beat those niggers.' People were saying it everywhere."

Crispus Attucks was led by the great Oscar Robertson, who in 1954 was a six-foot three-inch sophomore forward. Attucks was a strong, savvy, and spectacular team, a year away from invincibility. Milan raced to a strong first-half lead, but the effort exhausted Plump. At halftime he was seized by cramps in both legs and broke into a cold sweat. Wood wrapped him in a blanket and told him to stay in the locker room, the others would hold the lead.

Bobby Plump scores against Crispus Attucks High in the 1954 semi-state. Oscar Robertson watches, facing Plump. (Courtesy Bob Plump)

When Wood walked upstairs for the second half, Plump was already out on the floor warming up. His twenty-eight points led Milan to a 65–52 victory.

The next weekend, when the team fired up the Caddies for the state finals in Indianapolis, nine hundred of the town's eleven hundred residents went with them. Milan swamped a fine Terre Haute Gerstmeyer team in the afternoon game but still entered the evening showcase against Muncie Central as definite underdogs.

Muncie Central was — and still is — a big school with an intimidating tradition. The Bearcats had won the state championship four times, more than any other school but one. Muncie played its home games in a gym that could hold seven times the entire population of Milan. But the pressing problem was that Muncie's front line averaged six feet four inches; by contrast, Milan's Gene White jumped center at five-eleven.

Wood thought carefully about the job ahead. Nervousness would not be a problem. These kids had played together since childhood, and they weren't the kind to scare anyway. And nobody had taken them seriously enough for the fear of failure to enter in. But there was just no way a conventional approach could offset Muncie's height and muscle. Wood decided, for the first time, to try the spread offense — the Cat and Mouse — for a whole game.

The strategy worked like a charm for the first half, and Milan took a 25–17 lead into the locker room. Now all they had to do was stay calm and hit the shots that surely would come once Muncie started to press. But the third quarter was catastrophic: Milan failed to hit a single field goal and entered the final eight minutes of the game tied 26–26.

Most Hoosiers over fifty can tell you where they were during the final period of that game. Statewide television coverage of the finals had begun only three years before, but there had been a sophisticated radio network since 1921, and of course Butler Fieldhouse was jammed with over fifteen thousand Hoosiers. The state stood still that Saturday night, and the dream shimmered.

Muncie pulled ahead by two points in the opening seconds. Gambling that his veteran team would prevail in the frenzy that was sure to come, Wood stuck to his game plan. He told Plump, just as if they were playing Osgood for bragging rights to Ripley

County, to stand there and hold the ball until someone came out to get it.

So for four minutes and thirteen seconds Plump stood with the ball cradled under one arm, the other hand on his hip, staring at Jimmy Barnes, the player assigned to guard him. Barnes stared back, knees flexed, arms extended in a defensive position.

Most of Indiana thought Wood was insane, and many Hoosiers were furious. As the clock wound down, it sounded for all the world on the radio like Milan was *quitting;* Wood seemed to be mocking everything that every father told every son. They were *behind*, for Christ's sake, and they weren't even *trying* and the dream was ticking away.

Plump recalls those moments: "I kept looking over at the bench and Marvin Wood was sitting there as if he was out on the porch. He had his legs crossed, kicking his foot. If he would have told me to throw the ball up in the stands I would have done it, I had that much confidence in him. But when I'd look at him he'd just put his hands up, like 'Everything's okay.'"

Jimmy Barnes was likewise glancing over at Muncie coach Jay McCreary, who, ahead, was quite content to let time expire. "We wanted to go out and guard 'em, but coach said to lay back," recalls Barnes. "I wanted him to put the ball on the floor, 'cause I figured I could steal it from anyone."

With about two minutes left, the frenzy began: Wood let Plump shoot for the tie. He missed, and Muncie got the rebound, but then Milan's zone press forced a turnover and Ray Craft tied it at 28–all. Muncie coughed the ball up again, and Plump put Milan ahead with two free throws. Muncie's Gene Flowers retied the score at thirty. With all of Hoosierland on its feet, ear to the radio, eyes on the tube, or in the berserk fieldhouse itself, Plump and Craft brought the ball downcourt very slowly for the last time.

With eighteen seconds left, Wood called time out. In the huddle, Gene White suggested that everyone move to one side of the court and let Plump go one-on-one against Barnes. Plump was a little surprised since he was having a terrible game, having made only two of ten attempts so far. Wood agreed. Plump was the shooter and it was time for a shot.

Ray Craft was supposed to inbound the ball to Plump, and then the entire Milan team was to shift to the left side of the court, out

The day Hoosierland stood still: Bobby Plump holds the ball for over four minutes as Muncie Central's Jimmy Barnes stands ready. (Courtesy Bob Plump)

of Plump's way. But Plump, who had felt jittery in the huddle, nearly blew the play right away. He took the ball out of bounds himself and threw it in to Craft, who somehow found the presence of mind to catch it and toss it back.

Then the nervousness disappeared. After all, it was the play Snort Grinsted had told him to perfect years before, and he had done it a million times out back and at Schroeder's and against Osgood and Cross Plains and Aurora.

Alone and with nothing to do but what he knew how to do better than anything in the world, Plump slowly worked the clock down to five seconds. Then he suddenly cut across the lane, stopped quickly at the top of the key, leaped in the air and flung the ball over Barnes's fingers and toward the hoop. As the ball sailed through, Goliath buckled, Excalibur slipped free from the rock, and Indiana's dream came true.

When it was over, the two hundred folks left in Milan rushed out to start a bonfire. It is fortunate that the blaze did not burn out of control, since twenty-one of Milan's twenty-four firemen were at the game.

To keep his team from being crushed by celebrants, Wood permitted a brief Cadillac parade, backwards, as it turned out, around Monument Circle and then sequestered the boys in the Pennsylvania Hotel while joyous fans maintained a vigil outside.

They fired up the big Caddies for the last time and headed for Milan after breakfast on a bright Sunday morning. The caravan was led by Pat Stark, an Indianapolis motorcycle cop assigned to the team. They were expecting a celebration in town, maybe a brief homecoming in the Square, and then some sleep at last.

They were tickled to see the curbside crowds in the Indianapolis suburbs and thrilled by the fire trucks from Greensburg and Shelbyville that fell behind them on two-lane Highway 101. There were flags in all the little towns. Planes circled overhead. Officer Stark could not believe what was forming behind him, or ahead, for that matter.

About thirteen miles out of Milan, at Penntown, the team began to notice cars parked along the two-lane highway and met the first hikers waving and cheering and carrying picnic baskets. The motorcade had become a convoy, and they were losing speed. It took thirty-five minutes to go the eight miles from Batesville to Sunman. This was unreal.

When Officer Stark, flanked by American Legion cars, nosed into Milan, there were forty thousand people waiting. He turned off the Caddie and they all climbed onto a makeshift stage across from the park. From the stage, looking straight ahead, there were people as far as the eye could see. Kids dangled from the boughs of the sycamores in the park.

Everyone got to speak, even Stark. The big-city cop dissolved into tears. Marvin Wood repeated the four characteristics of a champion, the ones he had listed before every Milan game. They were: determination to win, self-confidence, alertness and luck. Mary Lou Wood, Marvin's wife, concluded her brief remarks with a line Bobby Plump was to use in the many speeches he would give after that day: "It's nice to be important," she said, "but it's more important to be nice."

"Plump" was the headline in *The Indianapolis Star* the following morning, and indeed Plump became a household word in Indiana. In fact, he remembers receiving a letter shortly after the tourney addressed "Plump, Indiana."

But it was still hard to get a totally swelled head in Pierceville. When *The Star* tried to telephone Plump to inform him that he was the new "Mr. Basketball" — the best player in the state — he still had to take the call at Schroeder's store. The phone went dead, and he didn't find out for sure what they wanted until the next day.

Today Bobby Plump has his own insurance agency, one which provides nicely for his family. His first clients were college athletes, kids who were thrilled to meet him. He had impressive careers at Butler University — which he chose largely because he knew Tony Hinkle's fourteen two-man variations by heart, and he knew there would be lots of shots in it for him — and in amateur basketball, with the Phillips 66 Oilers. He very nearly made the 1960 Olympic team.

Hundreds of speeches and banquets and celebrity golf tournaments have forced Bobby Plump — it's Bob now — to conquer his fear of public speaking; he says if he can get an early laugh he actually enjoys these appearances.

The number of requests for engagements has skyrocketed since the movie *Hoosiers* was released in 1986. The film is based on the Milan story, though screenwriters augmented the basic David and Goliath theme by adding a coach with a haunted past (Gene Hackman), a love interest (Barbara Hershey), and a town drunk (Dennis Hopper).

Plump's character, whose name is Jimmy Chitwood, is a troubled, sullen boy who has quit the team apparently because he felt loved only for his pure jump shot. Plump sees few similarities. "I didn't identify with Jimmy at all," he says, "at least not until the last eighteen seconds of the final game. I would never have held out and not played on the team. To me it was an honor to have a uniform and even sit on the bench. And at the end, I would have never said in the huddle, 'give me the ball, I'm gonna hit it.'"

He says that celebrity has taught him that everyone, even corporation presidents, have basic insecurities. Though he still seems to have more fun talking about the pressure shots he missed than the one he made, he knows that he is forever consigned, like Don Larsen or Bobby Thompson, to recount his special moment in the sun.

As the incarnation of the Dream, he is careful to tell an interviewer the whole story, with nothing left out, and as colorfully as possible. From time to time he'll say, "Wait, there's another story about that," or, "I forgot to tell you this," as if an omission would be irresponsible. Especially when you get to those final seconds, the stories peel away like layers from an onion. But the core is surprising: he says he really can't remember what he was thinking or what it felt like to hold the ball and look at Jimmy Barnes, except to recall, "He certainly was intense."

Jimmy Barnes is today a parole agent for the California State Prison System. He played college basketball for a year and was invited to an unsuccessful tryout with a professional team in 1961. Barnes says that although his relatives kid him a little about Milan when he goes back to Indiana, the people of Muncie did not hold Plump's shot against him. "They blamed everyone else but me, for some reason," he says.

Each year the Milan teammates get together at Thanksgiving to retell the old stories. Milan's victory did more than provide memories for these players; nine out of ten received college scholarships, and eight graduated. Before that game almost no one from Milan had ever been able to afford college. "I asked my father one time," says Plump, "if I had not gotten a scholarship, would he have sent me to college. He said, 'No, I couldn't afford to send the other five. It would not have been right to borrow money to send you.' "

Plump is amazed by his enduring celebrity. One of his high school championship jackets is in the Indiana State Museum, as is the outdoor basketball goal that his father made for him in Pierceville. There are questions about Milan High School on Indiana History tests, and a new biography is in the bookstores. Again and again, whenever an anniversary of the game arises or a new angle suggests itself to a reporter, Bobby Plump, now fifty-seven and the grandfather of three, is invited back to the Fieldhouse to try the shot again. Sometimes he hits it on the first try and sits down. And some days, such as the day he missed eleven straight for ABC television, he couldn't throw a basketball in a lake. Some things, he laughs, don't change.

Hardly a day goes by when someone doesn't mention the shot or the movie. His wife Jenine has learned to live with the calls in the night and interrupted meals. The couple's three children, now grown, have each had their own experiences with their father's legend:

"I was waitressing at this restaurant in 1981," recalls Tari Plump, Bob and Jenine's eldest daughter. "We were at a bar having drinks after work one night, and I still had my name-tag on my blouse. There were two gentlemen sitting next to me with very pronounced foreign accents. One of them looked at my name tag and said, 'Tari Plump? Are you any relation to Bobby Plump?' I said, 'Yes, he's my father.' He got very excited. He said, 'I come to United States, arrive in New York, fly to Indianapolis. We talk about sports. All I hear is Bobby Plump, Bobby Plump . . . did he do something special?' "

Hoosier immortals, the 1954 Milan Indians: front row (left to right): Bob Engel, Ron Truitt, Gene White, Bobby Plump, Ray Craft. Middle: Roger Schroeder. Back row: Glen Butte, Ken Wendelman, Rollin Cutter, Bill Jordan, Assistant Coach Clarence Kelley, motorcycle cop Pat Stark, and Coach Marvin Wood. (*The Indianapolis News*)

Indianapolis
Crispus Attucks High School —
No Mountain Too High

It is with a spirit of profound reverence and thanksgiving that we hail the new high school basketball champions of Indiana, the Crispus Attucks Tigers. Persons unfamiliar with our State may believe that we are overdoing it in going down on our knees and giving praise to almighty God that this glorious thing has come to pass. But basketball — especially the high school variety — occupies a particularly lofty place in the Hoosier scheme of things. It is far more than a boys' sport — in fact, it is just about the most important thing there is.

— *The Indianapolis Recorder*,
serving black Indianapolis, March 19, 1955.

Wearing green and gold letter jackets, their hair still wet from showering, ten boys scrambled out of Butler Fieldhouse into a frosty night and pulled each other aboard a crimson fire engine. The mayor's limousine and eight police motorcycles waited till the last player was secure and then swung in front of the fire truck and out east onto Forty-ninth street. As sirens wailed, the players looked back on a great jumble of school buses and sedans slowly sorting into a line of vehicles three miles long.

The motorcade turned right onto Meridian Street, and raced downtown toward the heart of the city. White people stood waving in the open doors of big houses, the kind in which the players' mothers and aunts cleaned. Children ran out onto the lawns, shouting the name of their school.

The motorcade slowed as it approached the spire of the Indianapolis Monument Circle, where fifteen thousand celebrants awaited. They took a single lap around the monument, pausing briefly for the mayor to present their coach a key to the City of Indianapolis on the Monument steps while the vehicles remained idling. Then they reboarded and the sirens sounded again and they all swung quickly away from the crowd and headed for Indiana Avenue, the main artery of Indianapolis' black neighborhood. Patrons poured out of jazz clubs and restaurants and surged around the truck, bringing traffic to a standstill. Horns blared in chorus from one end of the Avenue to the other.

The procession crawled toward Northwest Park, where thousands were already chain-dancing around a twenty-five-foot-high bonfire. The coaches and players soon joined their classmates and parents and aunts and uncles and neighbors and danced until dawn to platters like "Kokomo" and "Tweedlee Dee" which trumpeted through speakers as police watched from the park's perimeter, blowing into their hands.

Sixteen-year-old Oscar Robertson found himself unable to fully enjoy the celebration. It was strange: his school, Crispus Attucks High, had just won the state championship, ending decades of humiliation and scorn, and he had dominated the game. All around him, people pounded his back and flung their arms around him and pumped his hand. He saw nothing but wide smiles and eyes filled with tears of emotion.

But something about the motorcade gnawed at him. The downtown part had been a charade. Attucks had just given Indianapolis its first state champion after a half century of losses. There was supposed to be a celebration downtown, where all people would mix, not here in this park where almost everyone was black like them. The police had swept them away from downtown as if they were lepers. They had barely gotten off the truck.

After awhile Oscar slipped away to his father's house. Bailey Robertson, Sr., was surprised to hear the key turn in his door. "I remember Oscar came home about 10:30," he recalls. "He got a sandwich and lay down on the living room floor. He didn't say anything for awhile. Then he said, 'Dad, they really don't want us,' and he went to bed."

In 1922, the year the Indianapolis Chamber of Commerce first issued a call for a "separate, modern, completely equipped and adequate high school building for colored students," there were about two registered members of the Ku Klux Klan in Indianapolis for every black male. Statewide, nearly 250,000 Hoosier males — 30 percent of Indiana's white male population — and over 100,000 females were Klan members. Indiana was known nationally as the stronghold of the Ku Klux Klan.

The Klan's explosion was engineered by a native Texan with an eighth-grade education. In 1920, when he was hired by national Klan officials to organize a Klavern in Evansville, twenty-nine-year-old David Clarke Stephenson was selling stock in Indiana coal companies to World War I veterans. Often, he warmed up his prospects by gathering them in the lobby of the Vendrone Hotel and telling them stories of his war experiences. Eyes closed and voice swelling, he gave them bloody scenes in which he, the fighting Major David Stephenson, had led them through the enemy lines at Belleau Wood. In fact, the closest that Second Lieutenant Stephenson had come to Europe was the Iowa National Guard armory.

Stephenson was a stocky man with a full head of blonde hair and a ready smile. He was a brilliant public speaker who seemed equally at home among farmers and money men. No one knew much about him; later, researchers found that after completing eighth grade, he had drifted around the Plains states, working sporadically as a typesetter in print shops. He was married at twenty-four, but soon abandoned his pregnant wife and set off again. He drank heavily. He had been involved in political campaigns, first as a printer, then as a strategist, since his late teens. Ideals didn't matter — by the time he took the Klan job he had worked for socialists, Republicans, and Democrats, and had campaigned for office himself on both sides of the Prohibition issue.

Stephenson quickly saw how the Ku Klux Klan could make him a king. In 1920 Indiana had the highest percentage of native-born white residents of any state in the Union. Most were Protestants. Staffing his Klavern with Army buddies, Stephenson set out to give them common enemies, "aliens" and "outsiders" that "One-Hundred percent Americans" could stand together against.

"I am the law in Indiana," crowed Ku Klux Klan Grand Dragon D.C. Stephenson, and in the early 1920s, before he was convicted of murdering and mutilating an Indianapolis woman, he was. (*The Indianapolis News*)

Intimidation was an important tool. They discovered a forgotten law, rooted in the mid-nineteenth century, which allowed common citizens to be deputized to chase horse thieves. No one had ever bothered to scrub it from the books. In a matter of months the Klan swore in thousands of "Klan Horse Thief Detectives," authorized to carry weapons and enter the homes of "suspects" who were detained without warrants.

After increasing Klan membership in Evansville tenfold within a matter of weeks, Stephenson moved to Indianapolis in 1922 and took over the Klan newspaper *The Fiery Cross*. He warned readers that a tide of black laborers was on the way North to take their jobs for a dollar a day and commit unspeakable crimes against their wives and daughters. He wrote that Catholics were willing accomplices in the Pope's plot to conquer the world, and that Jews had already organized an international banking conspiracy against gentile businessmen and farmers.

Quickly he created what one writer described as a "hysteria of belonging." Tens of thousands of Hoosiers bought Klan memberships for between ten and twenty-five dollars, depending on income, and of which Stephenson pocketed four dollars, regardless of income. White robes and peaked hats went for six dollars a set, of which Stephenson kept four and a quarter. Within eighteen months D.C. Stephenson had raked in more than two million dollars.

Overnight, common people — caring parents, good neighbors, community leaders — formed vigilante squads, terrorizing blacks, Jews, and Catholics, and tarring women they accused of being prostitutes. There were public floggings. Crosses soaked in kerosene blazed on hillsides. Billboards reading "Nigger, don't let the sun set on you here" cast long shadows at town lines. On primary day in 1922 Klan deputies rode in a motorcade through the black neighborhood of Indianapolis, firing their revolvers into the air to discourage black citizens from voting. One mob of fifteen hundred, stirred to a frenzy by a Klan speaker, met a train in North Manchester and demanded that the single passenger prove he was not the Pope travelling in disguise to Chicago. Luckily, he was able to show that he was a corset salesman.

As bigotry became respectable, more and more politicians signed on, first secretly and then openly. Stephenson ran Indi-

Citizens of Muncie pose for a nighttime photo in August, 1922 — a time when nearly one of every three white males in Indiana was a Klansman. (Ball State University, A. M. Bracken Library, and the W.A. Swift Photo Collection)

ana's Republican Party from an eight-room suite in the Kresge Building in downtown Indianapolis. There he seated himself behind a massive desk supporting a battery of phones — including a dummy line to the White House. He positioned his upholstered chair beneath a bronzed bust of Napoleon and received supplicants. In 1924 Ed Jackson, a Republican who had run much of his campaign from the back of D.C. Stephenson's Cadillac, was elected governor of Indiana, carrying ninety of Indiana's ninety-two counties. The Klan vote also elected dozens of legislators, prosecutors, judges, mayors, and local leaders throughout Hoosierland.

There was plenty of work to do. More and more black workers had arrived in Indianapolis from the South to work in defense plants during World War I, sending for their families once they got a foothold. White leaders, many of them Klan-elected, took steps to carve up the city into racial zones. Separate parks were created for "colored" residents, and a separate wing was proposed for City Hospital. In 1924 the Indianapolis city council passed an ordinance, later struck down, to divide the city into "white" and "colored" residential districts. Real estate companies and rental agents advertised their properties in newspapers as "white" or "colored." In one 1926 editorial, *The Indianapolis News* called for the pavement of streets in black neighborhoods "to make them so attractive that there will be no desire to get out of them."

In December of 1922 the Indianapolis school board recommended establishment of a new high school for black students and teachers. Funds for construction were authorized three years later by a board whose members had been elected in the Klan tide. Local black organizations, aided by the NAACP, sued to stop the school from being built, but lost, and lost again on appeal. They were at least able to stop the board from naming their school Thomas Jefferson High. They named it themselves after a black seaman who was the first American to die in the Revolutionary War.

On September 12, 1927, the doors swung open to Crispus Attucks High School. Thirteen hundred and eighty-five students, many of them children uprooted from their neighborhood schools and often walking long distances, filed through the doors and into the classrooms. It was nearly double the number expected.

The Klan's influence was fading by then, largely because Stephenson had two years earlier been convicted of kidnapping, molesting, and murdering an Indianapolis woman. "Ed Jackson'll pardon me," he had said, grinning, as they led him away. Twenty-five years later another governor did, on the condition that the sun never set on him again in Indiana. But there were still enough Klansmen around in 1927 for a massive show of muscle on the first day of school. *The Indianapolis Star* reported that "One parade on Washington Street, consisting of row after row of masked Klansmen marching slowly to the beat of muffled drums, took an hour to pass." In this atmosphere, the black children of Indianapolis opened their books.

∞ ∞ ∞

A few days after Attucks opened, three prominent black leaders, F.E. DeFranz, Reverend H.L. Herod, and F.B. Ransom — "The Big Three," as they were often called — met with Arthur L. Trester, Permanent Secretary of the Indiana High School Athletic Association, to seek Attucks' membership in the organization that governed high school sports. Membership would let Attucks compete against other member schools and play in the Indiana state basketball tourney. There was no better way to show all Hoosiers that Attucks' athletes belonged among them.

Arthur Trester was forty-seven, eleven years into his job, and at the height of a remarkable career. His organization, fat on revenues from the grandest-scale basketball tourney in the U.S., was the envy of similar bodies throughout the nation. He was a well-known and powerful figure in Indiana; reporters often referred to his puppet board of governors as the "Board of Controlled," and editorial cartoonists caricatured him as a man on a throne. Whatever Arthur Trester's racial views might have been, there was little for him to gain by taking a pioneering stand in the Indianapolis of 1927.

The meeting was brief. Trester explained that since Attucks was not a public school — only blacks could attend — his organization's hands were tied. Trester rose and the Big Three exited, furious and humiliated. It was the opening round in a struggle that was to last for fifteen years.

At first, Attucks' athletic squads were able to compete only against other segregated and Catholic schools throughout the

KING ARTHUR TRESTER

King Arthur Trester, the imperious ruler of the ISHAA in its glory days. For fifteen years Trester resisted appeals to allow black and parochial schools to play in the Indiana State Tourney. (Courtesy Dale Glenn)

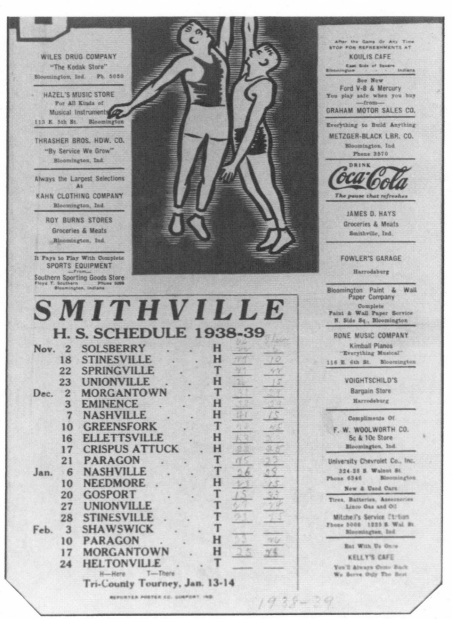

SMITHVILLE

H. S. SCHEDULE 1938-39

Nov.	2	SOLSBERRY	H
	18	STINESVILLE	H
	22	SPRINGVILLE	T
	23	UNIONVILLE	H
Dec.	2	MORGANTOWN	T
	3	EMINENCE	H
	7	NASHVILLE	H
	10	GREENSFORK	T
	16	ELLETTSVILLE	H
	17	CRISPUS ATTUCK	H
	21	PARAGON	T
Jan.	6	NASHVILLE	T
	10	NEEDMORE	H
	20	GOSPORT	T
	27	UNIONVILLE	T
	28	STINESVILLE	T
Feb.	3	SHAWSWICK	T
	10	PARAGON	H
	17	MORGANTOWN	H
	24	HELTONVILLE	T

H—Here   T—There

Tri-County Tourney, Jan. 13-14

REPORTER POSTER CO. GOSPORT IND.

1938-39

The 1938-39 Smithville High schedule. Note the December 17 game against "Crispus Attuck." For two decades, Attucks could find games only against tiny rural schools like Smithville and against segregated schools throughout the Midwest. (Courtesy Indiana Basketball Hall of Fame).

Midwest. Sometimes they travelled amazing distances. Once, athletic director Alonzo Watford raised four hundred dollars from local businesses to charter a bus to Tulsa, Oklahoma, for a football tournament. Knowing there would be few restaurants to serve them along the way, they packed enough food to last a week. The first snowflakes appeared in western Missouri. The driver pushed on until he couldn't see anymore, then eased the bus off the road. Darkness and Kansas engulfed them. Wind rattled the bus. Hours later the storm abated and they shouldered the vehicle back onto the pavement. Dressing on the bus, they made it to the stadium just before the coin toss and sprinted onto the field. A few hours later, having lost, they climbed back aboard and headed home.

In 1933 Attucks' principal, Dr. Russell Lane, convinced the athletic director of Ellettsville High, a small-town school north of Bloomington, to take a chance on a game with Attucks. As a precaution, the school's athletic director wrote to Arthur Trester seeking permission. Trester replied that he would allow IHSAA members to play Attucks in "contests in which not more than two schools should be involved at the same time." Lane saw it as the first break in the clouds.

The following season brought a few more games against tiny backwoods schools. Motor caravans formed in Attucks' lot on West Twelfth Street and followed two-lane roads out of Indianapolis until they reached the crossroads schoolhouses with oversized gyms blazing with light. Farm children gathered around the Attucks players as they emerged from the cars, gawking at the first dark-skinned people many had ever seen. Some shyly asked for autographs. To many, the Attucks players were like the Harlem Globetrotters, entertainers who had come to play an exhibition of some kind.

The games meant something quite different to Russell Lane. Lane was the son of a Baltimore attorney and a mother who had graduated with distinction from Brown University. The Lanes were Catholics, but the real creed in their household had been education. After three years on the faculty, Lane had taken over as Attucks' principal in 1930, determined to make the school a center of excellence in Indiana. Quickly he had recruited a top-notch faculty, including several Ph.D.'s from black colleges. Realizing that he was training a current generation of tailors and maids even as he optimistically prepared for a coming generation of engineers and teachers, Dr. Lane oversaw an enormous curriculum which included subjects from college algebra to tailoring.

To Russell Lane, each backwoods gym was a laboratory for progress and each Attucks player an ambassador. A game at a rural schoolhouse was a chance to show white fans, some of whom doubtless still owned robes and hoods, that black and white Hoosiers could mix without violence or incident. If they could see it in a gym, Lane thought, they would later come to believe in harmony in schools and neighborhoods.

Just as Branch Rickey later searched for a black baseball player who could withstand the abuse that came with being a pioneer, Dr. Lane personally oversaw the choice of players on the team, seeking well-spoken boys with very long fuses.

Lane constantly lectured his players not to commit fouls or protest calls, to ignore taunts, to avoid physical contact. They were to forget about showboat passes and behind the back dribbling. They were *not* the Globetrotters. As representatives of their race, they were to behave with dignity. Once the games began, Russell Lane worked his way methodically through the bleachers, introducing himself to farmers and merchants and housewives. Many found themselves warming to the short, bespectacled, genial man in a suit and tie who reached out for their hands and chatted with them until the final buzzer sounded, at which time he would settle up with the opposing athletic director and shepherd his players, glistening with sweat, out into the cars.

But sometimes it was hard even for Lane and Watford, deeply religious and optimistic men, to remain buoyant. They were so poor. Attucks' players dressed in hand-me-down uniforms that Watford had been able to salvage from a throwaway pile at Butler University. Students did their best to patch them up in Attucks' tailoring shop, but the tears and holes still showed. Since Attucks' gym had no seats, every game was an away game. Some school officials wouldn't even let Attucks' players shower in their locker rooms.

Worst of all was not being able to play in the state tourney. Each year March would come, and while the other schools were holding pep rallies, Attucks' players were cleaning out their lockers. Year after year DeFranz, Ransom, and Herod, along with a growing number of black and Catholic leaders and white liberals, crusaded for the admission of Indiana's Negro and parochial schools into the State Athletic Association, but Arthur Trester and his board just seemed to grow more stubborn.

It all came to a head at a meeting of the Indianapolis school board one evening early in 1941. After the roll was called, DeFranz rose to launch yet another passionate appeal for the board's support of Attucks' bid to compete in the tournament. DeWitt Morgan, the board's superintendent, cut him off. "I am sorry, DeFranz," Morgan snapped. "Not in my time nor in your time will this happen."

He was mistaken. That March, Robert Brokenburr, Indiana's lone black legislator, introduced a bill calling for state regulation of Arthur Trester's IHSAA and the admission of black and Catholic schools. Pastors sermonized in support, pointing out the hypocrisy of denying opportunities to students while their brothers and sisters were risking their lives for freedom in World War II. Editorial support in *The Indianapolis Star* gave the bill momentum. It passed the Senate handily and only a parliamentary maneuver kept it from passing in the House.

In December, with the handwriting clearly on the wall, Arthur Trester issued a matter-of-fact order which opened the IHSAA to all parochial and "colored" schools. It would still be several more years before the other public schools in Indianapolis would agree to play against them, but now they stood at the foot of the mountain. Here, at last, was a chance.

∞ ∞ ∞

In the winter of 1944, Mazelle Robertson ushered her three sons, Bailey, Oscar, and Henry, aboard a Greyhound bus in Nashville, Tennessee, and led them to the rear. She was leaving her home and family and the three hundred acres of cornfields that her grandfather had begun to sharecrop after the Civil War. Her husband, Bailey, Sr., had written that he found a job with the Indianapolis sanitation department. They should come on, now, he said. They could all stay with his sister.

Whatever Indianapolis was, it was North, and it had to offer more for the three boys than the one-room schoolhouse they attended in Tennessee. Unheated and without plumbing, it was a room in which a single saintly teacher named Lizzie Gleves taught every black child between first and sixth grade in Dickson County. The Robertsons believed their children deserved more than that room.

Sometime after midnight they pulled into the station in Indianapolis. They took hold of the one suitcase bound up with bailing wire that bulged with all their belongings and began to drag it down Illinois Street, asking for directions along the way, toward the address on the piece of paper. Sixteen blocks later, they found the house and waited on the porch until morning, when Bailey Sr.'s sister came home from work and let them in.

The neighborhood in which they had come to live was a collection of frame houses set within the flood plain of the White River. Some structures were merely squalid, cinder-floored shacks lined along the putrid waters of the Central Canal. Some residents lived without heat or electricity. The neighborhood was bisected from northwest to southeast by Indiana Avenue, a ribbon of taverns, jazz clubs and car lots, credit stores and clothing shops.

The best place to live in the neighborhood was a 748-unit federal housing project called Lockfield Gardens. There were three-room apartments, a central lawn, barber and beauty shops, and even a theater. There was a long waiting list for an apartment at Lockfield. For many boys, the best thing was a slab of cracked asphalt into which two basketball goals had been driven. There, on winter evenings and sticky summer days, black boys in Indianapolis waged war, teaching each other a form of basketball that bore little resemblance to the patterned game whites learned elsewhere in Indianapolis and in the surrounding towns.

Several months after their arrival from Tennessee, the Robertsons were able to put a payment on a small house on Colter Street, across from Lockfield Gardens. The basketball court was like a magnet to Bailey Robertson, Jr. With all the farm work there had been no time to learn sports in Tennessee, but here was something he was good at, and a way to gain respect in a new neighborhood. He became obsessed with getting better. He cut out the bottom of a peach basket and nailed it to a telephone pole in

Lockfield Gardens at the peak. Bailey Robertson shoots while brother
Oscar watches at center. Hundreds surrounded the court for these
summer games, while ice cream vendors patrolled the perimeter.
(Courtesy Indiana Basketball Hall of Fame)

the alley behind his house and played with Oscar and Hank, using a sock stuffed with newspaper as a ball. As the oldest and the biggest, Bailey had little trouble dominating the games.

Bailey was shocked when, on Christmas day in 1947, Oscar, then nine, opened a gift-wrapped box and pulled out a bright orange basketball. Oscar had begged his mother for a ball, but Bailey never thought she would take it seriously. How could she? Where would she get that kind of money? Mazelle explained that the lady she cleaned for had asked her what each of the boys wanted for Christmas. She had dutifully said that Oscar wanted a ball, and was as surprised as they were when the lady handed it to her, smiling, along with gifts for Bailey and Hank.

To Bailey, how it got there didn't matter. What mattered was that it was Oscar's ball. Oscar was now not only the only basketball owner in the family, but the only private ball owner in the *neighborhood*. Oscar made it clear to Bailey and Hank that it was not the Robertson Family Ball, but just his. In the mornings he took it out the door with him, and carried it with him wherever he went. At night, sometimes with Bailey looking on, Oscar soaped down the orange ball and placed it carefully beside his bed before closing his eyes. Here was something of his own worth having.

Ray Crowe grew up, the second of ten children and the oldest boy, outside a little farm town called Whiteland, twenty miles south of Indianapolis. His family rented and worked about two hundred acres of corn and alfalfa. The boys he worked with, fished with, studied with, played basketball with in haylofts and barns— in fact, almost everyone else in Johnson County but his family— were white. As a young boy he sometimes saw men and women in white robes and cone-shaped hats walking around the town square, directing traffic, sometimes just sitting and talking on the courthouse steps. His parents tried to explain and told him not to be afraid, and he wasn't. Why should he be? He recognized the men through their hoods as people had worked with in the fields, and with whom his family had shared harvest dinners.

Strong and athletic, he became a star guard on the Whiteland High basketball team. At first, Crowe didn't respond when whites tried to take advantage of his isolation as the only black player in a gym full of white people by shoving him around. At halftime of one game against Franklin High, Whiteland's coach, Glenn Ray, exploded. He threatened to bench Crowe unless he stood up to a player who had been literally pounding on him throughout the first half. When play resumed and Crowe got shoved he shoved back, hard, and then harder, and then before an astonished crowd and a delighted coach, Ray Crowe began to chase his tormentor up into the bleachers. Aggressive play brought respect; it was a lesson he never forgot.

From the time he was young Ray Crowe wanted to be a teacher. After he graduated from a small college in Indianapolis in 1939, it took him another six years to find a teaching job at Public School 17, next door to Attucks high. The problem had been that all the black teachers in Indiana were competing for a few jobs at the state's segregated schools.

Crowe had done his student teaching at Attucks while in college, and then, as now, he found it unsettling to be around so many black people. His first day he had simply stood across the street and stared at the hundreds of his people who were milling about the front of the school, cutting up, waiting for the bell to ring. He was embarrassed to be uncomfortable but he couldn't help it. Attucks was a different world from Johnson County.

Now he appeared each morning before his new math students at School 17 in a neatly pressed suit, often with a wide, double-breasted coat and pleated trousers, and with a well-organized lesson plan for the day. Many sized him up as weak. Some of the eighth-graders were already in their late teens, streetwise and bigger than Crowe. They talked and threw things and mocked him, and seemed to become bolder each day he didn't respond. The shop teacher carved him a paddle and urged him to use it. Crowe didn't want to; corporal punishment seemed an admission of defeat. Why should a student have to be bludgeoned into an education? He was in anguish. He thought about quitting.

Hallie Bryant, who later became one of Ray Crowe's star basketball players, remembers an early showdown. "This one math class, Ray left the room and then came back. This guy was showin' off for the girls. He had a Navy cap on. Hats were against the rules but he kept it on when Ray got back in. When Ray'd get mad in the classroom he wouldn't say anything, but you could see the muscles in his jaws poppin' out. He would sit up very straight. Usually the whole classroom would get quiet.

"But this guy kept at it. After awhile Ray rose and very calmly walked to him, took the cap off his head, stood him up by the collar, and whapped him horizontally across the face, vertically across the face, and in then whapped a little circle around his head. Then he stuffed the guy in his seat. The others were afraid to snicker. The kid sniffled, 'I'm gonna bring my daddy, I'm gonna bring my uncle.' Ray said, 'Please bring them *all*. I would love to meet your family.' "

Crowe organized an after-school intramural basketball league for the neighborhood boys. He was amazed by how little they knew about basketball. Living among whites, he had received years of training in the proper form and technique of shooting, passing, and dribbling. These boys just pushed each other around and threw the ball up. They had never played in organized games and had no heroes.

He taught them by playing with them, dribbling around them, shooting over them, slamming into them, picking them up, daring them to find a way to stop him from scoring. They adored him. He cared enough to challenge them, to give them goals, to show them how to do things. "He used to run up the wall, spring off it and slam-dunk," remembers Hallie Bryant "That used to impress us little kids. He'd come into your neighborhood and take you to get a soda. He'd visit your home and get to know your parents. He became like one of the family."

∞　∞　∞

The first mighty surge of Ray Crowe's Tigers, in 1951, aroused probably the greatest demonstration of genuine good feeling between whites and Negroes since the Civil War.

— *The Indianapolis Recorder*

Late in the 1950 season, Fitzhugh Lyons, the head coach at Crispus Attucks High, resigned abruptly. He cited poor health, but many believed he had succumbed to intense community pressure to make a winner of Attucks in the state tournament. Ray

Crowe, who had started coaching Attucks' reserve team the season before, took over. The team he fielded in 1951 was a hybrid of his intramural players — tough, hard-scrabble kids from the Westside like Hallie Bryant, Willie Gardner, and Bailey Robertson (whom everyone now called "Flap," after the way his wrist turned over when he shot) and a group of holdovers from Lyons' team.

The two groups represented conflicting philosophies within the faculty at Crispus Attucks High School, within the black community of Indianapolis, and in black America in general. In many ways, the 1950–51 Crispus Attucks High basketball season was about whether to make progress by presenting model sportsmen or young warriors.

Fitzhugh Lyons had been handpicked by Russell Lane. He had been the first black athlete ever to play on the Indiana University football team. In college his every move had been scrutinized, causing him to behave with caution even in a brutal sport. He and Lane stocked the Attucks teams with the well-behaved sons of a small black middle class in Indianapolis, young men who could be counted on to control their tempers in competition. The boys around Lockfield Gardens scornfully called them "Northsiders."

Lyons taught them a fastidious style of play. They were never to leave their feet when shooting, and they were to keep two hands on the ball except when dribbling. They walked the ball down the court and passed it deliberately, probing for a clear shot. They did not foul or complain when referees were unjust. They practiced a genteel style of defense in which players guarded zones rather than individuals.

If Ray Crowe had a philosophy about achieving racial progress through basketball, it was that everyone would gain from the experience of winning. Players would gain self respect. The black community would draw strength from a winning team, and whites would respect winners who carried themselves with pride and were not afraid to play hard more than they would good sportsmen who wilted in the heat of battle.

The contrasting philosophies were embodied in the two tallest players on the Attucks varsity. Bob Jewell, the starting center, had been Fitzhugh Lyon's pet project. A six-foot five-inch senior, Jewell was a fine shooter and rebounder, scholarly and reflective by nature. Jewell was the student council president, a thoughtful and diplomatic boy who was probably the most respected student at the school. His parents were together, and both worked. They had scraped enough together to pay for a home in a white neighborhood on the Northside. Jewell's older sister had been a top scholar at Attucks. The model of a scholar-athlete, Bob Jewell was Dr. Lane's Exhibit A. Ray Crowe thought him soft.

By contrast, Willie Gardner, a forward at six-eight, often came to school hungry. From time to time he dropped out of school to find work to help his mother, whose suffering he often dreamed about at night. He was reed thin, loose-limbed, and seemingly carefree. Sometimes in the heat of a game he would begin to laugh. No one knew why. Fitzhugh Lyons had viewed Willie Gardner as an embarrassment, the embodiment of the stereotypical undisciplined Negro from which they should all be striving to escape. Lyons humiliated Gardner repeatedly during practice, calling him "Drink of Water" and making him run laps alone while the others scrimmaged. "I don't know how many times he told me I'd never be a basketball player," Gardner later recalled.

Ray Crowe knew Willie Gardner as a deeply proud and rather private individual, and a phenomenal athlete. Gardner had been one of the first boys to play on Crowe's intramural teams at School 17. Fooling around one day, Crowe had demonstrated a standing back handspring and challenged a group of boys to try. Gardner, nearly a head taller than the others, was the only one who could do it.

When the 1951 season began, Crowe instantly placed Gardner in the starting lineup and gave him free reign to run and handle the ball. Midway through one early game, Hallie Bryant's long jump shot bounded off the rim and went straight up. Gardner, crouched beneath the basket, leaped up, cupped the ball in one hand high above the basket, and smashed it down through the hoop. The crowd was at first stunned, then ecstatic. In the Indiana of 1951 that dunk was a revolutionary move, a stylistic breakthrough something like those that Julius Erving would bring later.

Emboldened, Gardner worked out a pregame dunking routine. First he did a left-handed dunk, then a right-handed dunk, and then a two-handed over the head dunk. Often, opposing players,

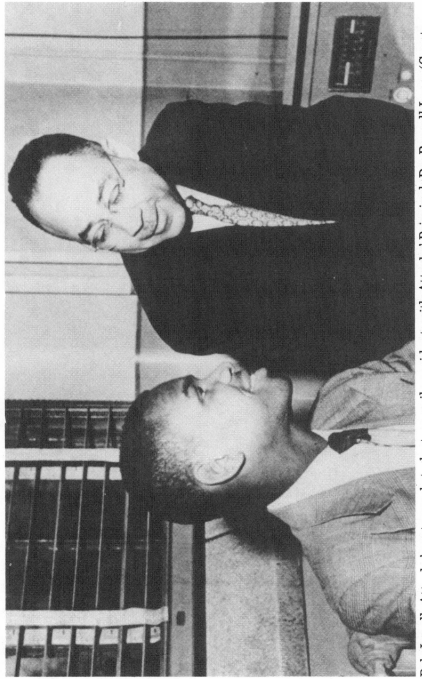

Bob Jewell, Attucks' center and student council president, with Attucks' Principal, Dr. Russell Lane. (Courtesy Angela Jewell)

Best friends Willie Gardner and Hallie Bryant, with their beloved coach Ray Crowe. (Frank H. Fisse)

especially those from the little towns which still made up much of the Attucks schedule, would stop their own warm-up drills to watch Willie Gardner dunk. Some coaches kept their players in the locker room until Attucks was finished warming up. It was a huge advantage.

After Attucks won the bitterly-contested Indianapolis sectional in 1951 for the first time, defeating several schools that still refused to schedule games against them, Ray Crowe and the Attucks players became community heroes. Store windows along Indiana Avenue blossomed with good luck signs for the second, or regional, round to be played the following Saturday at gigantic Butler Fieldhouse in Indianapolis. The tourney was televised for the first time that year, and during the sectional games neighbors had clustered around TV consoles in bars and hotels, squinting to make sense of blurred images on the little screens.

Their first regional opponent was Anderson High School, one of the established powerhouse teams in Indiana. It was by far the biggest game in which Attucks had ever played. The contest would be attended by fifteen thousand fans and broadcast and telecast throughout central Indiana. To Ray Crowe's annoyance, Dr. Lane now attended every practice, stopping play from time to time to orate on the importance of good sportsmanship. Crowe noticed that some of his players seemed to be suffering through these speeches, shifting from foot to foot, looking around. Bob Jewell seemed raptly attentive.

It turned out to be a game for the ages. "I saw the greatest high school basketball game I've ever seen last night . . . " began *The Indianapolis Times'* sportswriter Jimmy Angelopolous' account the morning after the game. "I saw a great Anderson team overcome odds in physical superiority. I saw Crispus Attucks demonstrate to critics that courage and the will to win will overcome tremendous odds and poor officiating."

Attucks was behind in the game by ten points with less than four minutes of play remaining. Hallie Bryant and Willie Gardner led a furious charge, stealing the ball time after time and driving hard for the hoop. Anderson began to buckle. Collapsing too was a belief, widely held among whites, that black athletes routinely collapsed under intense pressure. With eleven seconds remaining, Attucks pulled to within a single point, 80–79, and was in possession of the ball. Ray Crowe called time out and set up a play for Hallie Bryant to take a final shot. He also put in Bailey "Flap" Robertson, who had barely played in the game.

When play resumed the inbounds passer tried to force the ball to Bryant. The pass was deflected to Willie Gardner, who saw Bailey Robertson standing alone in the right corner. Gardner whipped the ball to him. "I jumped as high as I could and just let the ball go," Robertson later said. Accounts of what happened next differ. Oscar Robertson, then thirteen and in the Butler bleachers, recalls his brother's shot as a "Hail Mary," one that struck the rim, bounced up, and plunged straight down through the net. Hallie Bryant recalls it as rattling around the hoop before dropping through almost of fatigue. Bailey Robertson would have none of that. "Nothin' but net," he recalled, nodding firmly, a few months before his death in 1994.

It was a defining moment in his life, and in the lives of his school and community. "Later people told me their relatives died of heart attacks," he said. "One lady said she started to go into labor when the ball went through. Ever since, I've asked myself, why me? Well, there's no answer. I wasn't even on the starting team. I guess that fate — and Ray — just said, 'go in, Flap.' "

The miracle comeback made some whites curious about the Attucks players as individuals. Anyone watching closely could see the victory was not simply the product of sheer natural athleticism. The Tigers had shown discipline and heart. Some Attucks players seemed to have distinctive personalities. Hallie Bryant looked to be exuberant, Willie Gardner laconic, and Bob Jewell poised.

After the Anderson game Jimmy Angelopolous wrote a long feature piece for *The Times* about the Attucks team, portraying the players as ordinary young people with rather typical hopes and dreams. "This might as well be the story of any basketball team — in Podunkville, in Quail Creek, in Twin Forks — somewhere in Indiana," he began.

That story was little short of revolutionary. Soon Angelopolous' telephone number became an inviting target for crank callers, some with menacing messages. After writing a similar piece for

The Indianapolis Star, a young reporter named Bob Collins was repeatedly branded a "Communist." "That was a big word then," he recalls. "You did something outside the bounds, no matter what it was and people would call you a Communist."

The following Saturday Attucks won the third, or semistate, round of the tournament and, late in March, the players began to prepare for state finals — one of four teams remaining from 759 entrants, carrying on their shoulders the hopes and dreams not only of black Hoosiers, but of many whites in their city. It was a burning embarrassment that no school from Indianapolis had ever won the Indiana championship. After decades of ridicule, many whites were quite willing to have Attucks put an end to the ordeal.

Being so close to the summit after so long a journey filled Russell Lane with emotion. As the players were pulling on their jerseys at Butler Fieldhouse before their game against Reitz High of Evansville, Dr. Lane entered the dressing room to address them. As usual, everyone fell silent. It was a familiar theme: You are representing much more than your school, he told them. You *are* black Indianapolis. This time, the whole state is watching. More important than winning is that you must demonstrate good sportsmanship. Be gentlemen.

Willie Gardner remembers trying not to pay attention to Lane. He wanted to win more than anything. But for Bob Jewell, the speech was a balm of sorts. It was what Fitzhugh Lyons had always told him and it was what he believed. That he had never fouled out of a game in his life was a source of great pride. The state tourney *was* about sportsmanship as well as winning. The game was a nightmare from the start. They were out of synch, in a dream world. No one could hit shots, and Evansville Reitz couldn't miss them. Jewell was in a special hell. He found himself guarding the first really mobile center he had ever faced, a superb outside shooter named Jerry Whitsell. "I couldn't reach his shots," Jewell recalled. "He'd go out to the corner, out where I'd never guarded anyone before, and the ball would be up over my head before I could react."

Attucks lost 66–59, and the season was over. Jewell, blaming himself, went home alone, sank down on his bed and sobbed. He was still crying a few hours later when Dr. Lane called, ordering him back to Butler Fieldhouse to attend the game for the state championship that evening. There was a chance, Dr. Lane explained, that Jewell might win the Arthur L. Trester Award, given to the player on the four finalist teams who best exemplified the ideal of a scholar-athlete-citizen. It didn't matter to Lane that the award bore the name of the man most responsible for keeping Attucks out of the tourney for fifteen years. What mattered was that Jewell could be the first black player to win it.

Jewell pulled himself together, returned to the Fieldhouse, and, when his name was called, walked onto the floor to accept the award, still fighting back tears. He felt that he had let everyone down. The math was unforgiving. He had scored six points and his man had scored nineteen. His team had lost by seven. There was no one to talk to, no source of comfort in his reserved family, no friend or girl friend or teammate with whom he could share his grief. Ray Crowe was not really his coach, and his relationship with Fitzhugh Lyons left little room for emotion. "If I could have given that award back and we had won the game I would gladly have done it," he said softly, forty years later. "It was a Band-aid on a gaping wound."

The 1951 Attucks team galvanized black Indianapolis. They had done better in the tourney than any other Indianapolis team, even the ones that still wouldn't play them. One of Attucks' cheerleaders had made up a song that rubbed the new pecking order in everyone's faces. Called the "C-R-A-Z-Y" song, Attucks fans would begin to sing, weaving back and forth, once the game was firmly in hand. *Oh, Tech is rough / And Tech is tough / They can beat everybody / But they can't beat us / Hi-de-hi-de, hi-de-hi / Hi-de-hi-de, hi-de-ho / That's the skip, bob, beat-um / That's the crazy song.* The earlier the song began, the sweeter the goad.

And now younger kids in the neighborhood had heroes. Oscar Robertson began to challenge Hallie Bryant to one-on-one games at Lockfield, using his orange ball as bait. At first reluctant, Bryant saw Oscar's special talent and became a tutor. "We'd get out there before everybody," Bryant later recalled. "Just the two of us. Oscar was always asking, 'How'd you do that?' I'd show him and he could do it right away. I could see me in him. He could do anything I could do. I told people he was gonna be great."

Ray Crowe spent much of the summer reliving the loss to Reitz. He thought it was his fault. He blamed himself for letting them back down when the prize was theirs for the taking, and thought he had let Russell Lane weaken them. He vowed not to let it happen again. "It was the way they had been brought up," he later said. "They felt they shouldn't knock heads the way you have to if you're going to be a winner. I came up playing against white kids. I went to school with 'em. I knew."

But there had been other victories in Crowe's first year of coaching at Attucks, known only to the players and their families. He had put food in their bellies, kept them in school, sometimes found clothes that fit them. He created pressure to study by posting their grades on his classroom bulletin board. He arranged for them to get at least one free meal a day at the school cafeteria. "I remember once he called us together and said 'I don't want anybody to go all day at school without eating,'" recalls Willie Merriweather, a star on the Attucks teams of the mid-fifties. "He said, 'If your mother doesn't have any food in the house, let me know. I'll make sure you have something.' I never went hungry."

As his players got older they drove his car when they got licenses and wore his suits to the prom. When they dropped out of school to take jobs that could help feed their families, he tracked them down and patiently offered them reasons to return to Attucks, explaining that an education was the only real path to money.

"I remember once, after I quit my job and went back to school Ray gave me his socks, I remember that so well," says Willie Gardner. It didn't matter that the socks were way too tight for the boy, who by then was nearly a foot taller than his coach. The smooth, dark hosiery that had once been selected carefully to match one of Mr. Crowe's fine suits was evidence that this great man loved Willie Gardner. In turn they meant that Willie Gardner must be worth loving. He looked at the socks at night, and took special care of them. In the end, the decision to re-enroll at Attucks wasn't even close: no job was worth as much as a place in Ray Crowe's heart.

∞ ∞ ∞

Early in the 1952 season four members of an overflow crowd, unable to get into a sold-out game between Crispus Attucks and Cathedral High School, began to lob rocks through the windows of the Cathedral gym. The newspapers put a racial spin on the incident, since three vandals were white and one black, but the real problem was that no high school gym in Indianapolis could hold everyone who wanted to see Attucks play.

Attucks' athletic director Alonzo Watford searched desperately for a bigger place in Indianapolis. Finally as a last resort, he agreed to put three hundred dollars down to rent Butler Fieldhouse in the season's next to last game. It seemed like extortion.

On Wednesday, February 23, more than five thousand fans showed up at Butler for a game between Attucks and Dunkirk High, a team from a farm town with about twenty-nine hundred residents near the Ohio line. It was the biggest crowd ever to witness a non-tournament game in Indianapolis.

Everyone got their money's worth. Willie Gardner bounce-passed the ball between his legs on fast breaks and hung on the rim after rebounds. Hallie Bryant broke Gardner's one-game city scoring record of forty-two points, mainly because, once Bryant got close to his record, Gardner, his best friend, simply refused to shoot. Attucks won 104–54.

While the Dunkirk players moved around the court in patterns as if there were square dances and ballads running through their heads, Attucks seemed to play a form of jazz. Players improvised their attack at high speed, based on Ray Crowe's fundamental knowledge of fast-break basketball. As he saw it, the Attucks players didn't even play fixed positions. On an ordinary team, Willie Gardner, Attucks' tallest player, would have been called a "center." His job description would have required him to plod down the court, muscle his way close to the basket and wait for someone to throw him the ball so he could pass it back to a cutter or throw up a shot himself. But Gardner was the best passer on the team and he ran like the wind. Why hobble him? Likewise it made no sense to treat a player of Hallie Bryant's creativity as a "forward." Instead, Crowe encouraged Bryant to attack the hoop without a set plan and wait until a defender reacted to a particular fake and presented a fatal opening. Then he would score. To many it looked "natural," but each decision was based on an ex-

Crispus Attucks High teams changed forever the way basketball was played in Indiana. Their opponents seemed to have square dances running through their heads, while Attucks played jazz — fast, soaring, and improvised over a sound structural knowledge of fast-break basketball. (*The Indianapolis Recorder* Collection, Indiana Historical Society)

tensive body of experience and knowledge developed at Lockfield and at Attucks.

The morning after the Dunkirk game Alonzo Watford went to a bank and deposited a three hundred dollar check into a new account which he titled "Attucks Athletic Fund." Attucks' share of the gate at Butler was the first profit Attucks had made in a quarter century of competition. It seemed a strange thing to do, he later said, but it sure felt good.

Attucks entered the 1952 state tourney having lost only once and ranked third in the state by the Associated Press. They had beaten their opponents by an average margin of nearly twenty-five points. Once again black Indianapolis saw this as the breakthrough team that would win the state championship and deliver the respect they deserved. The players were mobbed everywhere they went the week before the tourney began. Study was impossible. Ray Crowe moved the team members out of their homes and into the Senate Avenue YMCA, where he could control what they ate, when they slept, and who they saw.

After narrowly defeating Cathedral high in the first game of the sectional, Attucks faced Indianapolis' Arsenal Technical High in the final game. Tech was Attucks' archrival, the last school that refused to schedule a regular-season game against them. Fights in the bleachers were common, and there had even been death threats against players. The contest was close throughout and its outcome rested on a final play. With Tech leading 61–60 and forty seconds remaining, Bryant tipped in Flap Robertson's missed shot for what appeared to be the winning basket. The goal was waved off by an official who blew his whistle to report a foul far away from the basket. Tech held on to win by a point. Attucks fans were certain the referee's call amounted to pure bigotry.

Once again, Ray Crowe found himself looking for silver linings in the season after the tourney had gone sour. One was clear: the Indianapolis school board had finally started a junior high basketball program. One reason no Indianapolis school had won the state tournament was that the city's players began competing later than everyone else. By ninth grade, when Naptown players had their first game, players from rural schools had been compet-

The Indiana-Kentucky All-Star game got plenty of attention in the 1950s, and when Hallie Bryant was threatened, it was big news in *The Indianapolis Star*.

Attucks' star players were household names in Indiana. Here the editors of the staunchly anti-Communist *Indianapolis Star* decided to give a written death threat against Hallie Bryant equal billing with the execution of Julius and Ethel Rosenberg, who had been convicted as Soviet spies. (*The Indianapolis Star*)

ing for three years. They knew each other's mannerisms and moves by heart, and had the local coach's system down pat.

Early in the year Crowe began to hear about Flap Robertson's younger brother, Oscar, now an eighth grader at School 17. According to his coach, Tom Sleet, Oscar was the leader of the team and was by far the best young player in Indianapolis.

Crowe drove to Tech High to see the first city-wide junior high tournament. Oscar Robertson was a tall, slender boy with large, slightly protruding eyes and a quiet manner. During the game he controlled the basketball as if it were on a string attached to his fingers. He directed his teammates around the court by pointing out spots for them to go, and rewarded their obedience with feather-soft passes that allowed them to score easy baskets. It was as if the others were playing checkers and Oscar Robertson was playing chess. He never seemed to make a move unsupported by the logic of basketball.

At the end of each quarter Oscar bounced the ball patiently, his body crouched between his defender and the ball, looking up at the scoreboard clock until only a few seconds remained. Then he squared his body, paralyzed his defender with two or three quick fakes and dropped the ball easily through the hoop just before the buzzer sounded. There was an element of contempt in his total control of those final seconds. "He just *ran* the game," Ray Crowe later remembered, smiling. "I had never seen any kid like that."

By the first month of 1953 everyone wanted to play Attucks. It was the color of money that mattered most, and the numbers were simple: whenever two Indianapolis schools played at Butler Fieldhouse, the gate was split evenly. Since Attucks always attracted thousands of fans, a game against Attucks at Butler could pay for new uniforms, freshly painted bleachers, maybe even a raise.

Alonzo Watford's phone rang constantly. The very men who had snickered when Watford had begged them for a game just a few seasons before were now wondering politely whether Watford might have an available date in January or if perhaps a double-header might be arranged during one of Attucks' Butler dates. Sometimes their voices would crack. It was too sweet. "One game with us could mean the whole year for them," Watford said later, his frame shaking with laughter. It got so I could play *Podunk* and make money. Man, what a great feeling!"

By year's end the Attucks Athletic Fund contained $25,000. Watford bought the players white uniforms for the road and home green and golds for the Fieldhouse. He gave them caped warm-up jerseys with snarling tigers and sent them around Indiana in double-deckered busses called Scenicruisers. And at last Watford could book games against big schools that could prepare Attucks for the state tourney.

Once again in 1953 the entire season came down to a minute. After winning the first two rounds, Attucks played Shelbyville in the semistate final. Shelbyville's coaches slowed the game to a standstill to try to keep the score close. With fifty-eight seconds remaining and the score tied at forty-four, Hallie Bryant rebounded a missed shot and broke free toward Attucks' basket. Suddenly two Shelbyville players converged upon him and knocked him to the floor. The three players went down in a tumble of limbs. When he was able to look up, Bryant saw referee Stan Dubis pointing a finger at him. A Shelbyville player struggled to his feet and hit two free throws to win the game and end the season.

Attucks fans were certain they had been robbed, and for the same old reason. How, they asked each other, could Bryant have charged into an opponent if there was no one in front of him? It so happened that the topic of bigoted referees was fresh on everyone's mind. Four days before the Shelbyville game a black referee named Bernard McPeak had been denied admission to the Indiana Officials Association, a trade group for referees. McPeak had seemed the ideal candidate to be the first black admitted, having fifteen years experience and having officiated four Pennsylvania State basketball final games. The Association's president, Clayton Nichols, offered a simple explanation, which found its way into news accounts. "It was because of his color," Nichols said. The vote had been forty to seven against McPeak.

None of this came as a surprise to Ray Crowe. From his first year as a coach Crowe had assumed that Attucks would be cheated in any close game. His game plan was always to get off to the fastest possible start and maintain a wide lead. This was one reason he let his players dunk in warm-up drills; he hoped opponent would still be intimidated during the first few plays of the game. In the locker room before each game, Crowe and the players would join hands, look into each other's eyes and say in unison, "first ten points for the refs . . . the rest are for us."

But Attucks couldn't always get far enough ahead, especially not against good teams like Shelbyville who slowed the game down. There was an element of despair in an editorial which appeared in *The Indianapolis Recorder* after the Shelbyville game. "Is it always going to be true," the writer asked, "that officials will take the close games away from Attucks, the close fights away from Negro boxers? Has a person with a dark skin got a chance for fair play?"

∞ ∞ ∞

Shortly after noon on Monday, May 17, 1954, Earl Warren, Chief Justice of the U.S. Supreme Court, began to read from an eleven-page opinion whose first words were, "We unanimously conclude that in the field of public education the doctrine of 'separate but equal' has no place." The landmark decision outlawed segregated schools as a violation of the Fourteenth Amendment's "Equal Protection" clause. Observers predicted that the ruling would soon change the lives of twelve million schoolchildren in seventeen Southern and border states and four northern states — including Indiana — which permitted segregated schools. But Indianapolis moved to its own clock. It would be another seventeen years and another court order before the first white student attended Crispus Attucks High. "Impeach Earl Warren" billboards sprouted throughout the city.

The Attucks players and their families still lived within the cocoon of their near-Westside neighborhood. They rarely ventured south of the Sacks Brothers Pawn Shop at the foot of Indiana Avenue, or beyond the City Hospital at the north end (later in the fifties City Hospital became Marion County General Hospital, and is now Wishard Memorial Hospital). They attended the three churches which stood like pillars at the intersection of Senate and West streets. Sometimes on warm days when the doors were open, the voice of Mazelle Robertson could be heard leading the Mount Zion Baptist choir in one of her own gospel compositions.

Now black children in Indiana had heroes of their own, in this case
Oscar Robertson (left) and Willie Merriweather. (*The Indianapolis
Recorder*)

A jubilant Oscar Robertson after a tournament win. Robertson was perhaps the first black Hoosier whom many whites wanted to know as an individual. (Frank H. Fisse)

Almost all restaurants and downtown stores and theaters in downtown Indianapolis were segregated. Betty Crowe, who married Ray in 1951, was allowed to walk rapidly through the L.S. Ayres department store's Tea Room to visit her father, the chief cook, in his kitchen office, but she could not sit down to eat. Once a year, on "Negro Day," black children were allowed to enter Riverside Amusement Park, but only if they presented fifty bottle caps from the Polk Milk Company.

The only whites the Attucks players encountered off the basketball court were a few sportswriters and the Jewish merchants who owned finance companies, pawn shops, clothing stores, and car dealerships along Indiana Avenue, and the gamblers like Isaac "Toughy" Mitchell, boss of the numbers game in Indianapolis, who sometimes rode around Attucks in a convertible, handing out dollar bills until Russell Lane would run him off. "We sort of modelled ourselves after the store owners," Attucks' guard Bill Scott would later recall. "We would see the Jews in their Cadillacs, their casual open collars and nice silks and mixes. You sort of trust people who are successful."

The white man they knew best was Harold Stolkin, the genial owner of Indiana Finance, on the Avenue's five-hundred block. Stolkin had financed Ray Crowe's first car and the two had soon become fast friends. For reasons the players never quite understood, Stolkin and his young son Mark sat on the Attucks bench with the team, cheering loudly and wearing beanies with Attucks colors on their heads.

Stolkin identified deeply with the Attucks players. His father had come to Indianapolis from Philadelphia early in the century to open a restaurant and, like other Jews, had been forced to move his business to the Avenue during the Klan years. Later he started ed a finance company, specializing in no-money-down car loans to black residents, and turned the business over to Harold in the forties. Though Harold Stolkin did not live in their neighborhood, he considered himself to be, like the Attucks players, an outcast.

Stolkin found the players jobs in the summer, and paid them to pluck dandelions from his lawn. Sometimes he ushered them into the Broadmoor Country Club for steak dinners or seated them at restaurants owned by his friends. They were among the first black non-employees ever to enter such places. They remember the bus boys and caddies smiling and giving them thumbs up when they recognized the Attucks players. It was a heady new world, one that took some getting used to. "I remember once he took us to the Italian Village at Twenty-second and Meridian," recalls Bill Scott. "Harold kind of stuttered. He said, 'you wanna pizza pie?' We thought he said 'piece of pie.' We were thinkin' about 'tater pies, apple pies, but we all ordered 'round the worlds' 'cause that was the biggest thing on the menu. When they came we opened the box and smelled those anchovies. We said, 'Man, what *are* these things?' Some of us couldn't eat them."

Ray Crowe had to rebuild his team almost from scratch in 1954. Hallie Bryant and Bailey Robertson were now on college squads, and Willie Gardner was now a member of the Harlem Globe-trotters' starting five. Gardner had travelled to Chicago for an open tryout, competing against hundreds of other young black men. When his turn came to shoot layups, he did his Attucks pre-game dunking routine. When he finished he was signed on the spot.

The best new prospect was Willie Merriweather, a six-foot five-inch junior. Merriweather was one of an emerging group of black players who had chosen to attend Crispus Attucks. In 1949 the Indianapolis school board, still years away from its first black member, had devised a plan to divide the city into school districts. Attucks, however, remained a racially segregated school. The few white students living within the Attucks district were granted "transfers" to go to white schools in the city. Black students living outside the Attucks neighborhood could choose between Attucks and their neighborhood school.

The arrangement set off a wild scramble for talented black players who lived outside the Attucks district. The year before, Mazelle Robertson, now divorced from Bailey, Sr., and well-established as a beautician, had bought a home at Thirty-fourth Street and Boulevard Place, within the Shortridge High School district. Though Oscar and Hank sometimes slept over with their father, who remained in town, they lived with their mother. Shortridge athletic officials promptly claimed Oscar and Hank as their own, but the boys insisted on staying at Attucks. At one point the discussion became so pitched that Mazelle simply threatened to move back to Colter Street if they didn't leave her sons alone.

Willie Merriweather's mother had saved just enough money as a cook and a maid, combined with her late husband's Social Security check, to purchase a home in a neighborhood barely in the Shortridge district. Willie had gone to an all-white grade school and had already enrolled to be a freshman at Shortridge, which had a national reputation for academic excellence, when he began to think about Oscar Robertson.

Like Ray Crowe, Merriweather had been at Tech High the day that Oscar led his team to the first junior high championship. After the game he had introduced himself to Oscar, who said little, but something about the encounter etched itself in Merriweather's mind. Totally immersed in the Attucks community, Oscar Robertson communicated to Willie Merriweather a sense of racial pride. Nothing Shortridge could offer was as important as that identity. He wanted to feel like Oscar. "Meeting him, seeing him win that championship . . . I just had a yearning to be around my people," he later explained. A few days before school started, Merriweather withdrew from Shortridge and enrolled at Attucks.

Crowe's other new players were center Sheddrick Mitchell, an introverted boy recently from Mississippi; Bill Brown, a mighty rebounder; and two junior guards, Bill Hampton and Bill Scott. Scott's circumstances were tragic even by neighborhood standards. Two weeks after their arrival in Indianapolis from Alabama, Scott's mother had been pulled from a streetcar, dragged into an alley, raped, and murdered. His father had long before disappeared. The boy lived in a converted garage with five others, including an uncle who drank heavily. As much as anything, Bill Scott saw basketball as way out of the garage.

Oscar Robertson was now a sophomore and eligible for the varsity. Over the summer he had developed tremendously, working with his brothers on his grandparents' Tennessee farm. They spent most days in the fields, sunup to sundown, planting and plowing with their grandfather. He wore no watch, but when the sun was high he would look up and declare it time for lunch. Together they would sit beneath a tree and open stained brown sacks bulging with chicken and greens and poundcake. In the long, slow evenings after dinner, their grandfather would recite from memory beautiful passages from the Bible. Sometimes they would sing together. Also living in the home was their great-grandfather, Marshall Collier, who had been born into slavery. During Reconstruction he had sharecropped until he had saved enough to purchase the farm in the hilly country west of Nashville. Nearly a century later he still stood ramrod straight and still said he was able to recall the day he was sold at auction.

It was a trip the three boys made every summer, and after three months of country food and outdoor labor, they always returned to Indianapolis physically and spiritually stronger. But in the early autumn of 1953 Oscar Robertson, barely fifteen, came back a man. Now he stood nearly six-feet-two, with arms and shoulders rippling with work-hardened muscles. Just before Hallie Bryant left for his sophomore year at Indiana University, the two played again at Lockfield. Though Oscar had not touched a ball since spring, he was now able to win most of the games. The reversal was not easy for Hallie. "I stopped playing him when I knew he could beat me," he recalls. "I struggled with it for a while, and it hurt. But after a time I was just proud of how good Oscar had become. It was like part of me was doing good, that's how I rationalized it."

The first hint of the glory that Oscar Robertson would bring to Attucks came in a December game between Attucks and Shortridge for the city championship. Playing before nearly nine thousand fans in Butler Fieldhouse, Attucks fell behind 22–9 in the first quarter and seemed overmatched. In fact, they were stuffed. Earlier in the day Ray Crowe had dropped the team off to eat lunch at the Indiana University Medical Center and gone on to run some errands. When he came back, he found that they had helped themselves to seconds, then thirds, and that his bill was nearly sixty dollars over budget.

At the beginning of the second quarter, Oscar, clearly disgusted, began to clap his hands and demand the ball. His teammates gave it to him and he hit shot after shot. When defenders inched forward to stop him from shooting, he faked and drove through them to the basket. With a minute left, Oscar hit a layup that put Attucks ahead for the first time, but Shortridge tied the game and sent it into overtime. After Attucks fell behind, Oscar stole the ball and drove again to send the game into a second overtime. He finally won it with a jump shot. The Shortridge game caused two changes: before, newspaper reporters had referred to Oscar as Oscar "Little Flap" Robertson. After that it was just "Oscar." And there was the matter of food: "Next time we went out there for the sectional," Willie Merriweather recalls, "all Mr. Crowe would feed us was boullion."

Attucks lost four games during the regular season in 1954 and again reached the third round of the state tourney. Playing without Willie Merriweather, who had broken his leg late in the season, they were defeated convincingly by Milan High School, en route to becoming the smallest school ever to win the Indiana championship. It would be, with one quirky exception, nearly three years before any team defeated Crispus Attucks High again.

∞ ∞ ∞

By New Year's Day in 1955 it was clear to basketball fans in Indiana that Oscar Robertson and his teammates were a once-in-a-lifetime team. Never had so many wanted to see a high school team play. Seven of Attucks' first thirteen games were moved to Butler Fieldhouse to accommodate ticket demands. One Wednesday evening game against Shortridge attracted 11,561 fans, a gathering that local papers called "possibly a world's record crowd for a non-tournament game." Attucks' share of the take for that game alone was thirty-two hundred dollars. By mid-season Alonzo Watford had enough money in his account to finance printing presses and engineering equipment for the school.

To Russell Lane and Alonzo Watford, the 1955 team was the product of twenty-eight years' hard labor. Brick by brick, season by season, they had built a mighty fortress of a team. The whole community — pastors and legislators and merchants and parents and fans — had been involved from the Klan days forward. Together they had won the right to play and learned how to win. Together they proved to whites in Indianapolis in the most public of forums available that black people did not require their guidance to accomplish substantial things. All that was left was a state championship. Now, in the 1955 team, they had the hammer to drive home the spike.

Though the surviving players recall that they had little sense of the struggle for civil rights which was building in the South, they had a sense of deep, intense local history. They knew that they represented tens of thousands of black Hoosiers. They had grown up at Butler Fieldhouse watching heroes win and lose glorious battles for a righteous cause, and it had given them the sense that their deeds were magnified.

They were welded together by shared experience. Most of them had been born in the South and most could remember a bus or train trip in their early childhood. By now there was tradition even in the uniforms they wore. Oscar Robertson wore his brother's number forty-three. Hallie Bryant had personally bequeathed his legendary number thirty-four to Bill Hampton. "I can see I picked a good man," Hallie had told him. "When you graduate, you pass it on to a good man."

They were heroes in their own community and well-known throughout the town. "Everywhere I went on the street it was 'Scotty, let me buy you a sandwich,'" recalls Bill Scott. Most went steady, though serious romance was hindered by Ray Crowe's strict nine o'clock curfew. A few players had access to cars, Merriweather his late father's '51 Olds 98; Scott an immaculate '35 Chevy with dark curtains in the rear window; and Oscar a '51 Mercury four-door. Radios tuned to WLAC in Nashville, where Randy's Record Mart brought Ray Charles and the Platters and LaVerne Benson, they cruised Eddie's Drive-In at Udell and West, Al Green's on the Eastside, and even the white-owned TeePee on the Northside. "They'd let us go there as long as you stayed in your car," Bill Scott recalls.

In contrast to the obliging Hallie Bryants and Willie Gardners of two years before, some of the 1955 players had cultivated a sense of cool, of studied reserve. Constantly Ray Crowe urged them to talk with reporters but Oscar in particular would remain in the dressing room after the others, avoiding reporters and photographers. His reserve fostered ever more curiosity, which became almost obsessive as the season progressed. White fans found themselves wanting personal information about a black Hoosier, wondering who he dated, what he ate, about his grades and dreams and where he was going to college. When cornered he answered politely and usually in very few words. The word writers most often used to describe him was "serious."

There was a cockiness to the team that had not been there before. At times, Crowe had to get tough to maintain control. During one practice, Oscar angrily berated a substitute who had muffed a pass that caused his squad to lose an intersquad game. Players fell silent as Ray Crowe walked slowly to his star. The moment remains vivid to Willie Merriweather. "Mr. Crowe walked over to Oscar and said, 'I am the coach of this team. Nobody will get on a player except me. You understand?' Oscar said yes and then when Mr. Crowe went away he mumbled something. Mr. Crowe grabbed him and turned him and smacked him. Told him to go down and take a shower. Oscar was kind of sniffling. We all looked at each other. We said, 'Shoot, if he'd hit Oscar he'd *kill* us.' Nobody messed with Mr. Crowe."

Late in January the team, undefeated and barely tested after sixteen games, played at Connersville High, one of the few small-town schools remaining on the schedule. Though the Attucks players took it lightly, it was the game of the year for Connersville. The gym was far too small to seat the thousands who arrived for the game, so officials broadcast the game into the school auditorium and roped off the court, seating spectators along the margin of the floor. It seemed more like a heavyweight fight than a basketball game.

By halftime, Connersville, by holding the ball for minutes at a time, led 24–21. During the intermission, officials threw open the gym's doors to ventilate the stuffy room with fresh winter air. When play resumed a thin veneer of ice coated the floor, which had been laid over a swimming pool. Connersville continued to play keepaway, using up time while Attucks players slipped and flailed in their increasingly desperate attempts to get the ball. By the end of the third quarter, Connersville had built a ten-point lead and held on to win by one point.

There was silence on the bus ride home. They were no longer undefeated and they would no longer be ranked first in the state. They watched the back of Ray Crowe's neck from their seats, and they knew there would a price to pay. The first installment came the next day. After a nonstop, five-hour long practice, Crowe assembled the varsity and reserve squads together on bleacher seats. "From now on," he said, addressing the varsity, "no one has a guaranteed spot on this team. You have to earn your position every single game."

No team again came closer than fourteen points until they played against Muncie Central in the championship game of the semistate tourney at Butler Fieldhouse. The Attucks-Muncie Central game was a battle of heavyweights. All season long the two teams had traded the number one and number two positions in the polls. Each team had lost only once. *The Star* called it "the Game of the Century." For many, Muncie was the White Hope, probably the only team in Indiana capable of beating Attucks.

It was also a game over which a great deal of money changed hands. Attucks games had long been heavily wagered, with racial passions causing fans to bet with their hearts rather than their heads against a black team. In the days before the Muncie game, long lines of cars formed at the Cities Service gas station at Sixteenth Street and Senate Avenue, the hub of basketball betting. Paychecks were wagered in the Chrysler and Allison factories of Indianapolis, and major sums were staked in "pea shake houses," named for a local game, along Indiana Avenue.

Attucks clung to a six-point lead with little more than a minute to go in the game when Willie Merriweather fouled out. Muncie quickly stole the ball twice, scoring two field goals and a free throw, and had the ball out of bounds behind by one point with fifteen seconds remaining.

The game, the season, and nearly thirty years of progress now hung on fifteen seconds. The referee handed the ball to Muncie's Gene Flowers, who held it over his head and prepared to throw it inbounds. Oscar Robertson, crouching and hidden behind another player, watched Flowers' eyes closely, searching for a clue as to where the pass was headed. When Flowers released the ball, Oscar sprang forward and caught it, then dribbled around the court in circles until time expired. In an uncharacteristic display of joy, he flung the ball high into the Fieldhouse rafters and leaped aboard his jubilant teammates.

∞ ∞ ∞

The victory over Muncie Central threw Indianapolis officials into a state of panic. Who the next state champion would be now seemed a foregone conclusion. None of the other three teams remaining in the tourney, Gary Roosevelt — also a segregated school — New Albany or Fort Wayne North Side, seemed to stand a chance. Clearly, Indianapolis would have its first state champion, and, like it or not, it would be an all-black school.

They had one week to get ready. Dr. Lane was among the first to understand that the city was preparing not to crown them, but to sequester them. "The week before the finals, I got called into the superintendent's office," he later recalled. "There were representatives from the mayor's office and from the police and fire departments. The mayor's man said, 'Well, looks like your boys are going to win next week.' I said, 'We think so.' He said, 'We're afraid if they do, your people will break up the city.' I said 'There will not be one incident.' "

Dr. Lane spent much of the next week addressing the student body. Once again he found himself preparing black students for contact with the white world. This time he was explaining the rules which governed joy. "I told them that if a white student turned over a car in jubilation it would likely be regarded as good-natured foolishness. But if a black student did the same, it could be held against them all as evidence of the Negro's violent nature."

As the Saturday of the state finals approached, city officials pulled sixty extra patrolmen from the day and late shifts and detailed them to Monument Circle, where there would be a brief ceremony. A hundred and twelve Civil Defense police and all the city's court bailiffs were assigned to traffic detail. Detectives were staked to Butler Fieldhouse.

The problem was that Indianapolis, in which people with dark and light skin had been kept apart for so long, now had no collective experience of mingling together on a large scale in public. It might have been easier to prepare for a demonstration or a boycott; at least there were rules of engagement. But how did whites prepare to thank black people publicly, especially in front of stores and theaters in which they were not allowed free movement? What would happen if white girls and black boys danced together, what if blacks got cocky and whites resentful, and people got drunk? No one knew, and Alex Clark, the youngest mayor in Indianapolis' history, was not about to take chances. Approving the emergency forces, and diverting the celebration to the black neighborhood were, as he saw it, responsible actions. "We really didn't know what was going to happen," he said later. "Those police were a booster shot."

On the Saturday morning of the finals, the team had breakfast at Ray Crowe's home, and then headed for Butler Fieldhouse, where they defeated New Albany in the first game. Gary Roosevelt slipped by Fort Wayne North in the second semifinal game. It would be an all-black state championship game.

Under heavy police guard, the Attucks players were taken to a dormitory at the Fieldhouse to rest between games. Officers guarded the front building and hallway entrances. Bill Hampton remembers leaving his room to go to the bathroom, and finding himself accompanied by a police officer. "What are you doing?" asked Hampton, startled. "Orders," his companion replied.

They were certain of victory. They had played together for years with this game in mind. By now Butler Fieldhouse felt like a home court to them. And since all the players on both teams would be black, for once the referees' racial attitudes wouldn't matter. "We thought the refs might even give us a break, since we were from Indianapolis," recalls Willie Merriweather. "That afternoon we were sayin' those rings are *ours*. We'll just go out there and beat those guys up."

And they did. Gary Roosevelt had a fine team, featuring Dick Barnett, who was later to star for the New York Knicks, but they were hopelessly overmatched. Oscar Robertson was a man among boys, scoring thirty points on a precocious assortment of shots. When he was double-teamed he always seemed to find an open man. He tossed soft lead passes to teammates Merriweather and Sheddrick Mitchell for flying layups. Attucks won the game 97–64, scoring thirty-two points more than any Indiana champion had ever scored. Fans started singing the "C-R-A-Z-Y" song early in the fourth quarter.

In a brief award ceremony at the Fieldhouse, each player was awarded a championship ring, and Oscar and Merriweather, as co-captains, hoisted the championship trophy above them for all to see. They had become the first state champions from Indianapolis and the first all-black team in U.S. history to win a major championship tournament.

After their brief and uneventful lap around the Monument Circle, they celebrated at Northwest Park. While Oscar Robertson felt uncomfortable and left early, most others danced the night away. "It didn't bother me that they didn't want to help us celebrate," recalls Bill Scott. "I was happy to get back into the neighborhood and share this with my people. This was the first time two all-black teams coached by black coaches had played. I said to myself, 'This is ours, not theirs.' I think most of my teammates felt that way.' " Asked by a reporter to describe his feelings, Ray Crowe answered in a single word. "Relief," he said.

In 1968 the Indianapolis Public Schools were ordered by a federal court to integrate all eleven high schools within the system. It took another six years for the first white students to earn a diploma from Crispus Attucks High.

Today, Crispus Attucks Middle School, recently reopened after a major renovation, stands as a sort of island in a concrete sea. The school's pillared front doorway now looks out on an entrance ramp to Interstate 65, which pierced the neighborhood in the seventies. Most of the houses in which Attucks' students once lived have been gobbled up by a hospital and a university campus. A wrecker's ball demolished School 17, much of Lockfield Gardens, and many of the buildings along Indiana Avenue, where condominiums now stand. It took the concerted, last-ditch efforts of black and historical organizations to save Attucks itself.

There were even bigger blows. In 1969 the Indiana legislature passed an act known as "Unigov" which consolidated under one government the neighborhoods of Indianapolis and the suburban townships of surrounding Marion County. The city's total population doubled overnight, but the percentage of the city's black population was cut in half. Decades of hard-earned black voting strength disappeared in a flash. Overall enrollment in inner-city schools decreased by a third between 1968 and 1979, but black enrollment increased. White-flight turned into a stampede, and many black professionals joined the rush to the suburbs. To some,

The 1956 Crispus Attucks Tigers, hoisting Ray Crowe after devouring Lafayette Jefferson for the state title. This was the first undefeated Indiana champion, and up to then, maybe the best high school basketball team ever. (Frank H. Fisse)

Unigov served to accomplish what D.C. Stephenson and his contemporaries had set out to do decades before.

Attucks won two more state championships after 1955, becoming Indiana's first undefeated championship team in 1956, Oscar Robertson's senior year. It was a team which could have beaten many college squads. Oscar Robertson went on to become one of history's greatest collegiate and professional players. More than a few Attucks players received college scholarships in those years and still others were able to parlay their local fame into good jobs. Before his death in 1992 Bob Jewell built an outstanding career as a chemist at Eli Lilly and Company in Indianapolis. Ray Crowe retired from coaching in 1958, a move he quickly regretted, and was rejected when he later applied for coaching jobs at several schools, including Shortridge High. "For the record he amassed," Oscar Robertson later remarked in disgust, "he should have been coaching at Indiana University."

Many who lived in Indianapolis in those years believe the Attucks teams changed their city. "The success of Attucks' basketball integrated the high schools of Indianapolis," says Bob Collins flatly. "They became so dominant that the other schools had to get black basketball players or forget about it."

Others say that Attucks players and coaches integrated city restaurants and softened resistance to the presence of blacks in downtown stores. Not long before his death, Russell Lane said simply, "Things got a lot better for blacks around here after those teams."

The legacy is hard to measure exactly. It is found most clearly in the spirit and memory of those who passed through those years together. The teams gave African-Americans a public basis for pride and self-confidence in a generally unwelcoming city. Above all, it bound them together forever.

Marcus Stewart, a former editor of *The Indianapolis Recorder*, was seventeen on the night that Attucks defeated Gary Roosevelt. His parents had struggled to make it to a neighborhood where the children could go to Shortridge, but as he felt the heat of the bonfire in Northwest Park that night he found himself envying the Attucks students. "I kept thinking, Attucks means black,"

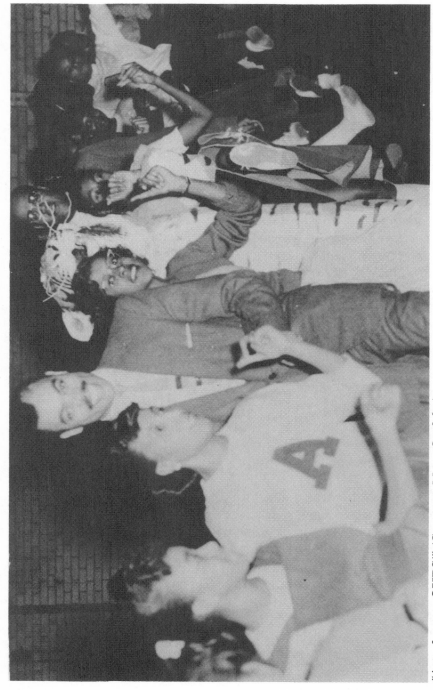

"Attucks was OURS!" (Courtesy Mary Ogelsby)

Stewart recalls. "Attucks means us." Attucks had turned the tables in a sweet, special way, through basketball, a way that maybe only people in Indiana could understand. The feeling was indescribable. "That was the happiest day in the lives of a whole generation of blacks in Indianapolis," Stewart recalls. "It was like when Joe Louis would knock someone out and the Avenue would be full of people. But this was better. Joe Louis belonged to every-one. Attucks was *ours!*"

Judi Warren
and the Warsaw Tigers —
Into the Front Court

Patricia Roy's office walls are covered with glossy photos of a high school girl with her hair in a bowl cut, but with the ends turned neatly under. She is steering what seems to be a huge basketball around and through much bigger girls. Her body seems almost horizontal to the court, she is driving so hard.

Commissioner Roy has been in charge of all girls' sports programs for the Indiana High School Athletic Association since 1972. She pushed hard for a girls' basketball tournament, and its success, whose magnitude not even she could have imagined, is due in large part to the girl whose image fills her walls.

"I thank God for Judi Warren," Roy says of the girl. "She's our Billie Jean King. She's the spark that ignited girls' basketball in Indiana. It was scary to start out in what had been a boys' program, but she was a little kid with a lot of fire. She caught people's imaginations. We were lucky she started when she did."

Girls' basketball has become a major force in Indiana. The state championship game routinely draws nearly fifteen thousand fans, the largest tournament crowds in the U.S. The TV ratings are impressive and growing. In several communities, girls' teams outdraw the boys' teams, and major stars have emerged. One Thursday night in January of 1995, seventy-one hundred fans wedged into a gym in East Chicago to see a girls' game between East Chicago Central and Lake Central high schools, both nationally ranked. The scores of reporters, the crush of the crowd and the noise left the players stunned at first. "When we came out for warm-ups I couldn't stop looking around," said Central guard Monica Maxwell. "This is something I'll tell my kids about," agreed her teammate, Kizzy Buggs.

Girls have forced their brothers to share the driveways and the boys' coaches to share the keys to the high school gym. Their knees are braced, their hair is pulled back from their eyes and their ankles are taped. Now they suffer torn anterior cruciate ligaments rather than skinned knees. Their mothers no longer wash their sweaty T-shirts — now their road greys or their home whites get tossed in the team's laundry bin. Many girls will not waste time or risk injury — and the loss of a scholarship — by playing other sports.

It wasn't always this way. Girls first played basketball in Indiana in 1898, wearing bloomers, middy blouses, and high cotton stockings. Sponsors cautioned the girls not to roll their stockings down — thus exposing the knees — when their legs got hot and itchy during a game.

Since competition produced excitement and sweat, men were not allowed to watch girls play in many towns. Experts cautioned that the exertion required to play basketball could prove dangerous to young women. "It must always be remembered that the fascination of the game is so great . . . that there is temptation to play at the time of menstruation," wrote Dr. J. Anna Norris. "It is accepted by most authorities that there should be no basketball during at least three days at that time."

For most of the century, girls played basketball as a form of tranquil exercise staged in a largely social setting. Smiling girls faced off for the center jump standing erect, one hand raised above their heads, as if they were pairing off for a ballroom dance. "Better than winning honor in basketball is deserving credit for ladylike conduct," explained the Hobart, Indiana, *Gazette* in 1915, "not only in the game but before and after."

Little girls who enjoyed playing ball were called tomboys. Those whose enthusiasm persisted into high school entered rougher waters. *They* became "jocks," and it was assumed that boys who dated them did so because they couldn't get anyone else. Some women coaches who spent a lot of time with their players were called "dykes," and more than a few were driven from Indiana schools like witches in Salem.

Jump ball at Winona High, circa 1916, when, as one Hoosier sportswriter put it, "Better than winning honor in basketball is deserving credit for ladylike conduct . . . " (Courtesy Herb Schwomeyer, Hoosier Hysteria and Hersteria, Inc.)

When Judi Warren and her Warsaw High teammates first started, there were few competitive female role models, few resources available to them, and little encouragement. But they didn't think about it, at least not at first. Like thousands of young people in Indiana, they were in love with basketball, swept up in the fun of a game involving a ball and a hoop.

"Enthusiasm without hysteria" was the goal of Miss Senda Berenson, who introduced Dr. Naismith's game to America's colleges in 1893. Applied to basketball in Indiana, that is a contradiction in terms. One dramatic winter night in 1976, Judi Warren and the Warsaw tigers proved to all of Indiana that "Hoosier Hysteria" is gender-free.

Judi Warren had a problem: the Lions Club had chosen her "Miss Claypool," queen of the fair, and there was no way out of it. She didn't want to be "Miss Claypool," she didn't feel like "Miss Claypool," but there she was, and they had to do something with her hair.

This required a team meeting. Cindy Ross, the team's center and co-captain, went with her to a beautician, for this was not a job for a barber. Before, Judi had just gone to the barber with her dad on a Saturday morning and had her hair cut straight. She wanted it simple, for she had no time to bother with curlers.

Janet Warren had long ago given up on making a homemaker of her younger daughter. Judi wouldn't come in for piano lessons, dropped band, and seemed to drift away from housework. At least Janet *had* put her foot down on 4-H. A girl should be able to cook and sew, and besides, Janet Warren was the Claypool 4-H leader and her own daughter was going to be there.

Not that Janet hadn't liked sports herself. She had played a little basketball at Claypool High, six girls on a team. With only fourteen students in her class, she had done everything else, too: led cheers, blown horns in the band, hammed it up in the school plays. "The class just wouldn't have functioned if I hadn't been there," she says.

But all Judi had ever seemed to want to do was play ball. As a little girl, when she got mad or moody, after dinner or before dinner, she'd take a ball out to the driveway and practice throwing it against the chimney and catching it. Then she started heaving it up and into the basket. Then, when her elder brother Jack's friends came over, she'd play with them. Even though she was six years younger and a girl, they all seemed to love her, partly because she'd chase the ball for them all day long. It worried Janet that Judi wasn't meeting any girls. It was good that she was dedicated to something, but this didn't seem, well . . . *rounded.*

Despite her misgivings, Janet Warren was above all a devoted and supportive mother. She made time to see Judi's games and arranged meals around her practices. As a Hoosier, and having herself married Layne Warren, a slick guard from Claypool, she had seen enough basketball to know that Judi was good. Judi was smaller than everyone else, but she seemed to get up and down the court twice as fast as the other girls. She had always been exceptionally well-coordinated. There had been no training wheels on Judi's bike; one day she'd just pedaled off to kindergarten.

While Judi was in grade school, all the Kosciusko County schools, Claypool and Atwood and Leesburg and Silver Lake, were consolidated into Warsaw High School, absorbed like provinces into a central soviet. "Our towns disintegrated," Janet said. "The towns became shambles of communities. When you take the teenagers out of a community there's not much left." Though she had been condemned to go to high school in a faceless institution, Judi amazed her mother by remarking one night at dinner that she was happy to be going to a school that had a sports program for girls. It was hard to figure her out.

And when the time came, just as her mother had predicted, Judi found Warsaw High to be a lot different from Claypool. It was so big that Judi told her she couldn't find the john until the third day. To Janet's relief, she did find girlfriends, although there was a catch: these girls were as crazy about sports as Judi.

Actually, Lisa Vandermark, Cindy Ross, and Cathy Folk had known about Judi Warren for a long time, for Judi's Claypool grade school teams kept beating theirs. In fact, Judi had met Cindy by falling on her in a sixth-grade basketball game. Judi swears Cindy tripped her.

Cindy was a head taller than Judi, with long blond hair. All through grade school, Cindy had worn short pants underneath her skirts, so she could whip off the skirt and play tag and dodgeball with the boys at recess.

The Rosses lived in town. Cindy's parents encouraged her desire to be an athlete. Bill Ross was a cheerful and muscular man who followed sports but who had himself started working too early in life to try out for the high school teams. He told his daughter that the main thing was to love something, learn to do it well, and not to quit when the going got tough.

The whole family played twenty-one and shot free throws in the driveway, mom spinning them up underhanded and dad overhanded and the three younger brothers heaving them up any way they could. On the day Cindy announced that she had entered the local AAU track meet as a javelin thrower, they were delighted. All six piled into the car and drove to the park for a Sunday afternoon of javelin throwing. It didn't matter at all that no one had a clue how to throw a javelin.

Judi, Cindy, Lisa, and Cathy ran track and played badminton in the fall, tennis in the spring, and basketball in the winter. They spent all their free time together. Their parents began to get to know one another, too, as the girls stayed at each others' homes on weekends.

They spent their winter Saturday afternoons like boys throughout Indiana, watching and listening to basketball games, munching chips, and tugging on sodas. If they didn't like the announcer on TV, they turned the sound down and listened to a second game on the radio.

At halftime they ran outside and practiced the plays they had just seen. UCLA was their favorite team, because the Bruins ran and pressed and played the whole court, just as their junior high coach, Vivian Eigemiller, had taught them to do. They worked on the timing of their own low-altitude version of the alley-oop pass, with Judi as Greg Lee and Cindy as Bill Walton.

At night they went out and cruised around in Judi's older sister Jill's red and white 1971 Olds Cutlass. They hit the Village Pizza Inn after the boys' games on Friday nights, and when there was no game they went downtown to the Lake Theater to catch a movie.

The night they went to see *Love Story,* there wasn't enough tissue for the whole squad. "Judi cried the whole time," says Cindy.

"Everyone was snifflin' but Judi had to bite her thumb to keep from getting loud. We were all sentimental girls. By the end Judi had about bitten her thumbnail off. The girl dies. We ended up bawlin'. What else can you do?"

At school they were branded as "jocks." Girls snubbed them, and they felt the boys they knew best — mainly other athletes — were a little intimidated by their closeness to each other. They wore little makeup — maybe just a little blush, except for Margie Lozier, the manager, who was into mascara — and, as Cindy Ross put it, "It took at least a funeral to get us into a dress." They all had boyfriends off and on, but they weren't oriented toward dating, except around prom time. "I think right then we all got a little sweaty," remembers Cindy. "Everyone wanted to go to the prom."

"We weren't the ones the guys wanted to be with," Judi Warren recalls. "We weren't the cheerleaders and high society girls all the other girls looked up to. It wasn't cool to date a jock. At times it was discouraging, but we weren't trying to impress anyone or stand out as a group. We just went out and had a good time.

"At that time, my teammates were closer to me than my own family. We knew each other very well. We understood each other. We became a unique group. We would do anything in the world for each other. We would do anything in the world to keep one of the others from going down."

Even though the girls had a team, basketball at Warsaw High meant boys' basketball. Warsaw High was a county seat school with a long-standing tradition of winning big games. The boys' basketball team attracted sellout crowds every home game and made enough money to pay for all the girls' programs and the rest of the boys' sports as well. Any question about expanding girls' sports would have caught the men who ran Warsaw's athletic program by surprise; the girls should have been grateful they even *had* a team.

The girls saw things differently: Warsaw High was their school, too, and they didn't even have uniforms. They practiced in grade schools at inconvenient hours while the boys practiced in the Warsaw gym right after school. And besides, going into their senior year they had lost only four games in three years. That was a lot better than the boys had done.

The girls believed that their chief oppressor was Ike Tallman, the boys' head basketball coach. Tall, stocky, and given to dark suits, he was an imposing figure. A decade before he had coached a Muncie Central High team to the Indiana boys' championship, which only added to his intimidating stature. But they felt they had to confront him if anything was going to change. One evening after school Judi, Cindy, and Lisa entered Warsaw's athletic office, hearts hammering. Without speaking, Lisa handed Tallman the list of demands they had drawn up, including uniforms and laundry service, buses for the games, cheerleaders, and above all, equal access to the Warsaw High gym for practice.

Tallman studied the list for a moment, then looked up. He did not appear angry. Well, he told them, to succeed you'll have to promote yourselves. First thing you'll need is tickets. He told them that he would have his secretary print up some orange tickets, the school's color, and the girls should see if they could sell enough of them to fill the gym. When they could fill the gym, like the boys did, then they could share it. He turned his attention elsewhere. Lisa, who had organized the event and written the list, grew livid. Cindy burst into tears.

When the secretary delivered the tickets, they didn't know what to do with them. They decided to try to sell them. Friends and relatives and people at church bought them faithfully, but few showed up at the games. This wasn't going to get them anywhere.

In their senior year the girls were granted permission to practice in the high school gym after the boys were finished. It was a bittersweet victory. Judi lived too far away to go home for dinner and then return to the school for practice. Instead, she would stay in Warsaw, study for an hour or so at school and then stroll with Lisa to Burger's Dairy Store for a couple of jars of baby food. Somehow "Fruit Delight," a mixed fruit, had become the official training food of the Warsaw Tigers.

Then they'd walk back to watch the boys practice. Judi studied the drills carefully and tried them herself when the boys' practice was over. She found she could do anything they could except dribble between her legs on the run. At five-one, her stride wasn't quite long enough for that.

It was usually nine o'clock by the time practice was over. With luck, Jill would be waiting in the Cutlass. By the time she got home, Judi had just enough energy left to stumble into the shower and roll into bed.

"I can remember Judi coming home and telling me she had talked to the coach," says Janet Warren, "and I said, 'Judi, you shouldn't talk to your superiors like that.' Looking back, the girls knew what they were doing. I just wasn't in on it. What I knew was that she was never home because she was always at practice. That was kind of upsetting, because it's hard to work around a family when one member is gone so late. We are a family that likes to sit down and have our meals together. It was a sacrifice for everyone."

In 1975, the summer before the girls' senior year, the IHSAA took over the administration of the girls' basketball program and announced that the first girls' state tourney would be held that March. It would be just like the boys' tournament, with all teams in one tourney regardless of enrollment.

That same summer Cindy's dad, Bill Ross, died suddenly of a stroke. He had been a part of the team, a constant source of encouragement and cheer since they were freshmen. Shattered, Cindy decided to quit the team. The others wouldn't hear of it. Cindy was the center, their rebounder, their enforcer, their intimidator.

But it was more than that: losing Cindy would be like losing a limb. "Judi and those guys said I couldn't quit because I was part of them. They said, 'We wouldn't know how to act without you.' We each knew what the others could do. They said, 'You gotta stay, for us.' So I decided to stay, and we started thinkin' that we could go to state and prove to people that we were legitimate athletes. We knew that having a dream wasn't good enough unless we worked and got it. My dream was to win the tourney to honor my father, because of the time he'd given me and what we'd done together." Together, they decided to win the first state championship for Bill Ross.

As the tourney approached, Cindy's life became even more complicated — she had fallen in love. Mike Knepper had asked her out that summer and they knew it was real almost from the start. But she had little time to see him and she wouldn't skip practice. It was a classic Hoosier conflict: love vs. training.

Faithful but lonesome, Mike would wander over to the Rosses' house and hang out with Cindy's mom and brothers until she came home from practice. Then they'd sink down onto the living room couch or go out for a quick drive. "This basketball is getting old, Cindy," Mike would say. "You never have time for us." And Cindy would throw an arm around him and soothe him with the words that Hoosier boys have whispered to Hoosier girls for nearly a century. "Mike," she would say, "the season won't last forever."

The Warsaw Tigers were good, and Judi was the spark plug. She may have been short but she was also aggressive, an intuitive passer and jet-fast. She had the quick hands of a pickpocket, constantly batting the ball away from dribblers and intercepting passes, which led to Warsaw lay-ins. The team's strategy was simply to outrun and wear down everyone else. They pressed from end to end and fast-broke at every occasion, with Judi penetrating and passing the ball off to Cindy, Lisa, Cathy Folk, or a gifted sophomore athlete named Chanda Kline. In seven of their fourteen pretournament games, Warsaw scored more than twice as many points as their opponents.

They entered the tournament undefeated, barely known and pitted against 359 other schools. Fifty or so relatives and close friends watched them win the sectional final against Plymouth High, 52–38. As sectional champions, they again demanded better uniforms and cheerleaders. The administration consented to let the junior varsity cheerleaders go with them to the regional tournament.

When they won the regional tournament the following week, the school began to take notice. Posters appeared in the halls. Kids began to stop at their lockers to wish them good luck. It felt weird but good. Judi was dating a guy already in college, and they all got a little misty when roses arrived after the regional title. "He was a jewel," recalls Judi's mom.

The fifty Warsaw fans became fifteen hundred for the semistate final in Fort Wayne. Hoosiers were Hoosiers, and this was one fine basketball team, and it had been here right under their noses all along. Most of the Warsaw fans wore orange T-shirts. The team won the semistate, too, making them one of four teams remaining in the tourney, and now there was real, high-voltage excitement. This was the first girls' tournament, after all, and the Bicentennial year. Warsaw's girls could be pioneers.

One afternoon, in the week before the state finals, the school held a pep rally for them. Lisa, Cindy, Judi, Chanda, Cathy, and the others sat in folding chairs in the middle of the court, staring self-consciously at bleachers filled with their schoolmates, students who just a few weeks before wouldn't have passed up a dogfight to see one of their games.

Near the end of the rally, Ike Tallman rose to his feet and walked slowly across the polished floor to the microphone. The gym was silent. The girls had no idea what he was doing, unless he was going to steal *their* moment to remind everyone that the boys' tournament was starting soon.

For a moment he said nothing. Then, looking at Lisa, he began, "Some of you have been after me to share this gym and I said no, not until you can fill it. Well, I owe you girls an apology." He paused and swept his hand in an slow arc around the room. "Because now I see you *can* fill this gym." Cindy Ross's voice breaks in telling that story. "After that," she says, "we got a whole lot of respect for him. It took a lot for the head coach of the Warsaw boys to say he was sorry to a team of girls."

Their first game in the state finals in Indianapolis was to be against East Chicago Washington, all of whose players except one was black. This was a totally new and forbidding prospect for small-town girls who rarely encountered African-Americans in their everyday lives.

The players on the boys' team, now eager to help, reported that the typical East Chicago crowd was a crazed mob given to tipping cars over and setting them ablaze. Even more sobering were accounts from the Rochester High girls who had lost to them the week before. "Rochester told us that they would probably draw

Judi Warren drives against a defender from East Chicago Washington. The game marked the first time most of the Warsaw girls had played against black players. (Courtesy Indiana High School Athletic Association)

knives on us," says Cindy. "We really believed it." But there was more. The Rochester girls reported that the East Chicago players didn't just knife you right away. They cussed you out first. Every dirty word in the book.

Knives were one thing, but coach Janice Soyez was not about to let her players become unnerved by dirty words, not having gone this far. So they created an obscenity drill in practice, to simulate a game situation. Two girls, an offensive player and a defender, worked their way down and back up the court, with the defender cussing out the offensive player. "We didn't know what to say," recalls Cindy. "We were all church-goin' girls. But we figured they'd call us 'honky' all the time. So one would dribble and the other would say, 'You bunch of damned honkies.' "

"Never having been around that many blacks, we didn't know how to handle it," says Judi. "We had always looked upon blacks as pretty rough people. We walked into the game and we were thinkin', Oh, my God. They were big and they were black." They were also unarmed, businesslike, and very good. One of East Chicago's forwards, freshman LaTaunya Pollard, was a wonderful shooter who was later named the outstanding woman collegiate player in the U.S. East Chicago jumped off to a quick eight-point lead, and Cindy committed three fouls in the first two minutes. "I was astounded," Cindy says. "I thought, This has got to be wrong, this isn't how it was written. So we dug in deeper."

In the second quarter Judi ignited the team by stealing the ball again and again, threading her way through defenses and hooking passes over her head for easy baskets. Chanda was hitting every shot she tried. Warsaw turned the game around and opened up a big lead in the fourth quarter.

"They turned out to be good, aggressive players, nothing short of that," recalls Cindy. "They really didn't talk to us at all . . . . color didn't make any difference at all." After the game, Warsaw tried to walk over to shake hands, but officials intercepted the girls from both teams and herded them downstairs and into their locker rooms.

Over five thousand people had seen the game, nearly half of them from Warsaw. Just as important, thousands more had watched the game on TV. Probably many viewers had intended to watch for just a moment or paused to watch between other programs. Given the strong ratings that game drew, quite a few must have taken their hands off the dial and sat down to watch it. Many in the Indianapolis area decided to drive out to Hinkle Fieldhouse for the championship game.

That night, when the team burst out of the dressing room and up the stairs, down through the hall behind the bleachers at Hinkle Fieldhouse where Oscar Robertson had run before taking the floor against Gary Roosevelt, where Bobby Plump had hit his shot, the tradition of it all, the cameras, the three thousand orange-shirted fans who had caravanned from Warsaw to see them go for it, gave them gooseflesh. It hit them all. This was it. This was for the state championship.

That night there were more than nine thousand people in the stands and a huge prime-time TV audience. The game, against Bloomfield, was close until the final minute. But once again Judi took over at the end, slashing again and again down the lane, scoring or passing to Chanda for assists, drawing fouls and shooting free throws.

Though Judi Warren was the smallest player by far, she somehow magnified herself in concert, as all great performers do. It was plain to see that here, too, was Hoosier Hysteria, packaged differently but radiant and authentic. At the end she was on the line, hitting free throws one after another, pulling her hair, jumping up and down and clapping, embracing her teammates, thrusting her fists in the air, shimmering like a hummingbird. This wasn't palm slaps and whacks on the butt, this was something new. These girls were excited, and they showed it. They led their own cheers during time-outs. That night Hoosierland melted.

When it was over and they had won, and Judi had won the Mental Attitude Award, and the last strands of the net had been snipped and all the cameras packed away, they slipped on their coveralls, climbed back into the Winnebago van and headed home for some sleep. They hoped someone would stay up to meet them and drive them home.

The van pulled into the school lot at 3:00 A.M. When they drew the curtain back, they were looking at a cop. When they opened the door, he said, "Better run, I don't think we can hold them back any longer." They were slapped on the back and borne into the

Judi Warren magnified herself in concert, as all great performers do.
(Courtesy Indiana High School Athletic Association)

The first Hoosier girls' champions, the 1976 Warsaw Tigers, hold the championship trophy aloft — except for Judi Warren, who can barely reach it. Cindy Ross is at Judi's left. (Courtesy Indiana High School Athletic Association)

gym, which people had again filled for them, but this time completely, the stands, the floor and the halls leading in. No one in Warsaw had gone to bed. When Judi and Cindy hoisted up the trophy, a mighty cheer filled the gym. "You know what I was thinking?" says Cindy. "I was thinking I wouldn't get to play ball with these guys next week."

∞ ∞ ∞

On an early November afternoon in 1994, ten high school girls run through a half-court scrimmage, blue jerseys against yellows, at Carmel High School just north of Indianapolis.

The yellow team's best shooter, Lisa Williams, sprints beneath the basket from one side to another, blond ponytail streaming straight behind her. She runs her defender into a pick, and bursts free, waiting, wide open, body squared for a shot, fingers aching for the ball. No teammate sees her. *"There she is!"* screams Carmel varsity coach Judi Warren. They freeze. Coach Warren slowly drags her fingers through close-cropped, feathered brown hair and steps forward. She takes the ball so that everyone will focus on her. "It floors me, ladies," she says slowly, "how you can play this game without talking. And I know you will start talking the minute practice is over. HELP! BALL! PICK! These are the words we've *got* to use. You've *got* to talk to each other."

Twenty seasons after she led her team to the first girls' state championship, Judi Warren is now the coach of a major girls' program in Indiana. She is one of a growing number of Indiana women who are returning to their game. After games, opposing coaches sometimes tell her that she was their girlhood heroine. She thanks them and feels old.

Some of the problems that Judi and her coach at Warsaw, Janice Soyez, grew up with are behind her. While Soyez coached for next to nothing, Judi earns about seven thousand dollars, roughly what the boys' coach makes. Carmel High provides both boys and girls practice jerseys, uniforms, warm-up clothes and shoes. Each year, Judi and the boys' coach work out a schedule to share after-school practice time on the varsity court, alternating weeknights.

At least two Carmel girls will receive full scholarships to major colleges this year. One of them is Lisa Williams, bound for the University of South Carolina after balancing forty scholarship offers. "I started thinking about playing college ball when I was a kid," she says. "Now I can move on to bigger dreams."

Lisa says that at Carmel no one calls her a "dyke" or a "jock" because she's an athlete. "I remember when I was seven or eight, my brothers and sisters said they didn't want me to play basketball because that was a 'dyke sport.' I think that's gone, now. For awhile we all kept our hair long just so the comments wouldn't get made. Now it doesn't matter anymore. Some of the best looking girls at Carmel are on the ball court."

Some hurdles remain. One is game scheduling. Girls play on schoolnights while boys play on weekends, which allows them to sleep in the next morning. "But we've learned good time-management skills," Judi says. "In the past few years, only two or three of the girls on our teams have not been honor roll students."

About three-quarters of the coaches of girls' teams in Indiana are men. Inability to find or pay for child care remains a major obstacle for women who want to coach. Judi, a single mother, gets up at dawn, eats breakfast with her fourteen-year-old son Andy, and then drives off to teach physical education to as many as five hundred and fifty elementary students in a week. Then it's practice and games and supper with Andy, and then often his games. Sometimes even then the day isn't over. Her players turn to her with their problems. Often they come over to talk. "Coach Warren is important to me," says Lisa Williams. "I trust her. She cares about me as a person, not just as a ballplayer who's gonna be gone soon. She'll know what I'm doing in five to ten years. She'll be there for me if I need her."

Each year Judi is honored as a pioneer at one event or another, which means she has to endure once again the film of her 1976 championship game. She sits in the dark, sometimes covering her eyes, mortified by their matador defense and the passes she didn't see and the layups they all blew. She thinks the level of play has progressed so much in twenty years that she could no longer start on the team she coaches now. Her players, who have also seen the film, disagree. "She'd still be tough," says Lisa Williams. "Even in practice, she sees the floor well. She had the moves and she was really fast. Everyone I've talked to says she was good. Everybody knows who she was."

Lisa is asked if the members of the Carmel Greyhounds girls' basketball team think they owe their coach anything. She pauses. They haven't even played their first game yet and it seems too early to be talking about doing anything for anyone. "Well, mainly our goals are personal," she says, pushing a blonde strand back into place. "But we've talked. There is something we'd like to do for her, and for all of us. We'd like to be the team that takes Coach Warren back to the final four."

A hundred and twenty days later they did, and then nearly won the state championship. "Don't ask me how we did it," said Judi, still hoarse a week after the final game loss to Huntington North. "They just decided to do it and no one could stop them."

They grew into each other week by week. Around Thanksgiving E.B. Larson settled in as point guard. By Christmas they had all decided in a team meeting to attack with a controlled offense than trying to win by running. "Around the holidays we got closer as a team," Judi says. "I'd see them together more, and staying after practice to shoot with one another."

They went into the tourney unranked and having lost their last three games. But they were adaptable and determined, led by experienced players and a fine coach. Every game in the tourney had a different script. They nearly blew a twenty-two point lead in their sectional final but staggered to a one-point win. They used three players and nine fouls on Anderson Highland's best scorer in a regional game and shut her down. They held the ball for the final two excruciating minutes to protect a slender lead against Ben Davis in the first semistate game. Then E.B., Lisa, and Betsy Palicek poured in free throw after free throw against Rushville in the semistate final, and Judi Warren was back in the final four.

Judi feared they would have nothing left for the finals, which were held at Indianapolis' Market Square Arena. She was nearly right. Dead on their feet, they fell behind by nineteen points and somehow found the energy to surge back and win by a point in the afternoon game against Washington. "One sportswriter told me it was the best game he had ever seen," says Judi.

Coach Judi Warren huddles with her Carmel Greyhounds, 1994 State Finalists. (Phillip M. Hoose)

Almost fifteen thousand attended the final game. Among them were nearly all of Judi's old Warsaw teammates. Judi asked Cindy Ross to speak to her players in the locker room before their championship bid. Cindy told them that she had been through a lot of ups and downs in the twenty years since she had played, but that she always carried in her heart the love of her teammates. Though she rarely saw them or spoke to them, it was always there. It was a bond she would never forget and that could never be broken. "It was just a wonderful speech," Judi says. They hung in well against Huntington North, but lost the championship by four points. They were exhausted, and proud. "I really liked the way they were after that game," said Judi. "They cheered while the winners got their awards. Their heads were up."

A week later Judi's phone was still ringing with calls of congratulations and interview requests. These were gratifying conversations, full of the flattering questions that all coaches hope to be asked at some time or another. Except for one. "You know what drove me crazy?" Judi asks, indignant. "At one point or another, almost everyone said, 'Well, now that you've won it as a player and made the final game as a coach, are you gonna retire?' I couldn't believe it! I mean, I'm thirty-six. I love kids and I love basketball. My mother still thinks I'm unbalanced, and maybe I am, but I've never found a better way to help young people. No, I'm not gonna retire . . . I might do this till I drop."

Fathers and Sons —
The Mounts of Lebanon, Indiana

In the late sixties a drive up Highway 52 from Indianapolis or down from Chicago took you through Lebanon, Indiana, population 9,500. At the town line, right beside the rack of service club emblems, the Lions and the Elks and the Rotary and the Kiwanis, draped there like medals on a general's breast, a second sign stood taller and truer. It read, "Lebanon, Indiana, Home of Rick Mount, Mr. Basketball 1966."

The biography of that roadside sign tells us the story of Rick Mount's basketball days. Erected after his senior year in high school as a monument to what was then the most publicized career in the history of Indiana basketball, the sign was ripped from the highway by a jubilant mob and carried thirty-five miles up the road to West Lafayette after Mount's jump shot put Purdue University in the NCAA Final Four in 1969. Hours later, Lebanon police roared up, recaptured it and returned it tenderly to its habitat. Several years later, after Mount's professional career had fizzled to a premature conclusion, the sign was discreetly removed.

But the sign tells only part of the story, a third to be exact, for it could just as easily have been planted there to commemorate the feats of Rick's father, Pete, as a way of marking the town for the Studebakers and Packards flying by at a mile a minute, or to celebrate the heroics of Rick's son Richie.

This is the story of three generations of a family which has lived in the same town, gone to the same school, and whose males have been the main producers of their town's principal export — points. Adored, resented, and celebrated, three towheaded Mount teenagers have eerily repeated a very personal script throughout much of this century. Each has been able to throw a leather ball through an iron ring better than anyone else in Lebanon, or Indiana—or in Rick's case, for a while, maybe the world. Each son learned from his father.

Each has borne the constant scrutiny and judgment of his neighbors. Each has been measured against his father in countless barbershop conversations. The three Mounts have spent years trying to beat each other in private one-on-one games, elbows flying, manhood at stake, calling fouls, bearing grudges until the next game. Each Mount has briefly allowed his talent to carry him away from Lebanon. Each has returned. The story of the Mounts of Lebanon, fixed points on the Hoosier compass, is, as much as anything, the story of a changing Indiana.

Lebanon is the seat of Boone County, a flat brown horizon of corn and soybean fields broken by dark groves of beech and maple, by farmsteads, ranch houses, and small towns. Back down gravel roads, past flagged mailboxes and backyards with satellite dishes that catch all of Purdue's games, a few barns still show "Chew Mail Pouch" painted on the side, only now beginning to fade.

Boone County was established by an act of the 1830 Indiana legislature. The following spring the governor appointed five commissioners to locate and name a county seat. An early account describes their quest:

Three of them met near the center of the county on about May 1, 1831. They were required by law to locate the seat within two miles of the center of the county. They finally chose a tall, dense forest where no one lived, not even Indians. They drove a large stake in the ground where the courthouse now stands. But they couldn't agree on a name for the town.

Mr. A.M. French, the youngest of the commissioners, lay nearby, quietly sleeping, unconcerned by what the name might be. He was aroused and told that the others had failed and had left the name solely up to him. He gazed up at the tall trees around him and he thought of the tall cedars of Lebanon in sacred history — he thought of the River Jordan — here were the tall trees, a little way off was Prairie Creek; thus the name was evolved in his mind — he shouted "Lebanon!" The name was fixed. Lebanon it has henceforth been.

Lebanon is within an area of perhaps a thirty-mile radius that was Indiana's first basketball hotbed. Schools from within this area won the first eight Indiana high school basketball tournaments. In 1911, the Lebanon High School Tigers finished second to despised Crawfordsville in the first tournament, but then won three of the next seven. Lebanon can stake some claim to being Indiana's first real basketball power.

Those vintage teams played their home games in the second floor of a hotel. The games took place in a small square room with a potbellied stove in the corner and a few hundred seats around the court. The instant the doors were opened, townspeople stampeded in out of the cold, stomped and brushed the snow off, and huddled together until the room became warm enough for shirt sleeves and coveralls. One house painter named Tom Dawson watched from outside the hotel, perched atop the stepladder which he propped against the building. There he would remain for an hour or two, nose pressed flat against the window, wiping the panes clear of steam with a kerchief and cheering into the winter wind.

John Mount, born in 1885, came to Lebanon from Kentucky around the turn of the century. He tried his hand at farming for a while, then found a better living pouring cement and smoothing out the streets and sidewalks of the growing town. Like nearly every other male in Lebanon, John lived for Friday nights. When he had sons of his own, he walked them to the gym and told them how he wished he could afford a car to follow the Lebanon Tigers on the road.

Pete Mount, born in 1926, walked to the games by himself from the first grade on. "You didn't want to sit too close to my dad in a close game," Pete later recalled. "You were liable to get a rib full of his elbow all night." Young Pete saw it all: he was there the night the Zionsville fan went at the referee with a whiskey bottle. He was there when the Frankfort Hot Dogs came to town and the fighting began in the runway to the dressing rooms and spilled outside into the parking lot. It was most exciting when big teams like Lafayette Jefferson and Muncie Central came through. He loved to sit around afterwards with his dad and hear Doc Porter and Butch Neuman and the others tell the stories of the glory days, when it was *really* tough. He wanted to be a Tiger.

He grew up tall for the times, six-foot-one, lean at a hundred and forty-five pounds, and a terrific shooter, the kind who could always find the basket even through a tangle of arms. Pete Mount played constantly, shooting at peanut cans and goals nailed to barns and garages and telephone poles. Looking back, he said later, there really wasn't much else to do.

When the time came, Pete started on the Lebanon High basketball varsity as a freshman, a rare privilege granted historically only to a precocious few. Given his slender build, it helped that he was older than most of his classmates, having repeated the second semester of third grade. To maintain turf, Pete found he had to "let an elbow slip every now and then. "

Pete broke all the Lebanon High scoring records and nearly led the Tigers to the state championship. Once he outscored the opposing team all by himself, an event which was recorded as an "incredible feat" in a comic book with Dagwood Bumstead on the cover. In Pete's junior year, 1943, Lebanon got to the Indiana championship game for the first time since 1918 but lost by five points to Fort Wayne Central. Tigers fans, enthusiastic even in defeat, ripped apart the steps of buildings along Courthouse Square and snake-danced through town. For his effort, *The Indianapolis Star* named Pete "Star of Stars" for the 1943 state tournament. A local paper called him, "the greatest prep athlete to dribble 'n' shoot in modern times."

Pete never got another chance to play. He was called for active duty on March 1, 1944, three weeks before the state finals. As it turned out, Lebanon was upset in the sectionals anyway — and off to war he went, or at least so he assumed.

There were few foxholes and shells in Pete's war stories: when he reported to Indianapolis' Fort Benjamin Harrison, he learned that his sergeant had already signed him up for a basketball tournament in Indianapolis. He played in California, then at Fort Riley, Kansas, then at Fort Sill, Oklahoma, where he once scored forty-three points in a game.

They shipped Pete's unit to Germany, but the war in Europe had ended by the time he got there. They were sent home for thirty days to rest up for the final assault on Japan. While he was in Lebanon, Pete married his high school sweetheart, Katie McLain, with whom he had gone steady since he was a freshman. A few days later Pete was back with his unit, ready to leave, when they heard that something called the atomic bomb had changed their schedule again.

In April of 1946 Pete was discharged. He and Katie took the Pullman together from Fort Jackson, South Carolina, to Indianapolis, with plenty to talk about. Teams of all kinds were tugging at Pete. Indiana, Purdue, and Clemson wanted him to play college basketball. The Indianapolis Indians wanted him to play minor league baseball.

Pete began the summer laying cement with his dad. Butch Neuman, his old coach, hounded Pete to stay near home and go to college at Purdue. But Katie was pregnant, and the couple needed money. One day when Butch happened to be out of town, Doxie Moore, coach of the Sheboygan Redskins of the new Basketball Association of America — a forerunner of the NBA — came through and offered Pete a contract. Pete wasn't sure, but Moore, later lieutenant governor of Indiana — was a persuasive man. He offered Pete no bonus but a fifteen hundred-dollar salary, plus more for exhibition games. It sounded like a fortune. When Butch returned, Pete was already gone.

It was a mistake from the start. Pete had always been a center, but now he had to play guard. He had to learn to shoot facing the basket, to set his feet and twirl up a two-handed set. Almost everyone in the league was bigger and more experienced. His loose elbows underneath didn't impress the likes of George Mikan. Pete was released at the end of the season and went back home to Lebanon. Anyway, it was time to quit fooling around; Pete and Katie had a son.

If ever a boy was born to score baskets, it was Rick Mount. The hands that pulled him into the world and whacked the breath of life into him belonged to Richard Porter, the very same Richard Porter who scored twenty-six points for the Tigers in the 1912 state championship game, a final game record that held for more than thirty years. And of course the child was Pete Mount's son. It was as though all the forces of the town's history had gathered on that day to produce a marksman.

Pete started his son out with a peanut can, just like the one he had used, cut out at the bottom and supporting a string net dipped in wax. When Rick got bigger, Pete nailed a goal to the garage and bought Rick a ball. Each night when Pete would come home from work at a defense plant in Indianapolis, he'd wash up and find Rick out back, shooting.

Before long their shooting contests turned into games, games that Pete made sure he won. "It'd make Rick mad 'cause he couldn't win," Pete later recalled. "He'd drive under the goal sometimes, and I'd say, 'No, you're not going to get that baseline on me,' and I'd put him up against the garage door and he'd quit doin' that. He'd keep movin' back, of course, but I could shoot farther with my two-handed set. But then he started stoppin', and jumpin' and poppin' 'em on me, you know." Rick would run inside crying after losses to his father, burning to beat him, causing his mother to turn on Pete. "What are you doing to that kid?" became a household refrain in those years. When Rick finally won, Pete looked briefly at his son, his face contorted. "Well, I guess now you're ready," he said finally, and went inside.

Those who lived in central Indiana at the time began to hear stories about Rick Mount when he was in junior high. It was as though another Mozart had been discovered in a cornfield. Hundreds of people followed Rick's fifth- and sixth-grade teams all over Boone County, just to watch the prodigy play. In his final years John Mount took to telling fans, to Pete's annoyance, that Rick would make people forget all about Pete.

Jim Rosenstihl became the Lebanon varsity coach during Rick's eighth-grade year. "Rosey," as everyone called him, and Pete were longtime friends, having played against each other in high school. Rosey's first chance to see Pete's kid for himself came in a summer league he set up for his seventh and eighth graders — forty games on sweltering asphalt from mid-May through August. As Rosey often put it, a kid whose desire wilts in hot weather is not the kid

Rick Mount, the pure jump-shooter, 1966. (Courtesy Jim Rosenstihl)

you want with the ball in his hands for the Lebanon Tigers with a game on the line.

One look told all. The slender boy was already an accomplished long-distance jump shooter. Every aspect of his form was perfect. He must have learned it on his own, too, Rosey thought, because Pete had never learned to shoot a jump shot. Rosey began to showcase Rick at coaching clinics. During a shooting workshop at one statewide coaches' conference, Rosey trotted Rick out to demonstrate the "minute drill." Before more than a hundred astonished coaches, the boy drilled twenty of twenty-two long-distance jump shots within a minute.

When the Lebanon High School season began, Rosey put Rick in the starting lineup as a freshman, just as Pete had been a freshman starter a quarter-century before. Like Pete, Rick was a year older than the others in his class, having repeated second grade. Rick averaged over twenty points a game and quickly began to receive statewide attention.

Part of Rick Mount's appeal was the way he looked. He was long and lean, perfect in a pair of pegged jeans, with killer blue eyes and high cheekbones. He had a sense of style. He wore his collars and sleeves up. His blond hair was cut in a burr, except for two carefully-managed rows of longer hair which converged into a butchwaxed curl dipping down onto his forehead. He called it the "Cobra."

He grew to be six-four, tall enough to be a high school center, but his was a marksman's game. He could shoot left-handed or right, and with defenders hanging all over him. He would dribble the ball at high speed, bounce it hard a final time and leap, delivering the ball at the height of his jump. He always seemed able to jump straight up, no matter how fast he had been running.

Rick Mount's jump shot came to be to small-town Hoosierland what Earl Monroe's spins or Julius Erving's dunks were to the cities: a perfect visual expression of the experience. There were long flat spaces and seasons and thunderstorms in Rick's jumper. It was a shot to be canned and preserved. The delivery was easy and light, the balance and trajectory sure and beautiful. Suddenly it seemed that all the great shooters of Indiana's history had done it wrong, but there had been no way of knowing this until someone did it right.

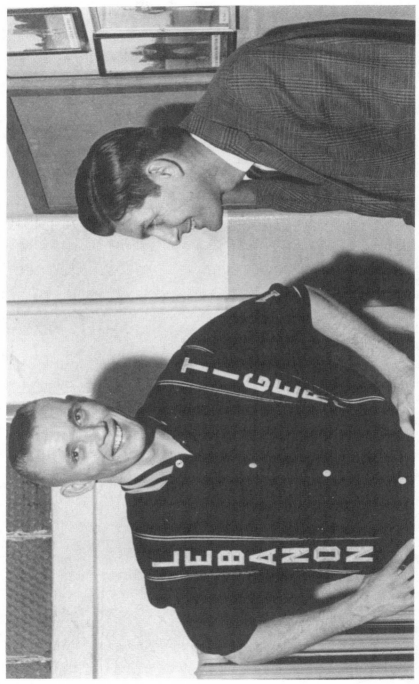

The best of times: Rick Mount as a Lebanon High star, with his promoter-coach Jim "Rosey" Rosenstihl. (Courtesy Jim Rosenstihl)

Jim Rosenstihl and Rick Mount were a match made in heaven, like Elvis and the Colonel. Rick was prodigiously talented, and Rosey, handsome, slow-talking, tireless, shrewd, and genuinely in love with basketball, was one of the great promoters in the history of the high school game in Indiana. Life was beautiful: Lebanon was winning games, and in Rick Mount, Rosey had the center-piece of the state. Offers from colleges were pouring in, including one feeler from all-black Tuskegee Institute.

There were all sorts of opportunities. One afternoon between Rick's sophomore and junior years, Miami University's basketball coach Bruce Hale showed up in Rosey's office with a gentleman who introduced himself as Aldo Leone, the nephew of the famous Manhattan restaurateur Mama Leone. He said he knew pretty near every basketball coach and player in the New York City high school world, which he kept calling "the prep scene." One of Aldo's friends was Jack Donahue, the coach at Power Memorial High School, who had a towering young center named Lew Alcindor. Rosey and Aldo started bantering about who would win a dream game between Rick the Rocket from the Hoosier cornfields and the Next Wilt. Aldo said he could get the ball rolling and sure enough Donahue called a few days later.

They agreed to try it in Indianapolis, where the crowds would surely be mammoth. They almost pulled it off. Tickets were printed, Butler Fieldhouse was rented, there were oceans of ink in the papers — and then the Indiana High School Athletic Association abruptly backed out, claiming the game would have been billed as a "national championship." To this day, Rosey thinks Lebanon would have won.

Rick's world at the time was circumscribed by the boundaries of his hometown. He had rarely been outside of Indiana, and he spent almost all his time alone or with his teammates, coaches, hunting pals, and the downtown merchants who sought to bask in his spreading fame. He had no brothers or sisters; his best friend was his special girl since early grade school, Donna Cadger.

Pete and Katie's marriage came apart before Rick's freshman year, and Pete moved out. All the hours of games in the driveway had not made Rick and Pete close. "He never would let me come to his junior high games," recalled Pete. "I think he was afraid I'd start yelling and make a scene."

"I didn't really know my dad," says Rick. "I looked at his scrapbooks, but it wasn't till I got older that people told me how good he was. I don't know why he didn't tell me. Maybe he didn't want to put any added pressure on me."

Rick seemed shy, withdrawn and often aloof to those outside his circle. He felt everyone's eyes upon him. "It's like you're in a little glass and everyone's peeking in at you," Rick recalls. "Anything I would do, people would say, 'Oh, that's terrible,' or 'That's okay.' It makes you kind of a loner."

Rick's summer habitat was an outdoor court in Lebanon Park, a couple of hundred yards from a pool where he worked as a lifeguard. Every few hours he'd whistle everyone out of the pool, drop down from the tower, pull on his sneakers and head for the court. "Hey, kid," he'd say to one of the boys who hung around him, "want an ice cream cone? Rebound a hundred shots and I'll buy you one."

Nights and weekends were for games. As his reputation grew, more and more players, especially black kids from Indianapolis, drove out to try their luck. Though they invited him to the city, Rosey kept Rick on his own court, where the rules were shooter's rules. At Lebanon Park the offensive player called the fouls.

Saturday night was date night. But if Rick had a date, he'd always drive past the court. "I remember once a date and I drove by the court on the way to the drive-in and I saw five or six black players out there. I didn't know them. I looked out there and thought, Hey, those guys are pretty good. So I told the girl, 'I got to take you home.' I took her home and she got out of the car and slammed the door. I got home real quick and got my shoes and went back. I never had another date with her but I got in some good games. How many guys would do that?"

Few Hoosiers who have become famous have made their mark in Indiana. Abraham Lincoln, who spent his youth in southern Indiana, made it big in Illinois and Washington, like Dan Quayle. The Jacksons left Gary to make it in Detroit and California; James Dean, Halston, David Letterman, Cole Porter, and Hoagy

Carmichael in New York. Among resident native Hoosiers, maybe only Wendell Willkie's presidential candidacy, John Dillinger's jailbreak at Crown Point, Larry Bird's senior year in Terre Haute, and Eugene Debs at the peak of his fame received the national attention Rick Mount attracted as a senior at Lebanon High School and a collegian at Purdue.

One event in particular changed Rick's life and briefly thrust Lebanon into the national spotlight. Midway through Rick's senior year, Rosey got a call from Frank DeFord, a writer for *Sports Illustrated,* inquiring about a story on Rick. Rosey cleared his calendar and soon, to hear Rosey and Rick tell it, Lebanon was like a movie set. For two weeks DeFord and photographer Rich Clarkson followed Rick everywhere. Clarkson snapped hundreds of pictures in the classroom, in the gym, in the town square. Rick says that once he saw Clarkson behind him as he entered the restroom at school. He turned around. "Anywhere but in here," he said.

"One of the shots they wanted to take, I don't know why, was with Rick downtown and by the poolroom," says Rosey. "He was standin' right out in the middle of the street with cars comin' by. I was standin' down on one end of the street makin' sure no one ran over him and DeFord was on the other end. Suddenly Pistol Sheets, the guy who owns the poolroom, came runnin' outside, wavin' a gun around, yellin', 'I'll shoot the first guy that hits him!' "

On February 14, 1966, Lebanon merchants gathered around the delivery truck that pulled up in front of a drugstore and tore at the string that bound the magazines. There was Rick on the *cover,* profiled from the waist up against a farmhouse, wearing his Lebanon High warm-up jacket, his lips parted in what appeared to be a bashful smile, the Cobra perfectly in place. It was the first time a high school basketball player had ever appeared on the cover of *Sports Illustrated.*

They devoured the article. DeFord proclaimed Rick to be perhaps the best high school player of all time, as good as Oscar Robertson had been. He was said to possess the moves of a cat, the eyes of a hawk, and the presence of a king. That sounded about right. On the other hand, he sent them up as hicks, which still leaves a bad taste in Lebanon whenever the subject of the article comes up. For his part, Rick, while suitably honored, wished maybe they could have left Oscar, his ultimate hero, out of it.

The state tournament started the following weekend. As usual, Lebanon easily won the sectional and regional tourneys, but they began the afternoon game of the semistate as heavy underdogs, billed as a one-man team against a tough Logansport squad.

No one who saw it will ever forget the Logansport game. Down 51–39 with eight minutes left, Rick decided he was at least going to go down shooting. He scored twenty points in those minutes, hitting seven bombs in a row in one immortal stretch. When the smoke cleared, Lebanon had won by a point, and Rick had scored forty-seven of his team's sixty-five points. Leg cramps destroyed Rick in the night game just as cramps had sidelined his father in the tourney — and Lebanon lost by a single point.

The following morning, sports editor John Whittaker wrote in *The Hammond Times:* "I've seen a few great things in my time. I was there when Red Grange went wild against Michigan. I saw the famous Dempsey-Tunney title fight. I watched the Babe call his home run shot . . . and now this performance by Mount."

When the headlines appeared announcing that Rick Mount had signed a letter of intent to attend the University of Miami, the people of Lebanon, and Indiana, were stunned. "People on the street wouldn't even speak to me," says Rick.

Given the reaction, Rosey advised Rick that, just to be safe, maybe he'd better also sign a letter of intent with a Big Ten school. Before long, Rick told Bruce Hale he had changed his mind and signed with Purdue. Lebanon was jubilant. One of every nine residents — including infants and the elderly — bought season tickets to Purdue's schedule in Rick's first year.

West Lafayette, Indiana, home of Purdue University, is just thirty miles from Lebanon. Rick never really took to college life. His girlfriend, Donna, was enrolled, too, and soon they were married and living in student housing, driving back to Lebanon on non-game weekends.

Lebanon never seemed to change. The downtowners were always coming up with some crazy scheme. There was still the sign with Rick's name on it at the town line, and now there was a life-size cardboard cutout of him in uniform at the bank. The court at Lebanon Park had been dedicated to Rick, with a sign of course, and Rosey now had a booklet out about jump-shooting which featured the shooting statistics of every game Rick had played in.

Purdue coach George King built an offense around Rick, with his big men leaping out like muggers to set picks. That was fine with Rick, just like Lebanon. And Purdue had real talent. Bill Keller and Herman Gilliam, both of whom later had fine professional careers, kept the defenses honest and set up the plays.

Rick was an even better collegian than a high school player. Three times he was an All-American, and, as a senior, he averaged about forty points per game in the Big Ten Conference. Such scoring was unheard-of. It was then that Al McGuire, John Havlicek and others started calling Rick the best "pure shooter" they had ever seen. For some reason, when you saw Rick Mount shoot, there was no need to explain what an impure shooter was.

The best night of his college career came as a junior in the NCAA Mideast Regionals against Marquette. Purdue, an underdog, found itself a point down and with the ball in the closing seconds. George King set up the obvious play, and it couldn't have worked better. Rick got the ball, drove his man through one deadening pick and into another and found himself sky-blue free in the corner with four seconds left. He swished his jumper, and Purdue was off to the finals.

It was after that intoxicating game that Purdue fans carried his highway sign from Lebanon up to West Lafayette and transplanted it near a fountain on a campus hill. Maybe on that night, too, Rick Mount, like his billboard, was liberated from Lebanon.

Early in March of 1971, after UCLA had throttled Purdue in the NCAA finals, professional basketball teams came panting after Rick Mount, just as they had come for his dad. This time the money was better, mainly due to a bidding war between the NBA and the newly formed American Basketball Association. Two days after his final college game, Rick signed with the ABA's Indiana Pacers for what was reported as a million dollars, chopped up into various investment schemes and deferred payments. The signing was televised live at six o'clock throughout Indiana.

At the time it was one of the biggest contracts ever. A physical education major, twenty-six credits shy of graduating, Rick quit school. He explained matter-of-factly to the press that he had gone to college not to learn to be a tennis coach but to play pro basketball.

Rick's pro career turned out to be every bit the disappointment Pete's had been, in part because the expectations had been so high. It took five years for the end to come. The Indiana Pacers were a championship team whose offense was concentrated in the front court. Tough veteran players like Roger Brown and Mel Daniels resented Rick's fame, and did not feel that they required a savior. For the first time in his life, Rick was not the center of the offense. Very few plays were set up for him. Often he wasn't a starter.

His confidence faded. He became convinced that his coach, Bobby Leonard, was out to ruin him. He badgered Leonard to trade him, and finally Mike Storen, the man who had signed him from Purdue, got him traded to Dallas and then on to Kentucky. There was one more trade, to the Utah Stars. When the Utah franchise's bankruptcy was announced, Rick was offered $16,000 for his fabled investment plan, into which few contributions had been made.

The end had come too soon. He was twenty-eight years old, a man who had devoted his life to a single, highly-valued pursuit — jump shooting — and who could do it as well as anyone else ever had. It was hard to understand or accept. Like his dad, he went back home to Lebanon. He too had a son.

"There was a big void in my life after I got out of basketball," says Rick. "You think to yourself, No more organized competition. Boy, it's an empty feeling for a long time."

Rick and Donna Mount have remained in Lebanon ever since Rick left the ABA. There has been no reason to leave; both extended families are there, and they prefer a small-town atmosphere.

Rick invested some of his Utah settlement in a sporting goods shop that went under in a few years. Since then, Rick has sold various athletic products and taught jump shooting at camps and

Richie Mount, Pete Mount, and Jim Rosenstihl, mid-1970s, after a Lebanon Tigers game. (Courtesy Pete Mount)

clinics, while Donna has held a job as a pharmacy technician at Witham Memorial Hospital in Lebanon.

Rick was once offered a head coaching job at a Lafayette high school, but his decision to leave college early came back to haunt him when the IHSAA disqualified his contract. He talked to Purdue officials about making up the credits but came home discouraged.

Rick loves to work with young players. He can teach almost anyone to shoot, adjusting an elbow here, shortening the stroke there, making sure the guide hand falls away so the shooter doesn't end up "thumbing" the ball. "I'm forty-seven years old and these kids still know Rick Mount because their dad told them," he says. "It really gives me a thrill if I can help kids shoot the basketball and get confidence in themselves."

Along with all the regular students, there was one special apprentice. Rick started his son, Richie, born in 1970, with the traditional family peanut can. As Richie grew, Rick schooled Richie in the guide hand and the planted foot, in the subtleties of backspin and arch.

Rick had more free time to work with Richie than Pete had had for Rick, and there was far more technical structure to this apprenticeship. But its essence was the same: intense competition between father and son. They played thousands of one-on-one games, as Pete and Rick had, in driveways and in Memorial park. As Richie grew, and the day of his first victory approached, their expressions and words hardened, and the action became rougher. A grimness set into the competition.

In the summer of 1984 the Mounts decided that Richie should repeat his eighth-grade year. "There are four reasons," Rick said at the time. "It gives him an extra year of maturity. It helps his schoolwork. It helps him mentally, 'cause he's my kid and he's probably feeling a lot of pressure. I had more publicity than my dad did, and now there's more emphasis on athletics. And it'll help him get a college education, an athletic scholarship." The Mounts reasoned that the extra year had helped Richie's dad and granddad, so why deprive Richie of the same chance? But Rick and Pete had repeated a year in early grade school, and both had been at best average students. It had just worked out that way.

This was different: Richie was a good student, and this was a calculated family decision.

Richie started his second year of eighth grade in Connecticut and returned home about two months later. Rick took Richie into the principal's office and tried to enroll Richie as an eighth-grader. The principal refused. The Mounts hired a lawyer and took their case to the school board. They argued that "red-shirting," as the practice is known, is an Indiana tradition. Rosey was able to cite seven kids who'd stayed an extra year at Lebanon High during his coaching career, and everyone knew of kids who had repeated grades for basketball in other Indiana towns.

By a 3–2 vote, in a packed and emotional hearing, the board granted the Mounts' request, citing the absence of a statute or policy forbidding such a move. The state educational bureaucracy asked the Lebanon board to reconsider, but the board held firm. Several months later, the IHSAA ordered schools to draw up rules and penalties against red-shirting in high school.

Rick Mount was news again. The school board's decision was featured on the front page of *The Indianapolis Star*. Television cameras rolled in for Richie's eighth-grade games. Lebanon's newspaper, *The Reporter*, backed the Mounts editorially, again citing the absence of policy, and published about a week's worth of letters — mostly unsigned — before announcing a moratorium on Richie Mount mail. Excerpts from some of them show the depth of feeling in Lebanon:

> *It absolutely amazes me that in our society it has become acceptable for parents to consider the primary function of going to school to be the enhancement of their child's athletic abilities . . . As a graduate of Lebanon High School, I am utterly embarrassed.*

> *I wonder why the practice is so wrong all of a sudden. Is it red-shirting that is wrong suddenly or is it wrong now because it involves a youngster named Mount?*

> *I have known Rick, Donna and Richie Mount for many years. They are basically good people, very interested in their son's well-being.*

Richie Mount puts a move on his dad, 1985, in one of countless, sometimes rough, one-on-one games. (Shoshana Hoose)

Is it fair that Richie gets this whole year to mature when al-most every other basketball player does not? And if it is fair, who makes the decisions on which player can repeat eighth grade and which cannot? What if every eighth-grader did this . . . would anybody ever graduate from Lebanon?

While the attention did not seem to bother Richie, the experi-ence heightened Rick's sense of estrangement from his neighbors. He believes, and probably with good reason, that had Richie been anyone else's son, or had Richie belonged to an earlier generation, the people of Lebanon would barely have noticed. Richie Mount made the Lebanon varsity team as a freshman, with Rosey as his coach, and averaged more than seventeen points per game. In one early game against the Frankfort Hot Dogs, rival fans wore red shirts and waved red towels whenever Richie got the ball. Richie hit thirteen of fifteen shots from the field, scoring thirty-four points. He thrust his fist in the air after every basket and Leba-non won by three. "That crowd really pumped me up," he recalls.

Resentments born in the mid-sixties flared up again in the Lebanon bleachers whenever Rick attended Richie's home games. Several of Rick's classmates had sons on the team, and the par-ents sniped at each other constantly. "I could hear them," says Richie. "I'd have the ball and someone would stand up and yell 'Pass It, Mount!' and I would stick one from the corner and my dad would get up and yell 'There's your pass!' He'd get so into the games that he'd have his elbow in my mom's ribs all night. Finally he quit going. He'd stay home and listen on the radio."

Richie graduated from Lebanon as the ninth leading male scorer in Indiana history and the third Mount to be a member of Indiana All-Star team. He also survived hundreds more one-on-one games with his dad, games in which they sometimes threw words, and balls, and elbows at one another. Neither would yield. Sometimes they went home separately and in silence. "My mom must have been the best mom in the world to deal with me and him back then," Richie says. Donna Mount said little, except to comment to a reporter, "If I were raising Richie by myself, he would probably play tiddlywinks instead of basketball."

The Mount family rite of passage came just after Rich's sixteenth birthday, on a summer day in which Richie beat Rick several times in a row. "Richie was pleased with himself," Rick said of the day. "He wouldn't smile but I could tell he wanted to."

Like his dad, Richie began his college career at Purdue. Many speculated that it was a mistake, that Richie was not a good Division I prospect, that being the son of a Purdue legend would make it harder. Richie scored well in some freshman games, and played especially well against the Russian National Team as a sophomore, but found himself playing less and less. After a dispute over playing time with Purdue's head coach Gene Keady, Richie left. He transferred to Virginia Commonwealth College where once again he played little, but left only twenty hours short of graduation. He has mixed feelings about his college career: "The college game is gruesome," he says. "It's only about money. It was disappointing, but I had the chance to see if I could play at that level, and I got to see how people are. I made friends of all colors. I got tougher. It didn't break me. In a lot of ways, basketball gave me an education."

One Saturday morning in the winter of 1990, Pete Mount smelled smoke arising from the mattress in his small upstairs apartment in Lebanon. He made his way downstairs, found the fire extinguisher and struggled back up to fight the flames himself. Police found him a few hours later dead in the bathtub.

Among those who mourned Pete the most was Rosey. Until the end the two men often got together to eat lunch and talk about the Chicago Cubs, Pete's passion, and of course Boone County sports. Theirs was a friendship cemented by stories polished smooth in the telling, by shared opinions, common enemies, and scorn for weakness. It was a pure pleasure to listen to the two of them, especially when they got going about Rick, as they always did, for his time was the brightest the sky ever got around Lebanon. They often talked about when the carnival would come to the county each Fourth of July, and how Rick would wipe out the basketball shooting event every year, arching shot after shot through the small hoop until the carney ran out of teddy bears.

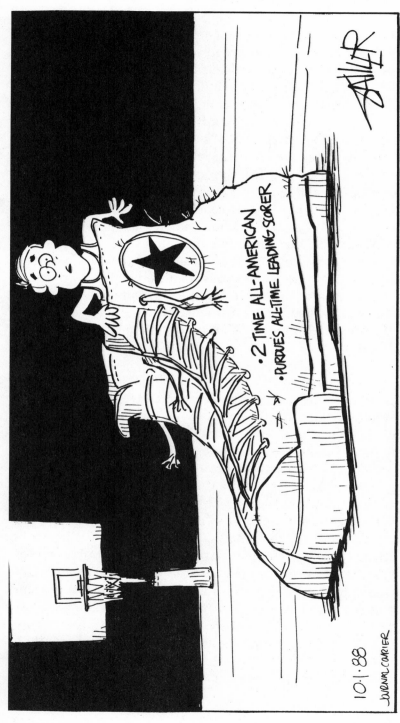

YOUNG RICH MOUNT AT PURDUE TRYING ON DAD'S OLD SNEAKERS

At Purdue, Richie Mount battled competitors for playing time and the ghost of his legendary father, as this 1988 cartoon shows. (Dave Sattler, *The Journal and Courier*, Lafayette, IN)

In the mid-eighties Rosey put together the "Boone County All-Stars" — seniors from county high schools — and took them to Clinton County to play against their best. With fifteen seconds left to play, Rosey stopped the game and sent Pete, Rick, and Richie out together on the floor, along with Brian Walker and his dad. "I'll let you play," he whispered to Pete, "but I don't want to see you runnin' up and down that floor." Pete nodded solemnly, then trotted out and called for the ball. He let fly a long one-hander as the buzzer sounded. No one on earth, Rosey thought, had ever been able to stop Pete Mount from getting in a shot.

Richie Mount is now an officer on the Lebanon Police Force. He rarely plays basketball, preferring instead to patrol the streams of Boone and Montgomery Counties for smallmouth bass. Weight-lifting is a special passion. Richie can bench press nearly three hundred and fifty pounds, and Rick takes pride in showing visitors snapshots that feature Richie's powerful upper body.

In 1994 Richie almost married a woman he met in Lebanon after a workout and whom he dated for most of a year. The relationship dissolved, but it gave him a chance to consider fatherhood and the prospect of a fourth-generation Mount someday pouring jumpers through the hoops for the Lebanon Tigers. "Well," he told a writer, "I wouldn't pressure a son to play basketball. He could turn out to be a football player and that would be fine. So the line could end with me. But if I ever have a son, whatever he wants, I'll help him. And my dad'll be around too."

That much seems assured, at least as long as deer and pheasant can still be found in Boone County and turkeys still scratch through the stubbled fields. Rick Mount, still trim at forty-seven, with not quite enough blonde hair remaining to fashion a cobra, bursts out laughing when he considers the next generation. "Another Mount?" he repeats. "Well, I'd like to see a grandson play, but I don't know if Lebanon fans would. I don't think Lebanon is ready for another Mount." He leans back in a lounge chair in the living room of his modest yellow house, less than a mile from where he and Donna both grew up, savoring the idea. "Another Mount . . . Another Mount might just short this town out."

Larry Bird —
The Guy Down the Road

Late one evening in the autumn of 1994 Jim Jones came home from a coaching clinic in Louisville. As he was catching his wife up on the day's events, she handed him a small UPS package. It had a Florida postmark. She was smiling and looking right at him. He tore the tape and opened an envelope. A ring fell into his hand. He looked at it, puzzled for a moment. It was huge, a gold ring with the number thirty-three fashioned in diamonds across an emerald face. There were thirteen diamonds in each three. There was also a note written in a familiar, loopy handwriting, thanking him for support that came a nearly a quarter century ago. It was from the best player he ever coached. It concluded, "I hope I made you proud. Larry."

Jim Jones was the high school coach of the best basketball player who ever grew up in Indiana, with the possible exception of Oscar Robertson. For years Jones picked Larry Bird up at dawn each morning, took him to the gym at Springs Valley High, fed him donuts and milk, unlocked the door, and gave him a chance to excel. He often told Larry Bird, as he has told hundreds of others, that no matter how badly he wanted to succeed, there was a guy down the road who wanted it more. If you're shooting a hundred shots, he said, the guy down road is shooting a hundred and one. And now, after thirty-two years of coaching, Jim Jones has a way to prove it to the kids he still picks up at dawn: he has a ring from the guy down the road.

Now that Larry Bird's basketball career is over, it seems easier to evaluate what he meant, and means, to Indiana. To people around French Lick he is a source of neighborhood pride. He honors them when he comes home with his family for a few months each summer. They still love to tell the stories about how he picked up his first MVP trophy wearing jeans and left it on his mom's refrigerator, and about the time he told the brass from *The American Sportsman* to call him back when they decided to fish the farm ponds of southern Indiana.

To Hoosiers statewide he is, among many other things, a throwback, an image from Indiana's past, a reminder of times when basketball was all there was in the winter and when it was played best by white players from small towns, boys who spent more time on the floor than in the air.

"I really don't need anyone to boost my ego," Larry Bird said during his NBA days. "I've already proven that a white boy who can't run and jump can play this game."

That had always been assumed in Indiana, at least until the 1950s, when black players began to transform the game into a faster, higher-flying form. Within a few years, most of the game's major stars were African-Americans, even in Indiana's high schools. Deep down, few in Indiana ever expected the best player in the world to look like Larry Bird again.

And yet, for awhile, before Michael Jordan raised the standard perhaps beyond reach, and before Magic Johnson found the peak of his game just as Bird's back began to deteriorate, there was no better basketball player on planet Earth than Larry Joe Bird, from a town of about two thousand in Orange County. Three times he was voted the most valuable player in the National Basketball Association. He led his Boston Celtics teams to two NBA championships and barely missed several others. When the U.S. Olympics Committee agreed to allow the best basketball team ever assembled to represent the country in the 1992 games, Larry Bird stood tall as its co-captain.

But how did it happen? Those who grew up with him point out that he rarely watched televised games as a boy. How did he learn so much without watching the game's greatest players? He played against competition mainly from small hill-towns in southern Indiana. Growing up, the only blacks he played against were the staff members at the local hotel, though he ended up playing in a league in which he was the only major white star. He became a superb rebounder without having superior leaping skills. Defense? Jim Jones laughs, "Even then, he couldn't guard anybody one-on-one. But he was the best team defensive player, the best anticipator, I had ever seen."

During his playing days, Hoosiers opened their hearts in gratitude to the man who put the Hoosier back on the basketball dollar. Streets in French Lick and Terre Haute were named after him. Days after he held up the NBA championship trophy on national TV and said, "This is for Terre Haute," they tried to wipe the donor's name right off the Indiana State University Fieldhouse and replace it with Larry Bird's. He stopped them with a modest but firm letter to the local newspaper.

But no one could stop Hoosiers from asking, as they still ask, how could a small-town boy whose team never even got out of the Bedford regional, who barely made the Indiana high school all--star team, become the best?

Parents wonder what, besides the value of hard work, they can teach their children by holding up Larry Bird as an example. How do you teach your kid to play basketball like a great pool player, a hustler who has already run the entire table mentally while a pigeon of an opponent tries to figure out the next shot? And how many other geniuses are walking down the street, looking ordinary or even dull, only because they have not found the game which brings out their special talent? There are some things that simply playing all the time can't explain. These days there are thousands of kids who play all the time. In the slow settling dust of Larry Bird's retirement Hoosiers still look back and wonder, Who *was* that man?

French Lick and West Baden, Indiana, are two sides of the same road sign, along Highway 56, in a valley to which Indians and white settlers alike were drawn by three springs of rank-tasting, foul-smelling waters that their animals seemed to love. This is the hill country of southern Indiana, springs and limestone quarries and fossil beds, the part that was piled up by the last glacier to come through.

In 1904 Thomas Taggart, mayor of Indianapolis, a genial Irishman who was doubtless cheered by the few cents he and his cronies made on every barrel of beer sold in Indiana, built a six-hundred-room resort hotel and mineral spa in the valley and named it the French Lick Springs Hotel. Located at the junction of the Southern and Monon railroads, it became one of America's preeminent resorts.

Twenty-one trains a day carried socialites and industrialists, politicians and entertainers, prizefighters, gamblers, and gangsters through southern Indiana and right up to the portico. There they were met by some of the more than one hundred black porters and busmen who wheeled their trunks over the sawdust walking paths, past the Japanese gardens, and into the great hotel itself.

They checked in, found their rooms and padded down to the baths — Turkish baths, Russian baths, electric baths, mud baths — expensive baths full of the same stuff the Indians' horses had lapped up. Taggart called it "Pluto Water," after the king of the underworld.

Taggart built a bottling plant across the street and soon was selling Pluto Water hand over fist. Pluto's twenty-two minerals were said to soften skin, cure rheumatism and arthritis, and clean the pores. And, especially after even more salts were added, it won rightful acclaim as a laxative. Guests found a jar of Pluto outside their doors each morning. "If nature won't," said the label, "Pluto will."

Leaders from all professions gathered there. Al Capone, the Pluto of his day, was a regular guest; he was perhaps the only one who relaxed with five bodyguards. It is a Bird family story that Big Al once tipped Larry Bird's grandfather a hundred dollars. The hotel was a popular site for political conventions. In 1904 Democratic National Chairman Tom Taggart ran Judge Alton B. Parker's faltering campaign against Teddy Roosevelt from the hotel lobby. In the same grand setting, the nation's governors squeezed Al Smith out in 1931 and brought in FDR as the party's new standardbearer.

French Lick Springs Hotel waiters in the 1930s. Hotel staff members and their children were the first black players Larry Bird ever played against. (Courtesy French Lick Springs Hotel)

Tom Taggart took womb-to-tomb care of valley residents. Almost everyone who lived in the valley worked either at the hotels — a rival sprang up in West Baden — or at the Pluto plant. Taggart built separate housing for the black workers who came up from Evansville and Louisville. They had their own church and school, their own restaurant and bar in the "Brown building." Even Joe Louis, who trained for several of his fights at the West Baden Hotel, was not allowed to stay in the rooms, although he alone among blacks was allowed to play on the French Lick Springs golf course.

Whites ran the grounds, the kitchen, the golf course, and the casinos. They worked year-round, nine hours a day. In the winter, they stayed outdoors, clearing ice from the trees. During the summer, the women who did not work in the dining halls got ready for winter, freezing meats, canning, getting the apples in. Three generations of people in the valley slipped out of their beds and into uniforms each morning and made ready to coddle the richest people on earth. It is small wonder that Larry Bird, the grandson of Tom Taggart's people, is content to pick up awards in the world's finest hotels in jeans.

The winter rivalry between the West Baden Sprudels and the French Lick Red Devils was red-hot even by Hoosier standards. Both towns were poor and small, and there was no breathing space between them. "They just despised each other," said Jack Carnes, sixty-one, a lifelong valley resident and longtime kitchen manager of the French Lick Springs Hotel. "You were just liable to get beat up if you went to West Baden or a West Baden kid went to French Lick. They fought over that basketball *all* the time.

"When I was a kid growin' up, there probably wasn't a ball game when there wasn't a fight afterwards. Our teams weren't that good, but whether you won or lost, you *had* to agitate the other team. The old West Baden gym had a balcony with four or five rows of seats, and I've seen people jump off of that balcony and onto a player. It was just *violent.*"

In the mid-fifties the two towns began to face pressure from the state board of education to consolidate their schools. West Badenites could see the writing on the wall from the start, for theirs was the smaller school.

In a series of rancorous public hearings, they first resisted the whole idea, then fought for a new building which would straddle the town line. But French Lick had almost 80 percent of the valley's people and almost all the power.

One thing was sure: West Baden parents refused to let their children play for, root for, or date French Lick Red Devils. So it was that in the fall of 1957, when the West Baden students crossed the line into French Lick, they went not as Red Devils, but as Springs Valley High Black Hawks.

The first Springs Valley basketball team must have been sent from heaven. Even today, valley residents invoke the boys of 1958 as the Irish recall cherished rebellions. They won twenty-five games in a row. In the tourney they massacred three teams from big schools, teams ranked among the top ten in Indiana. It actually looked like they might go all the way, until they were martyred in the state finals by a Fort Wayne team with a seven-foot-tall center.

Residents make it clear that it was the *team*, not the board of education, that consolidated the schools. They buried the hatchet in the skulls of common foes. Some of the players were from French Lick and some from West Baden, but when sharpshooters like Bob McCracken and Marvin Pruett started lobbing mortar from the corners and the fast break was on, there were no Sprudels or Red Devils, only Black Hawks and enemies. Such was the heat that coach Rex Wells, who had come from West Baden, spent much of his time calming his players. At halftime, he would sit the boys down, pass out oranges, and read them poetry.

Tickets became harder to come by as the undefeated string grew longer. The shortage became a drought, a matter that naturally engaged civic leaders like Shorty Reader, a midget who owned the poolroom downtown. "We was all in there one night, gripin' about how we couldn't get into the Shawswicke game," recalls Jack Carnes. "Next night Shorty had tickets for everyone, good seats, too. He said, 'Only thing is, be there when the doors open.' We thought it was funny that he didn't wanna go.

"Well, we got in first thing and before long some people came in wantin' our seats. We got in a big fuss, the police friskin' everybody, and finally they set up new seats for us on the floor. When we got back we told him all about it and Shorty said, 'I knew I didn't get the color quite right.' "

Today a great banner celebrating the Team of '58, one of the best teams ever seen in southern Indiana, hangs from the rafters of the Springs Valley gym. "If we'd had a losing season that year," says Jack Carnes, "we'd probably still be fightin' today."

The Birds, Kerns, and Nobles who settled into the valley came mainly from Ireland and Wales. Joe and Georgia Bird, married when Joe came back from Korea, produced six children, five boys and a girl.

Larry, born in 1956, was the third of the five boys. Like lots of younger brothers, Larry grew up fast, tagging along, younger and smaller, burning to play too. "When me and Mike were eight and nine, Larry was four or five," says Larry's brother Mark. "Every time we went some place, we had to take him along. We used to beat him up every day. He was a little smart butt. We used to send him home cryin' and then Dad'd come down there and beat me 'n' Mike up for beatin' up his baby. He'd come down with a switch or somethin', and me and Mike'd get it. Even if we just told him he couldn't play, he'd go home and tell Dad we hit him, and it'd be all over for us."

"Those brothers were so competitive, and they just pounded on the kid," says Jim Jones, who started coaching basketball at Springs Valley High in the early sixties. "Boy, he'd fight them tooth and nail, and he'd stay around and play after they'd leave. His will to win was the biggest thing. I remember in Little League, when he'd get beat he'd cry. They were just great, competitive kids."

Larry started his career on a basketball team in fourth grade. He is remembered locally as a skinny kid with a good eye and a quick temper. Once in junior high he was sent home from practice for fighting. On Friday nights while his brothers played for Springs Valley High — Mike as a part-time player and Mark as a high-scoring star — Larry stayed home.

The family had a hard time making ends meet. Joe Bird, Larry's father, was a laborer with a drinking problem, and Georgia Bird, his mother, worked at a variety of jobs, often as a waitress. They moved around a lot, sometimes living with relatives in the country. Joe was sometimes in the household, sometimes not. When Larry started playing for the school teams, he moved in with his grandmother, as Mike and Mark had done when they played. She lived only a block from the school, and, better still, she let the boys stay out as late as they wanted. Larry would play in the gym at night until they locked the doors and then play outdoors near a streetlight. "I used to drive by the park, and he'd be out there with a couple of friends until one or two in the morning," says Gary Holland, then Jones's assistant coach. Even after the others went home, Larry would stay out, whipping the ball against a concrete wall.

It was the way he practiced, as well as the amount of time he spent at it, that made him good. "Most kids are afraid to fail," Jones says, "but Larry wasn't. Most kids keep practicing what they're good at but Larry practiced on his weaknesses. He spent one whole summer doing things left-handed. He was obsessed."

Larry made the Springs Valley team as a sophomore, wearing Mark's old number, thirty-three. A guard, he stood six-one and weighed but a hundred and thirty-five pounds.

He was mainly a passer and rebounder on a team of good shooters. Slow afoot, he developed his own ways to help the team on defense. "He would let his man go and steal the ball from someone else," recalls Jones. "Or he would leave his man to steal the ball or block a shot. Somehow he could just anticipate what someone else was going to do."

In the season's second game, Larry broke his ankle in a battle for a rebound. He practiced shooting with the team, balanced on one crutch, until his cast wore off and then begged Jones for a chance to play again. Jones was never one to pass up a chance to issue a challenge. "We told him if he could play up to a certain level, we'd take him to the state tournament," says Jones. "I didn't tell him we'd already decided to take him. I said he'd have to run the suicide drill every day within a certain time, and he couldn't do it and get frustrated and almost cry. He practiced very hard, and dragged his leg around until he beat the time." He went to the sectional, got in at the end of the first game and won it with two free throws. Springs Valley was defeated in the second game.

Larry had a fine junior year as a six-foot three-inch guard, averaging about sixteen points, ten rebounds, and six assists a game. He spent much of the season feeding the ball to a senior named Steve Land. In the season's final game, Land entered the fourth quarter needing a few points to break the school scoring record. Springs Valley was far ahead, so Jones pulled the starters except for Land, who was supposed to stay in until he broke the record. But the subs couldn't get the ball to him. Pass after pass was intercepted as time ran down. "I remember Larry saying, 'Put me back in, coach, and he'll get it,' Jones says. "I did. Bang. Bang. Bang. Three or four passes later, the kid has the record."

A week later Springs Valley was upset by Paoli in the first game of the sectional. Many around town were beginning to think Larry might have a future as a small college guard.

No one was prepared for what happened. Over the summer, Larry shot up to six feet seven inches, and increased his strength by working out each day on the football team's new universal weight machine. Somehow he lost none of his exceptional coordination; instead, overnight, he became a guard in a center's body.

"I had been away at college, and I hadn't seen him play," recalls Mark Bird. "Once between his junior and senior years I was workin' with our uncle up in Gary and Larry and a friend came up to see us. Suddenly he was six-six and he'd put on some weight. I couldn't believe it."

Basketball had become his life. There is no reference to Larry Bird in his senior yearbook that does not relate to basketball, no clubs or prom pictures or senior trips, not even other sports. "Larry never paid much attention to girls growing up," says John "Beezer" Carnes, Larry's high school teammate and constant companion. "He was basketball-minded."

Beezer describes a typical Saturday during basketball season: "I'd probably stay all night with Larry. We'd sleep in till about noon and Larry'd like to talk about who we were gonna play that night. You couldn't keep him from talking about basketball. Then his granny — he has the most wonderful granny — would fix lunch and we'd go out and ride around." They didn't smoke or drink, says Beezer, and those with drugs "knew not to come around us." At night, they hit the drive-in or hung around the

Make my day: Larry Bird and the Springs Valley Black Hawks of 1974 put on their game faces. Beezer Carnes is at bottom left. (Randy Dieter, *Sunday Courier and Press*, Evansville, IN)

Shell station or shot pool at Shorty's. As Beezer puts it, "We were just typical kids."

Larry Bird's senior year at Springs Valley High had to be as good a year as any Indiana player has ever had, but, because Larry played in a remote part of southern Indiana, he received little statewide attention. Bird averaged about thirty-one points, twenty-one rebounds, and five assists per game and led the team in every other statistical category but free-throw percentage. He twice scored over fifty points and once pulled down thirty-eight rebounds in a thirty-two minute game.

That year Jim Jones quit coaching to become the Springs Valley athletic director — "one of the many, many mistakes I've made in coaching," he laughs — and Gary Holland took over. Holland had grown up in Paoli, ten miles away, where he had been a basketball star. "My father owned a store in Paoli," Holland says. "That first year, they shot his windows through with buckshot. I got calls in the night all winter long, people from Paoli saying 'traitor' and hanging up."

Holland inherited from Jones a team of fast, good athletes, and he simply turned them loose. "It was probably the most fun year I've had," says Holland. "I figured, If it's gonna be like this, coaching's gonna be great."

Larry's passing ability could be dangerous. "We used to tell them, 'Better have your head up, lookin' toward Larry,' " says Holland. "Even in high school, he made an average player great."

"The man could do everything," says Beezer Carnes, who, having played on teams with Larry since fourth grade, may have caught more of Larry's passes than anyone else. "He was the most unselfish man I ever played with. He could've scored any time he wanted to."

Asked if there was any single play that foreshadowed the Larry Bird of today, Holland, Mark Bird, and Beezer Carnes all mention the same pass. Against Corydon High, on a night when he scored fifty-four points, Bird was in the left lane on a fast break. He was racing toward the corner when a teammate lofted a pass to him from the opposite side of the court. It came down a little behind him. Instead of slowing down to catch the ball, Bird reached back and batted the ball behind his back with his left hand, sending it on one bounce to Doug "Turkey" Conrad, who was streaking down the middle and who laid it in without breaking stride. The next morning, Holland, Beezer, Larry, and several others ran the film clip over and over. "We just sat there laughing," says Holland. "Even Larry had to laugh."

Larry's self-confidence increased by the game. "Frankly," says Beezer, "I always figured Gary wanted me to be the leader, but after the second or third game it was clear who our leader was. Larry liked to joke around, but it was always *after* practice. He'd get his work done first. He could come down on you out there, too. I might be standin' around and Larry'd come over and say, 'You tired? Then why aren't you workin' helpin' us win?' "

On the days when the team had a 6:30 A.M. free-throw practice, Jones would swing by Larry's grandmother's house and try to wake Larry and Beezer up. "Larry probably didn't look too favorably on it, but he'd roll out and put his pants on and we were off." Beezer, on the other hand, often rolled back over.

It came back to haunt him in the tourney their senior year. After Springs Valley had won the sectional, Beezer found himself on the line for four last-minute free throws against Bedford with the regional championship at stake. He missed them all, and Springs Valley lost by three points. "After the game," Beezer says, "we went back to Shorty's, and Larry just laid it out to me. He said, 'Beezer, you should have got up and shot them free throws in the mornings.' "

It didn't take long for Gary Holland to realize that there could not be many better players in Indiana, if any, and he owed it to Larry to spread the word. In Indiana, the greatest honor a boy can get is to be named "Mr. Basketball," and, after that, to make the twelve-player All-Star team that has played a group of All-Stars from Kentucky each summer since 1939. The selections are made by *The Indianapolis Star*, and when Larry played, particularly by a promotions man named Don Bates, now retired. "When you die," explains Bates, "that's in your obit, that you were an Indiana All-Star. And it's usually in the lead paragraph. It's like your pedigree."

Larry Bird averaged about 31 points and 21 rebounds per game his senior year. Few outside of South-central Indiana had heard of him. (Courtesy Gary Holland)

Bates and his advisory committee always had a tough job. Half the coaches in Indiana were out to convince him they had an all-star. The lobbying is to this day year-round and intense, with letter-writing campaigns and violent fan reactions when their boys don't make it. Always, fans from both northern and southern Indiana have believed *The Star* has slighted — maybe persecuted — them.

With Larry, Holland knew he had an uphill fight. "Mr. Basketball" was out of the question — no one would believe he was that good. Larry had been a guard the year before, the number-two scorer on a team that hadn't even won its sectional. Now he was a hundred-and-sixty-pound center on a small, rural team, light-years from Indianapolis.

Holland called Jerry Birge, a respected sportswriter from nearby Jasper, who had seen Larry enough to know. Birge responded by printing hundreds of fliers and glossy action photos. He sent them to every newspaper and radio station in Indiana and hounded Don Bates and his colleagues at *The Star*. Birge had the feeling he was getting nowhere.

But early in the season Indiana University coach Bobby Knight began to show up at Larry's games. He'd slip in quietly, after the game had started, sit up there eating popcorn for a while and slip out again. He rarely spoke to Holland, or to Bird, but he sent three of his players — Steve Green, John Laskowski, and Kent Benson — to talk up IU over dinner at the Joneses' home. After the tourney, when he made his pitch, Larry signed, though his first choice was Kentucky. "We were all IU fans," says Mark Bird. "My dad was probably the biggest IU fan ever. He'd say to Larry, 'Boy, I seen this red jacket the other day, and I sure would like to buy it and wear it to one of your ball games.' "

"When he signed with IU, it really caught my attention," says Don Bates. "I thought, I'd better drive down and take a look at this kid. They were playing at Mitchell. I got there and they were warming up. Right away you could tell which one Bird was, shooting layups and jump shots. He had great hands, big hands. He scored about thirty-five points and had about twenty rebounds that night."

Larry made the all-star team, but, even after spectacular practices, he played less than half the time. When his coach sum-

Indiana high school All-Star Larry Bird dunks against a Kentucky counterpart. Note the placement of Bird's right foot. (Courtesy *The Indianapolis Star*)

moned him for action at the end of the second game, he refused to play, stating that he wasn't a mop-up player. Deeply proud and certain of his abilities, he was burned by the insult, and the memories still linger.

Asked by writer Ray Didinger in 1985 to explain "What do you think it is that drives you?" Bird replied, "I'm sure it dates back to Indiana . . . I didn't even make all-state my senior year [he didn't make the wire service teams] . . . I heard what they said about me: too slow, can't jump. Country kid, never had the big-city competition. I went to the state all-star game my senior year, and I got in the first five minutes. I wondered if I was really that bad.

"I look back and I realize I was the best player in the state. No one gave me credit for it. But maybe it worked out for the best. It kept me practicing four or five hours a day in the summer, and now it's a habit."

In the fall of 1974 Bird travelled to the IU campus at Blooming-ton with seventy-five dollars in his pocket. Overwhelmed by the campus ("thirty-three thousand students was not my idea of a school, it was more like a whole country to me"), he hitchhiked home after twenty-four days. Bob Knight, who later expressed re-gret for not supporting Larry, saw him play only once, briefly, at an informal scrimmage.

Within the next two years Larry found himself in turns mar-ried, divorced, fatherless, and a father. Joe Bird, divorced from Georgia and unable to keep up support payments, took his own life in 1975. The same year Larry married a high school sweet-heart and months later, convinced he had made a mistake, broke it off. The couple conceived a child during a brief reconciliation, then divorced. A daughter was born in August of 1977. At first Larry claimed the child was not his, but her mother went to court and won a paternity and child support judgment. She has since remarried and the family lives near Terre Haute.

Bird enrolled briefly in a local trade school, dropped out, then enrolled at Indiana State University in Terre Haute. Mark was nearby, as was an ex-Springs Valley teammate, Tony Clarke. Bird was ineligible for a year, then played for ISU, making an immedi-ate and overwhelming difference to the team. In those years he met Dinah Mattingly, a student at ISU, whom he later married. In his final year of play, he led Indiana State to an undefeated season and the final game of the NCAA tournament, where they lost to Magic Johnson's Michigan State team. He was voted the nation's outstanding collegiate player and drafted by the Boston Celtics, for whom, in a thirteen-year career, he won international fame as the greatest forward ever to play basketball.

During each of his Celtic years, Bird returned home in the summer, staying with his mother in West Baden. He would play golf and fish, and relax as he could nowhere else. His old friends grew accustomed to his impulsive calls, sometimes at odd hours. "I only got to see Larry once last summer," said Beezer Carnes, now a pipefitter, in 1984. "He just called me up and said, 'Let's go.' We just went out and drove around till four in the morning. I had to get up at five the next morning and I wanted to get one hour's sleep, anyway. He tried to talk me into cuttin' work the next day, but I have a mortgage on a new house I'm tryin' to pay off and I really couldn't cut . . . I told him, 'If you'll pay for the day,' and he just laughed."

Things are different in the valley now. Pluto Water stopped selling in the mid-thirties, a decade before the state police came in and boarded up the casinos. Shortly before he was murdered by a Capone mob member in Arkansas, the owner of the West Baden Springs Hotel donated it to a Catholic order.

But the French Lick Sheraton, as it is now called, is back on the upswing after decades of musty decline. Even in the lean times, the politicians still came: Nixon and Agnew, Ronald Reagan when he was governor of California. One morning in the late sixties Jack Carnes's pot washer walked out of the freight elevator, a vessel apparently overlooked by the Secret Service, and was startled to find Hubert Humphrey alone, writing, in the hotel kitchen.

When the Taggarts sold out, the towns had to grow up quickly. The Pluto plant, where Mark Bird worked for a while, today turns out bottles of Blue Lustre Carpet Cleaner. The Kimball Organ Company has developed a scholarship program to try to keep kids in the valley. Still, many of those who leave for college settle in Terre Haute, Bloomington, Louisville, or Indianapolis.

Larry Bird debuts as himself in the 1994 Hollywood film *Blue Chips*, which also marked the screen debut of former Indiana University star Matt Nover, seated beside Bird. The car is driven by Nick Nolte. (Kevin Swank, *The Evansville Courier*)

Local rivalries die hard in the Valley. The Springs Valley vs. Holland "Nostalgia Game" in 1990 was marked by a scrap between players who hadn't faced each other in a quarter of a century. (Tom Roach)

The sports rivalries remain hotter in the valley than in most parts of Indiana. It wasn't until 1984 that the Springs Valley Black Hawks finally felt things had simmered down enough to resume their rivalry with Dubois High, two towns over, after a quarter century's athletic estrangement. In 1990 Springs Valley played Holland High School in what was billed as a "Nostalgia Game" among ex-high school players who were now in their thirties and forties. The game was halted early in the second half when, just like old times, a fight broke out.

These days Larry Bird spends his winters in Naples, Florida, and returns to the valley each summer with Dinah and their two young adopted children. They settle into a splendid brick-and-shingle house on about ten acres down a country road. The house is custom-made for an NBA-sized owner, with oversized doorways and tall ceilings. Set in a huge front lawn is what basketball courts must look like in heaven, a patch of asphalt shimmering against the hills, with glass backboards, floodlights, and a gravel apron around the court. Few people seem to bother Larry as he jogs and bicycles down the country roads in the mornings.

He likes to play golf with Tom Jones, Jim's son, the pro at nearby Salton Ridge. The rods in his back make him stiffer off the tee, but, says Jones, that's not all bad. "Used to be he swung as hard as he could and hit it a long way, but he hunted for the ball a long time, too."

Larry Bird is probably most visible in Terre Haute. One of the city's busiest restaurants and convention centers is "Larry Bird's Boston Connection." The dining and meeting rooms are covered with hundreds of photos, magazine covers, and Bird memorabilia. The establishment's cordial manager is Mark Bird.

Terre Haute's hottest high school basketball team is Northside, ranked among the top five schools in Indiana throughout much of 1994. At times it seems as though the Springs Valley Black Hawks of the mid-seventies have taken over the school as a base of operations. The boys' coach is Jim Jones, now sixty-two, but still up each morning at five-thirty to round up his most dedicated players and drive them to the gym. The girls' team is coached by Tony Clarke, Springs Valley Class of '73. Jones' most active volunteer assistant is Mark Bird. Jones, Bird, and Clarke all live within a couple of blocks of one another. Larry visits when he can.

Years after Larry's final minutes with the Dream Team, Hoosiers, including those who know him best, still reach back, trying to remember games and shots and passes and events of his childhood that might have foreshadowed his greatness as an adult athlete. It is all so mysterious. "He'd make passes that you didn't even see were possible," says Jones. "You wondered, how'd *he* see them?"

Some think the explanation lies in where he grew up. Larry had only about three hundred classmates at Springs Valley High but there were sometimes three thousand fans in the gym when he played. It could only happen in small-town Indiana, goes this line of reasoning, where basketball was all there was to do and everybody cared . . . but then nobody else got that good.

Mark Bird holds to at least a partial genetic theory. "We were all good shooters," he says, "everyone in our family. They say that granddad Bird was just a tremendous baseball player. Dad quit school early to join the Navy, but Shorty Reader knew our dad real well, and he'd say, 'You kids *ought* to be good, as good as your dad was.' "

Gary Holland offers something quite different, something that speaks to Larry's success in the NBA. "Larry just seemed like he could adjust to the character of other people," he says. "Really, the game of basketball is getting along with other players. After he got out of high school here he signed at IU, and then he dropped out and enrolled in Northwood Institute up here for a while. We never had any blacks in school for him to play with, but at Northwood there were a few, some good players. I was amazed by how he could adjust to their style of play. It was rough play. He fit in real good. They really respected him."

Finally, Jim Jones just laughs. "How did Larry Bird get so good? He just has a God-given talent for the game. He loved it so and he worked so hard. There'll never be anyone just like him." In the end there really is no answer. Maybe the only explanation for Larry Bird is that somebody had to be the Guy Down the Road.

An Interview With Damon Bailey

During Indiana Pacer timeouts in the 1994–95 season, fans sometimes caught sight of Damon Bailey in the margin of the camera's eye. Respectfully dressed in slacks and a sweater or jacket, he was often craning forward from a seat behind the bench or standing at the outer fringes of the huddle to listen in on coach Larry Brown's strategy. He had the look of a man who did not wish to intrude, who did not presume to claim something he had not yet earned, and yet who wanted not to be overlooked.

In the madhouse excitement of the Pacers' post-season run for glory, it took such sightings to remind fans that Damon Bailey was on the roster. After having been chosen by the Pacers in the second round of the 1994 NBA draft, Bailey played in three pre-season games and then was offered a one-year contract during which it was agreed that he would undergo surgery on both knees. It was an unusual arrangement, but Damon Bailey is a special case. "It wasn't really a very hard decision," said Larry Brown. "I liked what I saw of him. Obviously he had been very well-coached and versatile. I look forward to a chance to coach him."

But there was more to it than that. Damon Bailey had been a legendary high school player and a four-year starter at Indiana University, and he had not been forgotten by Hoosier fans. More than twenty thousand had attended the 1994 NBA draft, held in Indianapolis. Many of them were there to see that Bailey landed with the Pacers.

Though there had perhaps been a very few high school players in Indiana's history as good as Bailey, no one had ever been so loved. Pat Aikman, who directs the Indiana-Kentucky All-Star

Damon Bailey, Indiana Pacer. (Courtesy Indiana Pacers)

game for *The Indianapolis Star*, remembers the moment when he fully understood the magnitude of Damon Bailey's fame. "It was the week before the game in Indianapolis in 1990," he recalls. "After practice we took the team to the Indianapolis Zoo. There was a dolphin show, and Damon was just hounded. People came up to him constantly and kept shoving paper in his face for him to sign. It was distracting and his teammates were being ignored and he seemed embarrassed. I asked him what he wanted to do. He said, 'I just want to get out of here.' So we got up and headed for an exit door. Damon pushed it open and right outside was a young couple strolling a baby. As soon as they recognized him, they picked up their baby, thrust it in his arms, and started snapping his picture. It was like he was one of the Beatles."

Growing up in a tiny town south of Bloomington, Bailey scored more points than any other Indiana player, played before bigger crowds, and led his team to almost unprecedented success. Patient with fans and writers, he proudly and politely represented the forgotten hamlets of Indiana whose schools were lost to consolidation a generation before. Songs were written about him, paintings of his jersey and shoes were commissioned, fans plucked blades of grass from his front lawn as souvenirs. His college coach, Indiana University's Bob Knight, was once asked if Bailey had become as popular in Indiana as had been his former star, folk hero Steve Alford. "There's no comparison," Knight said. "As popular as Alford was, he wasn't even close to this kid."

Damon Bailey was born and grew up in Heltonville, population about three hundred. It is a crossroads community of shingled houses with one general store, set in the limestone country of south-central Indiana, whose giant quarries produced the stone for the Empire State Building, the Pentagon, and Rockefeller Center. Its residents are timbermen, stoneworkers, farmers, and factory workers. Until the fifties, a railroad line backed up to the Heltonville Limestone Company, a mill which employed hundreds. Freight cars were loaded with slabs of freshly-planed stone and hauled off to Indianapolis and the world beyond. In those days Heltonville boasted three saloons, a hotel, and, most importantly, a high school basketball team of its own.

The Heltonville High Blue Jackets had at least one Bailey in the lineup during most of the years from 1925 on, including Damon's grandfather, great uncles, uncles, and cousins. Damon's father, Wendell Bailey, Class of '68, was a three-year starting forward for the Jackets and his mother, Beverly Case, was a cheerleader for rival Tunnelton High.

Heltonville and Tunnelton were among a group of tiny towns in Lawrence County whose residents were united in their burning resentment of Bedford, the county seat. Bedford was the home of the giant Indiana Limestone Company, which had been formed in the mid-twenties when Chicago bankers put up the money to buy out most of the small independent mills and quarries of the area. It was a source of pride in Heltonville that their mill had been large and prosperous enough to avoid the merger. The Bedford Cutters, as their basketball team was called, played in a gym that seated forty-five hundred fans and drew team members from a town of fifteen thousand. They always hosted the sectional. They were the ultimate Goliaths.

In 1974 Heltonville and six other little towns were forced to consolidate their schools along with Bedford High School into a regional monolith called Bedford North Lawrence. Though Heltonville High had never won so much as a sectional tourney in half a century, the loss of their school and its team was a mortal wound. The Blue Jackets had been the soul of the town in winter. Even today, many still remember commencement night in 1942, when the Heltonville school caught on fire and collapsed before the fire department from Bedford arrived. After everyone was evacuated, a few brave souls went back in to try to rescue the things that meant most to the community. Among the first items they pulled out were the basketball uniforms.

The consolidation meant that their children would go to school with Bedford kids who viewed them as hicks. Heltonville parents feared that their sons and daughters would become immersed in Bedford's faster culture and lose their identity. Worst of all they feared for the town's very identity. What did it matter that twelve grades had studied under one roof at Heltonville High? They had been family; aunts in the upper grades had walked down the hall to straighten the jackets and smooth the dresses of younger nieces on school picture day. Now they wondered, without their school, without a team to anchor them, would Heltonville simply blow away?

From the beginning, Damon Bailey was not only bigger than other boys his age, but unusually well-coordinated. After high school Wendell Bailey had continued to play basketball in local industrial leagues several nights a week. He took Damon with him down gravel roads and two-lane highways to old backroads gyms, still standing. Damon was devoted and attentive. He could heave the ball up against the backboard and down into the net at five. A few months later he could do it with his left hand. By third grade he was playing on his school's sixth-grade team.

At ten, Damon was regularly playing with his father in games against working men three times his age. They understood they were not to baby the kid. There was no praise from Wendell Bailey. Criticism was necessary. Sickness was not tolerated. Toughness and stoicism were valued above all. The transformation of Damon into a finished basketball player became the family business; each day his mother and later his sister Courtney rebounded the hundreds of shots he launched toward a driveway goal. Each morning began with weight lifting and running before school.

By the time Damon entered junior high he had played on several national championship Amateur Athletic Union teams. Word spread rapidly among coaches and basketball writers that a new Larry Bird lived somewhere south of Bloomington, not far from where the original had grown up.

Damon's life was changed forever by a single event in the late winter of 1986. One Monday evening Bob Knight, upset with the play of his team and particularly that of his guards, decided to drive twenty-five miles to see the eighth grader he had heard about. Locals first froze in the shock of recognition when Knight entered the Shawswick Junior High gym, then shyly pressed around him and finally left him alone as he absently munched popcorn and studied the boy. At six-one, Damon Bailey was half a head taller than anyone else on the floor, powerful, insightful, and fluid. The following morning Knight told his coaching staff, straightfaced, that, "Damon Bailey is better than any guard we have right now. I don't mean potentially better, I mean better

Bob Knight enters the Shawsick Junior High gym to watch eighth-grader Damon Bailey play. If Indiana were a church, this would be a scene on a stained-glass window. (Sanford Gentry)

right now." The remark was overheard by journalist John Feinstein, who reported it in his bestselling book, *A Season on the Brink*.

Overnight the Indiana basketball world flocked to see the backwoods child. Unlike Larry Bird, who escaped public attention until college, Knight's comment had served up Damon Bailey as an adolescent. Game after game, fifteen hundred fans packed into the stuffy little gym. As he entered his teen years, Damon Bailey began to sign autographs and his parents quietly took out an unlisted telephone number.

In some ways, the attention made Damon, already a sturdy individual, even stronger. He learned to zone out the distraction of fame and became a better and better player. He led Bedford North Lawrence High — or BNL, as it was called — to four consecutive state finals, the first Indiana player ever to do that. His peach-complexioned face with the wide smile showed up on TV at six and in sports pages throughout Indiana. He grew to be six-three and a hundred and ninety pounds. The weights gave him a body of steel. He was a white player who could dunk. He showed no fear. By the time he was a senior, he was almost as famous as Knight. He credited his teammates, he flattered his coach. Always, he identified his home as Heltonville, not Bedford. Signs sprouted at the town limits proclaiming Heltonville the home of Damon Bailey. Heltonville residents who had boycotted BNL games ever since their school had been erased scrambled to buy season tickets. They were back on the map.

By the morning of March 25, 1990, when the BNL players arrived in Indianapolis for Damon's fourth and final try for the state high school basketball championship, most of Indiana was absorbed in the story. Anticipating that Damon would bring in a greater crowd than usual, officials of the Indiana High School Athletic Association moved the finals to the Hoosier Dome (now the RCA Dome) a football stadium in downtown Indianapolis. They were astonished when 41,101 fans showed up for the two afternoon semifinal games, pairing first Concord and Anderson, and then BNL and Southport. It was nearly twice as many fans as had ever before attended a high school game in the United States. Damon scored twenty-five points and grabbed ten rebounds against Southport, giving his team a chance to play for the championship a few hours later. That evening, 41,101 returned for the championship game against undefeated and number-one-ranked Concord High of Fort Wayne.

The last two minutes and eighteen seconds of that game are simply dreamlike. Behind by six points, and with his last chance for a state championship slipping away, Bailey gathered his teammates beneath one goal and urged them to get him the ball and trust him with it. He then scored BNL's final eleven points, leading them to a three-point victory. When the buzzer sounded he fell to the floor with his teammates in a heap of joy, then sprang to his feet and plunged into the crowd, trailing cameras and cables behind him.

For a moment he disappeared into what must have been half the population of Heltonville, then emerged with his family. Organ music swelled throughout the stadium. While his mother dabbed her eyes, and his father's lips moved, and his sister wrapped her arm around him, Damon Bailey calmly began to field reporters' questions. Only one seemed to give him a few seconds' pause. It was about the man for whom he would play the following winter and who had thrust his family into the spotlight five years earlier with an offhand remark. "What about Coach Knight?" someone asked. "Well," Damon Bailey replied, "Up to now I haven't thought much about it. But I'm his boy now."

The spotlight grew even hotter at IU. In his first game, which was played in Hawaii, Damon scored only three points. The next morning's sports headline in *The Indianapolis Star* read, "Bailey has quiet game." To fans who had waited so long and hoped so hard he turned out to be a tantalizing and frustrating collegiate player. For long stretches he would seem to disappear, shooting rarely, then suddenly emerge to take over a game, making Big Ten players look like Concord High again. No one knew the real Damon Bailey. Knight professed puzzlement. When it was done, Damon had been a starter on four winning teams and was the fifth leading scorer in IU's long history. Playing with injuries, he was named a third-team All American as a senior and averaged nearly twenty points per game. Had he arrived in Bloomington unheralded, he would have left a god.

Damon Bailey first dunked as a seventh-grader. Opponents constantly underestimated his leaping ability. Marion's Jay Edwards (12) and Lyndon Jones (4) are in foreground. (Sanford Gentry)

Damon Bailey, here a high school freshman, who restored pride to forgotten hamlets like his native Heltonville, became the most beloved player ever in Indiana. (Sanford Gentry)

The force. (Sanford Gentry)

But many Hoosiers were disappointed, though they told each other they weren't. He hadn't been the second Larry Bird. Bob Knight praised Damon lavishly in the days after his senior season, calling himself Bailey's "greatest fan," and proclaiming him "one hell of a basketball player." A year later, Knight seemed to be offering a different appraisal. "I got less out of Bailey than anyone I ever coached," Knight told Robin Miller of *The Indianapolis Star*. "I didn't get it done . . . rarely have I felt that about a kid."

This interview took place in the Indiana Pacers' training room at Market Square Arena in Indianapolis in November of 1994, while Bailey was beginning a program of physical therapy after operations on both knees. Wearing red shorts and a Pacers T-shirt, he answered questions while reclining on a training table. Heat pads bore down on both thighs. From time to time a trainer arrived to adjust the heat and assistants delivered various objects for him to autograph.

At this writing Damon Bailey lives in a condominium in Indianapolis. He has been dating an Indiana Pacers cheerleader for some time. Recently he invested in a business which supplies parts to operators of heavy machinery. One of his first employees was his father. Bailey is a sturdy, shorthaired, clear-eyed man who considers questions carefully before answering in a voice that is lower and huskier than his boyish face would suggest. The words come through a heavy Hoosier twang. It is a Heltonville twang, not a Bedford twang.

∞ ∞ ∞

P.H.: Growing up, did you have the feeling that you were being groomed to be a basketball player?

D.B: Well, I was being groomed, but it wasn't like when I was born my parents said, "We're gonna make him a basketball player." My dad played a lot and as a kid I tagged along and I fell in love with the game. Once I showed that interest, my parents pushed me hard to be a player and gave me a lot of support.

P.H.: Did your father give you technical instruction? Did he say things like, "Damon, you have to come out to meet a pass," or "Here's a place to move when the ball's on the other side of the court?"

D.B: Some, but it was more like on-the-job training. The men my father played with really knew how to play this game. Mine was a hands-on education. I figured things out as I was playing. I would think, Hell, if I can't get the ball this way, I'll have to try something else. Little kids ask me all the time now, "What do I need to do to become a better player?" I tell them, "I don't know because I've never seen you play." Every player needs to work on different things. But if there's one piece of advice I could offer every kid, it would be to play with people who are older and better than they are. They will make you do things you don't want to do and that you've never done before. When I was young I couldn't jump over those men so I had to learn new ways to score.

P.H.: What was it like being so young and playing with men?

D.B: They didn't cut me any slack. If I was going up for a shot, they were trying to block it, and if they knocked me into the wall, they knocked me into the wall. They weren't trying to hurt me. They were trying to help me in the long run. They were trying to help me learn things that most kids didn't.

P.H.: Did you play against your father one-on-one a lot?
D.B: Yes, quite a bit.

P.H.: Do you remember the first time you beat him?

D.B: (Laughs.) It was just before my junior year in high school. We were in my driveway. We went to twenty-four points, by two. He was an inside player. He would drive in and find a way to score, however he could. I was taller than he was by then but he could always find ways to score. I thought I was a very good player when I was a freshman and sophomore in high school, but I could never beat him. When it happened, it was a close game, and it went into overtime, and I won.

P.H.: How did he react to the loss?

D.B: He didn't say anything. He just walked inside. I bragged a lot to Mom. He was very competitive. He was glad that I had become good enough to beat him but he hated to lose. Even now I don't think I could beat him very bad. He is a very smart player. People say you can't teach someone to be a smart player, but I think you can.

P.H.: How?

D.B: My dad was very hard on me when I was a young player. I won't tell you differently. He wasn't full of praise. He never told me I had played a good game until we won the state championship. I admire him for that. I thank him for that. There's no way I'd be the player I am if he wasn't the way he was. When I was a five or six I played on a Boys Club team, and I was bigger than everyone else. I was the best player. I can remember going to the Boys Club and scoring forty or fifty points, and my team winning by twenty or thirty, and then getting in the car and being in trouble. I'd get yelled at for the one time I didn't throw it to the kid who was wide open underneath the basket, whether the kid could catch the ball or not. After a lot of that you become a smart player. You understand. You learn to see things that most players don't see. It can be taught in a certain way. It wasn't like a classroom for me. My father never sat me down and said, "Here's what you need to do." It was from years and years of playing, and years and years of him getting on me for not making certain passes. After awhile you start thinking, "Hey, there's more to this game than just me."

P.H.: But are there any other lessons that get taught with this type of education? Is there a part of you that says, "Man, I can never please this guy. What's it gonna take?"

D.B: (Takes his time.) I don't want to say no because I don't want to lie, but I don't want to say yes because I really don't know. I won't pretend that there weren't times that I was thinking, Man, I scored forty and got ten rebounds and we won by twenty-five . . . What else can I do? But again, I thank and admire him because there is no way I'd be the player I am without him. I have a drive to be a good player, but I needed someone to kick me in the ass every now and then. As a high school player I got up every morning and went to the gym because I wanted to. I thought that playing and running before school would give me an edge. But there were times when I would wake up and think, I'm not gonna do it today. Sometimes that would last a week. But Dad was there saying, "Get up. Go down there." He knew that I wanted to do it, but he also knew I needed a kick. He made me understand that being good was not going to be easy. And that in life I would have to do things I didn't want to do.

P.H.: *Were you having fun?*
D.B.: It isn't fun becoming a good player. It's fun being a good player. I remember one time in junior high I was sick. And maybe by today's standards I was too sick to play. I didn't want to play. Dad made me play. I played very well. I remember him saying, "Do you think Dr. J. never played sick?" It gave me an edge.

P.H.: *Did that edge pay off in college?*
D.B.: There were times that I could barely walk. I had a side injury my senior year in college. I could barely straighten up. But I kept playing because I loved to play. If I couldn't play there was no sense in my being around. I had developed the toughness to block pain out. A lot of people wouldn't have got out of bed the day I played against Temple in the NCAA tournament. I had the tunnel vision, the focus to block it out. And it's been worth it, because there are a lot of things in life that you can't control but you have to keep going.

I just went out and tried to do my job the best I could. Sometimes my knees hurt, sometimes I was sick. People think that being a good player is all fun. It isn't. I love being where I am now. But there's been a lot of heartache. And a lot of sweat and pain put in, back when I was eight or nine, and now.

P.H.: *It's surprising to a lot of people how well you can jump.*
D.B.: I used to be able to. One reason my knees are so bad now is that I was doing squats with weights when I was twelve. That was too young. By the time I hit IU my vertical jump went down. I hope the knee operation will put it back to where it was.

P.H.: *Do you remember the first time you ever dunked?*
D.B.: Yeah. It was the summer after my seventh grade year. I was at my junior high. I could palm a basketball even then but I'd

never even been able to even come close to dunking, and then all of a sudden one day I did it in a warm-up drill before a game. My friends went nuts. So did I. After that it was a piece of cake. I just needed that one time, and then I could do it over and over.

P.H.: You said that your dad didn't praise you until your high school team won the state championship. When did he praise you then? After the game?

D.B.: No, it was the week before the state finals. He told me several times that I had worked hard, and now I was becoming a man, and I could see things now, as a player and a man, that I hadn't been able to see before. He no longer had to point certain things out to me. He said he was proud of me. That was the proudest time of my life.

P.H.: There was such excitement around Indiana in the week before your last chance to be a state champion. What was that week like for you?

D.B.: That was the most meaningful time in my life so far. It's hard to make people understand how much this dream has meant to me. I don't just mean playing professional basketball, I mean being able to be an idol to a lot of kids. To have people look up to me. To have my family play the biggest role in putting me in this situation.

P.H.: Everyone has fantasies of stepping in to snatch victory from defeat. But you actually did it, and in front of forty thousand people. What did it feel like? Was there a voice in your head at the turning point that said, "Hey, Damon, this game is slipping away . . . if you don't act now your dream will die?"

D.B.: (Sighs.) I'm very competitive. There was never a time when I thought we were gonna lose. We were down by six points with ninety seconds to go. Even then I didn't think we would lose. I wasn't gonna let that happen. I would do anything. Score points, play defense, knock a guy out. Whatever it took.

P.H.: But it's hard to imagine having the confidence to feel that you could just personally take over. Those were good players out there. That was an undefeated team. This was for the state championship. They wanted it too. It was their dream as well.

D.B.: Wanting is an art. Desire is an art. An average player who wants to win will beat a great player who doesn't.

P.H.: If you close your eyes and think about it, what can you remember about that last stretch?

D.B.: A foul had been called with about two minutes left. I got my team together underneath the other team's basket and told them, "This is it. This is what we've worked for all of our lives. We're not gonna lose. Get behind me and we'll do this." After that I really don't remember specifically how we won, play by play.

P.H.: Have you ever watched the tape?
D.B.: No.

P.H.: Never?
D.B.: Never.

P.H.: Why?

D.B.: I don't look back. I can do that with my grandkids when I'm sixty. When I'm done playing a game I don't have time to sit back and think, Boy, I was a great high school player. Every step you take is a bigger step than the one you took before. What happened before doesn't matter. The other Indiana Pacers don't care that Reggie Miller went to UCLA, or what he did last year. They care that we have a game against Houston on Wednesday. What matters is what's going on now. I've never watched a film of myself, except to learn. Never for the pure sake of enjoyment. At IU when I was in a shooting slump I watched a film of us playing against Kansas, because I had shot the ball very well in that game.

I don't like watching basketball, I never did. Even as a kid I rarely did. And when I do watch, I try to learn. I watch certain things. I don't watch a Michael Jordan dunk as much as I watch how people try to prevent him from scoring. The other night when the Pacers played Atlanta I was at home and I watched it. Mainly I focused on what Reggie was doing to get open. I was trying to learn. I was frustrated just sitting there. I wanted to be playing.

P.H.: Let's talk about Coach Knight. First, the moment when he walked into the Shawswick gym to see you when you were an eighth grader. Did you know he was coming?

D.B.: No. Actually he came two or three times. The first time I didn't know it until after the game, when the kids started talking about it. It was a thrill, but I wasn't in awe of him. I've never been in awe of anyone. I don't say this to disrespect him. I think Coach Knight is one of the greatest coaches ever. I enjoyed my time with him. But I was never in awe of him. I felt that I belonged there.

P.H.: When you finally did notice him, surely you knew what he was there for.

D.B.: Yeah, I knew what he was there for, but I was smart enough to know that if I didn't continue to work hard, that visit wouldn't matter.

P.H.: How did you find out about the quote in A Season on the Brink *in which Coach Knight tells others that you, an eighth grader, were better than the IU guards?*

D.B.: Right after the book came out somebody shoved the part about me in my face and said, "Here, read this." I had read about the quote in newspapers. I never read the book. Never read the part about me.

P.H.: Did you believe what he said? Did you think there was any chance that you were actually better than the IU guards?

D.B.: I was smart enough to know that it wasn't true. And now I can look back and it's even funnier when I think of how many times Coach Knight says things that he doesn't even mean.

P.H.: Did another Damon Bailey ever appear at IU while you were there? I mean, did Coach Knight ever say, "There's this grade school kid in Oolitic or somewhere that's better than any of you?"

D.B.: No. He never did that to us during my four years.

P.H.: What was your dad's reaction to the quote about you in the book?

D.B.: I don't know how he felt. He never said anything to me, but that's not surprising. You'll never see a quote from my dad, or any other member of my family. They've never given an interview. They just instilled in me what was right and wrong. I've made the big decisions in my life on my own. I never talked to them about going to Indiana University. I was the one who would be there for four years, not them. I told them. It would have been fine with them if I had gone to Purdue. They've stayed out of the spotlight.

P.H.: How did Indiana recruit you?

D.B.: Coach Knight started recruiting me early. There was no song and dance. He said, "This is what we can do for you and this is what you can do for us. If you wanna come, come."

P.H.: Did you visit anywhere else?

D.B.: I halfway went to Purdue. A buddy who was a Purdue fan took me to a football game up there and it was arranged that I would meet Coach Keady and the staff. We talked, but my heart was set on Indiana.

P.H.: What was Coach Knight like to play for?

D.B.: You can comb through any sport at any level and you will never find a person who is more competitive than Coach Knight. Pheasant hunting, fishing, coaching a game, he wants to be the best. That's why his players and teams are successful. They will find a way to win. I won't say it was all fun. Sometimes I woke up in the morning and wondered what the hell I was doing there. Sometimes I wondered whether it was worth it. Now I can look back and say I'm glad I stayed. I'm glad I went. Coach Knight made me a better player and a better person. I came to IU with a good work ethic and he drove it home. When I chose to go to college at Indiana University, people kept saying, "How are you going to handle Coach Knight?" I was never a bit worried, and to this day I have no hard feelings toward Coach Knight or anything he ever said to me, because there's nothing that Coach Knight ever said to me or did to me that had not been said or done by my father before I went to Indiana.

P.H.: There were times when you dominated your college games and then there were times when you seemed to be somewhat pas-

sive. You went long stretches without shooting. What was going on?

D.B.: Fortunately or unfortunately, depending on the way you look at it, I played with some great players at Indiana. Calbert Cheaney, Greg Graham, Eric Anderson. As a freshman, even as a sophomore and junior, I had to play behind those great players. There were times I made a personal sacrifice to make our team better. I could have averaged 20–25 points a game all through my career, even as a freshman, if I wanted to shoot enough. But my first year Calbert Cheaney was our go-to player. Somebody had to get him the ball. Nobody better than I, I thought. Every year I was there I led the team in assists. Coach Knight never told me not to shoot. I just played that way. I was thinking, If I shoot twenty times a game, how many shots does that take away from Calbert? Maybe by playing that way I didn't look like as good a player as people thought I was. I think my senior year I showed them. I averaged over twenty points until I hurt my side, and then it was hard to play. You can check me on this, but I think I was the winningest player ever to play at Indiana University. By that I mean I spent more time in first place in the Big Ten and have a better winning percentage. I know I'm close. I feel that I'm a winner. I don't want to be known as a great player or shooter. I want to be a winner.

P.H.: Are you confident that you can be a good NBA player?

D.B.: I think I can do whatever Coach Brown asks me to do. I read the other day that Reggie Miller said that if we win an NBA title he would retire. If that happens, and he does, I'm confident that I could step in and fill his role. If that doesn't happen, I'm confident that I could back Reggie up, or play the point and get him the ball. Sometimes success, and how you are judged, depends on the situation you are in. I'll give you an example: Calbert Cheaney was in a great situation. When he arrived at Indiana there was no star player. He was the best freshman and automatically he took over that role. No one else was gonna take that role until he left. And no one here is gonna take Reggie's role until he leaves. He's been here seven or eight years.

P.H.: Your fame in Indiana is like that of a rock star. When did that begin?

D.B.: I think that book really kicked it in. I've grown up with it. It's been part of my life for so long it's just there, like brushing my teeth. Every morning when I wake up I know that after I walk out my door people I don't know will come up to me. They will want my autograph. They'll want to talk to me.

P.H.: Does it ever just drive you nuts?

D.B.: It gets old. I try to do the best I can to live up to people's expectations. I try to be a role model.

P.H.: You haven't mentioned your mother in talking about growing up. What's she like?

D.B.: Very emotional. When you have people like my father and Coach Knight in your life, you also have to have a person who comes along and says, "It's all right . . . So they're mad . . . So they've lost it." I think that's what my mom was and I think that's what the assistant coaches at Indiana are.

P.H.: Moms?

D.B.: I think so. They're just there for when Coach Knight gets on you really hard. It gets to you. You get down. They are the ones who pick you back up. You can't have one without the other. Same with my mom. I don't think my dad could have been the way he was to me if it hadn't been for my mom, and I don't think Coach Knight could be the way he is to his players if it weren't for the assistant coaches. My mom was always there for me. She doesn't know all about the game, but she would rebound for me, in the driveway, and in the gym. My sister would too. My success is a family success.

P.H.: When your high school championship game was over you rushed into the stands and embraced your family. Had you decided to do that before the game or did it just happen spontaneously?

D.B.: It just happened. I had never seen anything like it on TV. I don't know what hit me. We had just won. I was in a big pile on the floor with my teammates when Bam! I just broke away and went to them. I thought, here is a way to really acknowledge my family and all we've done together. It would be better than just saying it to a reporter. Here was a way to show everybody.

P.H.: You played in a few games against NBA players before the decision to operate on your knees. What was your early impression of the level of play in the NBA?

D.B.: NBA players understand the game better than collegiate players. They're very intelligent about basketball. I don't think there's a great talent difference — some NBA players are definitely better than college players — but you don't have to be a great player. You just have to be very smart and understand the game and know what it takes to play at this level.

P.H.: What's your life like these days?

D.B.: I live in Indianapolis. I come in, I work out. I'm trying to work very hard, but I can't overdo it. So I'm pushing taking it slow (laughs). It's frustrating. It's hard for me to sit back and watch the guys practice when I want to be out there. I want to be there but I think watching can help me too. I can see what it takes to play in this league, I can understand things. I won't just be thrown into it. This will take a lot of the pressure off me and off the Pacers. No one will expect me to score thirty points or Coach Brown to play me forty-eight minutes in the first game.

P.H.: Is that what you think people expect of you?

D.B.: People expect a lot, both of me and the team. But nobody will expect more of me than I will. I know that I will do whatever it takes to help my team win — score points, distribute the ball, rebound, whatever. The people on the outside won't always understand that. They won't know what Coach Brown is asking of any player. This is a team game. It's not the Reggie Miller show or the Damon Bailey show or the Mark Jackson show. It's the Indiana Pacers show. It hasn't changed . . . People have always expected a lot of me and I've just gone out to help my team win. I've been a winner everywhere I've played. I think anyone can score points at this level, but only a few people are consistent winners.

Heltonville attractions. (Sanford Gentry)

P.H.: Every time you go to your home town, there, on a hill at the crossroads is a monument to you, with an inscription that says it was given with the love and gratitude of your neighbors. And you're, what, twenty-three? How does that feel? Is there any part of you that sometimes steps back and says "What a strange life I've led?"

D.B.: Heltonville is a special place to me. It's a place where I can go to relax and I can get away from most of the hoopla. My friends are there, and the people who helped make me successful. You can't find a person that wouldn't enjoy living the life that I live. There have been times that I've hated it. But there's not one thing in my life that I'd change. Everything that has happened, this surgery, even my sister having leukemia, has made me stronger. I'd give anything in the world for her not to have it. At the same time it's made me appreciate what I have all the more. The pain that I go through now is nothing compared to what she goes through with chemotherapy. Imagine what it must be like for a fifteen-year-old girl to lose her hair. I can't imagine how she feels.

P.H.: Do you think you're special in any way?

D.B.: Yes. I'm very levelheaded. I understood things early. I matured quickly. Some of it had to do with that book and the attention I was getting. My dad never let me get a big head.

P.H.: Do you consider yourself a chosen person or your success in any way miraculous? Everyone wants what you have, but you're the one who got it.

D.B.: I think to a certain degree I'm blessed with talent. But it was up to me to go out and develop that talent. It was a dream, but it wasn't a miracle. I've worked so hard. I think that people think I was born and could just play the game or that I woke up one day at thirteen and could play well. It didn't happen that way. It's a dream that my family and I had for many years. We made it happen.